Fringe to Famous

Fringe to Famous

Cultural Production in Australia After the Creative Industries

Tony Moore, Mark Gibson, Chris McAuliffe
and Maura Edmond

BLOOMSBURY ACADEMIC
NEW YORK • LONDON • OXFORD • NEW DELHI • SYDNEY

BLOOMSBURY ACADEMIC
Bloomsbury Publishing Inc, 1359 Broadway, New York, NY 10018, USA
Bloomsbury Publishing Plc, 50 Bedford Square, London, WC1B 3DP, UK
Bloomsbury Publishing Ireland, 29 Earlsfort Terrace, Dublin 2, D02 AY28, Ireland

BLOOMSBURY, BLOOMSBURY ACADEMIC and the Diana logo
are trademarks of Bloomsbury Publishing Plc

First published in the United States of America 2024
Paperback edition published 2025

A catalog record for this book is available from the Library of Congress.

ISBN: HB: 978-1-5013-3488-7
PB: 979-8-7651-1247-2
ePDF: 978-1-5013-3490-0
eBook: 978-1-5013-3489-4

Typeset by Integra Software Services Pvt. Ltd.

For product safety related questions contact productsafety@bloomsbury.com.

To find out more about our authors and books visit www.bloomsbury.com
and sign up for our newsletters.

Australian Government

Australian Research Council

This research was funded by the Australian Government through
the Australian Research Council (ARC). The views expressed herein are those of
the authors and are not necessarily those of the Australian Government or the ARC.

Contents

Acknowledgements

Books, as in most cultural production, are the result of collective effort, and networks of support and institutional enabling. *Fringe to Famous* is the principal output of an Australian Research Council Discovery Project that was nourished by the Faculty of Arts at Monash University and its School of Media, Film and Journalism. Over its duration, the ARC project employed three Research Assistants who we thank for their tireless and dedicated work on archive, interview and conceptual research and logistics – Louise Sheedy, Jasmine McGowan and Kyle Harvey.

We would also like to thank all the cultural practitioners who participated in the project through agreeing to be interviewed, and in many cases providing images to illustrate the book. *Fringe to Famous* would have been impossible without the enthusiasm and generosity of this creative community. Their many names can be read in the book's text and references. We particularly want to single out for acknowledgement in this regard and for sage advice cultural sector practitioners Steve Vizard, Andy Nehl, Courtney Gibson, Marcus Westbury, Julian Morrow, Peter Chellew and Reg Mombassa. Reg also kindly made available his artwork for the *Fringe to Famous* cover!

We also want to acknowledge academic dialogic colleagues who gave encouragement and critical feedback to earlier versions of our arguments, particularly Justin O'Connor, Stuart Cunningham, Kate Oakley, Catharine Lumby, Paul Long, Tony Bennett, Mike Grenfell, James Albright, Deborah Hartman, Jacqueline Widin, Victoria Durer and Dave O'Brien.

We would also like to thank the copyright owners of the images in this book, who kindly gave permission for their use in *Fringe to Famous* – their names are in the image credits. Finally a big thank you to the talented team at Bloomsbury for their value-adding ideas, hard work and patience in bringing this book to fruition, especially Katie Gallof, Erin Duffy, Stephanie-Grace Petinos and Alyssa Jordan.

Introduction: From art school to beer barn

In 1977, post-punk band Mental as Anything was formed by a group of budding visual artists at East Sydney Technical College, a hothouse for that sunny city's bohemian wannabes, their first gig being performed for fellow art students. Original members Chris O'Doherty (aka Reg Mombassa), Martin 'Plaza' Murphy, Andrew 'Greedy' Smith, Peter O'Doherty and Wayne 'Sea Bird' De Lisle were inspired by Dada and active participants in alternative and avant-garde cultural movements at the time. In the aftermath of punk, the 'Mentals' found a nurturing niche audience in the inner Sydney indie music scene, appealing to fringe youth subcultures and university students. Their early gigs alternated between raffish inner city pubs and undergraduate refectories, while their first music video was shot on a shoestring budget at the University of Sydney's Tin Sheds workshop, an autonomous art space that became legendary from the early 1970s as a site of aesthetic and political experimentation.

Yet the Mentals also struck a chord with suburban youth, allowing their songs to break out of university refectories and inner-city garrets to become beer barn standards and radio favourites. Notwithstanding their experimental arts provenance, songs such as 'Too many Times', 'Berserk Warriors' and 'I Didn't Mean to be Mean' were relatable, funny and often poignant, locating the human comedy in the suburbs and mediascape, much as Barry Humphries had done with his comedic monologues in earlier decades. With their catchy tunes, Pacific-tinged guitar licks and clever play on Australian slang, they heralded a succession of national top ten hits combining quirky pop with postmodern pastiche, fondly ironizing media culture and everyday life (Nichols 2016: 435–6). The Mentals' music became a cross-demographic soundtrack for the 1980s, finding its way even into Australia's most commercially successful film export, *Crocodile Dundee*. At the same time, the members of this most visual of bands never lost connection with their avant-garde art school origins. Indeed, Reg Mombassa's visual arts practice has outlasted his musical career, his

Figure 1 Paul Worstead screenprinted poster for a Mental as Anything gig, 1982. Courtesy National Gallery of Australia.

work being collected internationally and exhibited by institutions such as the Art Gallery of NSW and the National Gallery of Australia.

Mental as Anything was not unique in this fusion of fringe and famous. Another from an art school background was goth dandy Nick Cave, who migrated from the small, sweaty spaces of the post-punk pub-rock scene in Melbourne in the late 1970s to the status of international cult icon. In the twenty-first century, acts such as Courtney Barnett, Tame Impala and Bloods attained large popular audiences while retaining the 'Indie' identity of their origins. Nor is the phenomenon limited to music. In comedy, for example, a generation of

Figure 2 Boys Next Door, 1978, in Nick Cave's bedroom at his parent's house in Melbourne. Photograph by Peter Milne. Courtesy National Library of Australia.

student performers emerging in Melbourne in the 1980s from student revues and small comedy clubs gained mass audiences in the top rating television sketch comedy series *The Comedy Company*, *Fast Forward* and *The D-Generation*. The comedy cycle was still turning in the early 2000s, this time in Sydney, when the newly graduated University of Sydney pranksters behind fringe satire magazine *The Chaser* were commissioned to produce primetime TV hits for the Australian Broadcasting Corporation, the country's leading public service broadcaster.

Examples of such crossover can be found in many other fields. In fashion, the surreal, scatological designs of the artists associated with Mambo Graphics, including the Mentals' Reg Mombassa, have been transposed onto T-shirts and board shorts, taking an aesthetic spawned in subversive punk and protest poster art to suburban streetwear (McAuliffe 2017). In computer games, new ideas emerging from peer-to-peer conversations at Melbourne's independent games festival Freeplay have found their way into successful titles distributed around the world. And arising within some of Australia's most marginalized communities, Indigenous artists working across media, from inner urban Black theatre and dance companies to community-owned desert satellite radio and television networks CAAMA and Imparja, have produced widely acclaimed

Figure 3 Gina Riley, Jane Turner, Magda Szubanski and Marg Downey (L-R), shooting a parody of *Neighbours* and *Home and Away* for *Fast Forward*, *c.* 1990. Courtesy Steve Vizard.

films such as academy award nominated *Samson & Delilah* and neo-Western television series *Mystery Road*, whose 2020 second season scooped industry awards, dominated international 'best of' television lists and became the highest-rated Australian drama of the year.

The movement from fringe to famous is not unique to Australia. In the UK, a similar trajectory was traced by post-punk bands The Clash, The Specials, Elvis Costello and the Attractions, The Pretenders, Joy Division and The Smiths. Emerging in the wake of the Sex Pistols' challenge to mainstream pop, these groups went on to attract mass audiences, first nationally and then internationally. In comedy, an alternative scene that emerged in the 1980s from university revue, the Edinburgh Festival Fringe and punk performance culture gained mainstream distribution through television. Notable examples include *The Young Ones* ensemble – Rik Mayall, Adrian Edmondson, Jennifer Saunders and Ben Elton – and the creators of *Not the Nine O'Clock News* – Rowan Atkinson, Mel Smith, Griff Rhys Jones and Pamela Stephenson. In the United

Figure 4 *Samson & Delilah* film poster, 2009, directed by Warwick Thornton and featuring actors Marissa Gibson and Rowan McNamara. Courtesy Scarlett Pictures.

States, Blondie, The Ramones, The B-52s, REM and the Bangles jumped from boho venues like NYC's Max's Kansas City to College Radio and on to *American Bandstand*. From the late 1970s, several generations of American alternative comedians – including John Belushi, Dan Akroyd, Chevy Chase, Bill Murray and Mike Myers – found nationwide popularity via NBC's *Saturday Night Live*, with sketches morphing in the 1980s and 1990s into international hit films such as *The Blues Brothers*, the *National Lampoon* series and *Wayne's World*.

In *Fringe to Famous*, we investigate Australian examples of this phenomenon in music, design, comedy, Indigenous screen and digital games from the 1980s to the present day. The case studies suggest that there is far more exchange between marginal and mainstream cultural production than is generally recognized in scholarly studies, policy discourse and public commentary on the arts. They reveal that many things that we take to be 'pop cultural' have origins in small obscure scenes, often quite 'difficult' or 'avant-garde'. And vice versa: many things that we take to be 'high art' have been shaped by an encounter with large mainstream audiences. A not uncommon pattern is for a circulation by artists between fringe and popular production, and an exchange of aesthetics, ideas and practices between the two. Based on this evidence, we argue for the recognition of a generative hybridity between fringe and mainstream. This hybridity goes beyond the Warholian appropriation of pop culture into high art, to include generative exchanges between people, texts, sectors and audiences. It is a major source of cultural and economic value, making it a legitimate focus for policy thinking about culture.

Fringe phobia

The main obstacle to the position we want to develop in *Fringe to Famous* is a widely held idea that the only possible relation between the fringe and mainstream is one of radical difference or antagonism. It is an idea that is generally associated with a romantic tendency, particularly marked in the wake of the counterculture of the 1960s and 1970s, to celebrate a 'pure' fringe and to represent crossover with the mainstream as a loss or betrayal. We suggest, however, that it is also subtly embedded in an anti-romantic reaction that has formed since the 1980s as a critical counterpoint. Indeed, this reaction is now the more substantial problem. The suggestion may appear surprising, as the anti-romantic tendency has been defined precisely by a rejection of heady dramas played out around the themes of 'authenticity' and 'sellout'. Our argument, however, is that the dominant forms of anti-romanticism protest too much, their very vigilance against romanticism betraying shared assumptions. Rather than reconceptualizing the relation between fringe and mainstream, they remain haunted by an idea of the fringe that they are also committed to denying.

The problem was not evident in the initial challenge to the romanticism of the counterculture, which was indeed an extremely fertile moment for ideas of hybridity. This challenge might be characterized as interrogative, seeking only to trouble or complicate ideas of difference between the fringe and mainstream. In scholarly work, this was the moment broadly of the 'postmodern' cultural studies of the 1980s and 1990s, associated in Australia with authors such as Meaghan Morris, McKenzie Wark, John Hartley, Catharine Lumby and Adrian Martin. A key British example, and an inspiration for us in *Fringe to Famous*, was Simon Frith and Howard Horne's (1987) *Art into Pop*, a study of the contribution of the art school in channelling the avant-garde aesthetics and dispositions of visual artists into commercial pop culture, especially rock music and design. While Frith was later to become a scourge of romantic ideas of the fringe, particularly in relation to music, this direction was still developing and had not fully set. Even as it questioned the *absoluteness* of differences between small fringe scenes and the mainstream cultural industries, *Art into Pop* shared the conviction of the counterculture in the *significance* of these differences. It is this balance, more precarious than it may have seemed at the time, that opened the imagination to the idea of hybridity.

Our difference with the anti-romantic reaction is not so much with this early moment, therefore, as with a hardening of the position that has occurred since the 1990s and into the early decades of the twenty-first century. The key development has been an increasing determination not so much to trouble the distinction between fringe and mainstream as more systematically to *eliminate* it. In cultural theory, the tendency is captured most clearly in arguments, after Michel Foucault, that there is no outside to relations of power. These arguments, which became particularly influential in Australia during the so-called 'cultural policy' moment of the 1990s (Bennett 1992; Cunningham 1992; Bennett 1998), served to flatten distinctions between mainstream institutions and fringe cultural formations. While they succeeded in reducing the emotional and political charge of oppositions between fringe and mainstream, they did so at a significant cost. The response to the countercultural insistence on the purity of the fringe was not to moderate the concept so much as to liquidate it, making it impossible even to pose the question of relations between fringe and mainstream.

Two further examples are important points of reference for us in *Fringe to Famous*. The first is the 'creative industries' position of the early 2000s, for which, in an echo of the Foucauldian formula, there was no outside to economic exchange within fields of market relations. From this perspective, fringe arts practice should be understood as a site not of alternative values but of business innovation, a merely functional component of the mainstream economy. The second example is a conceptualization of the fringe, after Pierre Bourdieu, as a site for acquiring cultural capital. Here again, the motivations and forms of value within the fringe – or 'field of restricted production' (Bourdieu 1993: 39) – are effectively identified with those of the mainstream. However subversive or oppositional fringe arts practice may seem, it is consistent for Bourdieu with the logic of the mainstream cultural industries. Even the most radical gesture needs to be understood as ultimately a play for influence *within* the mainstream (Bourdieu 1980: 269). Fringe artists are seen as staking out positions that can later be cashed out in the 'field of large-scale production' [*la grande production*] (Bourdieu 1993: 39).

The Bourdieusian example is intriguing as the anti-romantic argument appears at odds with other aspects of the intellectual project. Bourdieu was clearly drawn to the field of restricted production, particularly its association with aspirations to 'autonomy'. One of his major legacies has been a rich set of resources for anyone seeking to understand small cultural scenes, bohemias and avant-gardes. This makes it all the more striking that he turns at crucial points so forcefully to deny their real independence. The pattern is one that can be seen more widely. Another reference point for us is a position, associated with writers such as David Hesmondhalgh, Kate Oakley and Justin O'Connor, that we call 'left culturalism'. It is a position that has resisted the reductionist tendency of anti-romantic arguments, particularly the creative industries insistence on representing all creative production in business terms. Like Bourdieu, left culturalism has sought to keep alive a belief in the possibility of practices that cannot be so represented. Like Bourdieu, however, it has also felt compelled to hedge this position to guard against romanticism. The result can sometimes come across as an academic Stockholm syndrome.

The general phenomenon we are identifying here is not restricted to scholarly debates. A reluctance to recognize a difference in the fringe can also be found in cultural policy, which has taken a resolutely utilitarian turn over the last twenty years. In Australia particularly, but also internationally, the arts are now conceptualized as an industry to be analysed according to metrics such as audience reach, employment and financial turnover. Within this framework, the prescription offered to artists and arts organizations is inevitably an improved business plan, leaving no place for recognition of the productive tension, important even for business itself, between business calculations and other ways of seeing the world. As a result, the specific contributions of fringe practices – such as risk-taking, experimentation and audience participation – are systematically overlooked.

But the tendency is perhaps most marked in centre-left politics, which has become increasingly intolerant, over the last twenty years, of fringe cultural formations. The social democratic government of Gough Whitlam (1972–75) engaged in significant dialogue with activist practitioners from the countercultural arts and overlapping social movements, dialogue that led to policies such as the creation of FM Community radio stations, the opening to youth of the national public broadcaster and the establishment of a fund for experimental film. From the late 1990s, by contrast, Labor governments at both state and federal level largely restricted policy dialogue to insider circles, preferring structured consultation with sectional interests, including the 'arts sector', understood on an industrial model. As in the case of British New Labour's big tent of 'luvvies', the model of outreach became corporatist, instrumentalist and elitist, excluding ground up fringe formations and much else (Moore 2003).

It would be unfair to suggest that Australian Labor has made no attempt in the twenty-first century to engage with the arts. Examples include the Australia 2020 Summit convened by the incoming Rudd government in 2008 and a series of 'virtual public sphere' events feeding into the development of the Gillard government's 2013 cultural policy, Creative Australia. But these efforts have skewed strongly to players with established mainstream recognition, such as Hollywood favourite Cate Blanchett, and have favoured arts bureaucrats over practitioners. Antipathy to fringe ideas is such that otherwise democratic and generous Labor leaders have sometimes struggled to understand or support more radical cultural and media activists operating outside a narrow centrist politics. For example, the imprisoned Australian head of Wikileaks, Julian Assange, had to wait for the election of Anthony Albanese as prime minister in 2022 before a serving Labor leader was prepared to criticize his detention in Britain or threatened extradition to the United States. The failure in relation to Assange is a potent example of a recent incomprehension and fear of overtly subversive countercultures by mainstream progressive political parties.

The closure to the fringe over the past two decades contrasts strikingly with the position of earlier generations of leaders on the centre left. An example is Prime Minister Gough Whitlam's appearance as himself in the 1975 film comedy *Barry McKenzie Holds His Own*, regally bestowing a damehood on Barry Humphries' character Edna Everage and playing along with a satire of his Periclean role in Labor's so-called 'Australian Cultural Renaissance' (Moore

Figure 5 Barry Crocker, Barry Humphries (as Edna Everage), Prime Minister Gough Whitlam and Margaret Whitlam at Sydney Airport, 20 April 1974, for the filming of *Barry McKenzie Holds His Own*. Courtesy News Ltd/Newspix.

2005: 48). Another is the participation by Prime Minister Paul Keating in a 1993 feature for *Rolling Stone*, peering over Ray-Ban sunglasses on the cover and being interviewed inside by Mental as Anything's Reg Mombassa and other artists about Labor's plans for arts policy (Corris et al. 1993). This is not to romanticize these twentieth-century leaders. Whitlam oversaw policies, such as a 25 per cent cut to tariffs on imports, that were strongly criticized from the left at the time. Keating was often accused of nothing less than 'hijacking' the labour movement (Jaensch 1989), setting Australia on a path to economic rationalism. The point is rather that a hard-headed approach to governing did not exclude an engagement with youth culture and independent music scenes (*Rolling Stone Australia* managed to resist the charge of 'corporate magazine' for a good deal longer than its American counterpart).

The problem with a closure to the idea of the fringe, whether in the academic, policy or political fields, is that it denies an important source of renewal around values. As we hope to demonstrate in later chapters, fringe formations are generators of ideas of the 'good' – not in an empty and abstract sense, but in the sense of concrete conceptions, forged through close interactions within small circles of peers and audiences, of what is funny, insightful, edgy, ethical, uncomfortable, beautiful or original. It is mistaken, in our view, to see such values as inconsistent with mainstream media and cultural institutions. It may be true that the formality, legalism and inertia of the latter prevent them ever from becoming, as they sometimes claim to be, 'values led'. Yet they nevertheless depend on ideas of value to engage audiences, sell products, enrol public sympathies, motivate their workforces and maintain legitimacy. Ensuring a porosity between fringe and mainstream is therefore important not only for the sake of 'the culture', but also for the economic and institutional health of the media and cultural industries.

Those who favour anti-romantic arguments often warn darkly of political dangers in admitting the fringe. It is certainly true that fringe formations can be disruptive, interfering with the smooth functioning of institutional processes. We might even concede that there were moments in the 1970s when such disruption fed into wider political instability. But in the 2020s, there is a strong case that the charges in relation to dangers should be reversed. The suppression of the idea of the fringe ultimately contributes to political cynicism. Any attempt to raise questions of value is seen as a cover for what we know, or *think* we know, are the 'real' motivations – making money or gaining social advantage. In the wake of the Trump presidency in the United States, Brexit in the UK and a widely remarked slide towards 'toxic' politics in Australia and New Zealand, this idea must surely now be recognized as the more significant threat to stable government. Taken seriously, it leads us to see social relations as a zero-sum struggle for advantage over others, corroding trust and negating the possibility of resolving differences through democratic processes. These are clearly bigger themes than a book on the cultural industries can fully address, but we hope in *Fringe to Famous* to make a contribution to reversing these tendencies.

Kirkpatrickism

Fringe to Famous is a book with multiple authors and there are probably points where internal dialogue has not been fully resolved. In the 1970s and 1980s, multiple authorship in the humanities and social sciences was often associated with the irruption into the academy of 'social movement' collective practice, similar in kind to the irruptions we trace for the cultural industries in the book itself. Examples include the work, famously, of the Birmingham Centre for

Contemporary Cultural Studies or, in Australia, of groups such as those around R.W. Connell on class and education (Connell et al. 1982). *Fringe to Famous* has emerged, by contrast, from the greyer world of 'project ecologies', as described by economic geographer Gernot Grabher. The book is an 'output', as scholarly works are now described, of a project funded by the Australian Research Council (ARC). Projects, in which participants are conceived as 'teams', are more institutionally constrained than collectives. In business contexts, from where the form derives, they are governed by what Grabher (2004: 1495) calls a 'service logic' – that of solving a problem for a client – and a 'management logic' – aimed at keeping the project within time and on budget.

But the differences between projects and collectives are not as great as they sometimes seem. The formal premise of a research project does require a certain alignment with Grabher's logics, sometimes involving imaginative conceits such as the idea – increasingly explicit in Australia in recent years – of the nation whose funding body underwrites the research as 'client'. The art of pitching a funding application is, in part, to convey a sense that the project has been fully conceptualized at the outset, needing only to be 'executed' to deliver outcomes in the service of the client's needs. In practice, however, there are countless unforeseen questions that need to be addressed in the course of the research, not only at an operational level, but also in refining the value horizon of the project – the shared understanding of what it is ultimately 'for'. Projects are therefore more internally dialogic than their externally facing appearance might suggest. Indeed, they could be thought of as one of the forms preserving a space for collective practices in the corporatized university.

So it has been with *Fringe to Famous*. Besides coordinating inputs to deliver on outputs, the project form has provided a platform for conversations among those involved. The latter includes others beyond the authors of this book – notably Louise Sheedy, Jasmine McGowan and Kyle Harvey who worked on the project as research assistants. The project has also been shaped by conversations with colleagues, particularly in the 'Culture, Media, Economy' research group at Monash University under the direction of Justin O'Connor. And beyond the academy, we have sought to involve our research 'subjects' as dialogic partners and first audiences for some of our ideas. One of the arguments of the book is that those who have negotiated the exchange between fringe and mainstream have some of the most acute insights into the nature of this exchange. They might be thought of, to use Antonio Gramsci's famous phrase, as 'organic intellectuals' whose perspectives have much to contribute to more formal academic interpretation and analysis.

In fact, the origins of *Fringe to Famous* itself were as much in practice-based as academic contexts. The ideas that led to the project began to form when Tony Moore was a television documentary producer and researcher at the ABC in the mid-1990s. The period was one of significant circulation between fringe and mainstream culture by alternative bands, graphic designers, zine writers, indie publishers, new wave comedians and short filmmakers – a process that occurred largely through electronic media. Moore was himself a participant in this process, advocating with others from within the national broadcaster for greater openness to crossover, particularly in relation to stylistic conventions in television. His first attempt to reflect in a more formal way on the relation between fringe and mainstream was a ninety-minute documentary, *Bohemian Rhapsody: Rebels of Australian Culture* (1996), which was also an experiment in the possibilities of the documentary form for national television. This led on only later to a PhD thesis, a scholarly monograph and the initial idea for the research project.

In reflecting on their practice, media makers are often drawn to the concreteness of historical writing over the more abstract register of cultural theory. The inspiration for *Bohemian Rhapsody* came initially from a history of the literary scene in Sydney between the wars, Peter Kirkpatrick's (1992) *Sea Coast of Bohemia: Literary Life in Sydney's Roaring Twenties*. Two things about the book were striking, for Moore, from the perspective of Australian media and culture of the 1980s and 1990s. The first was the similarity between the self-conscious bohemianism of the literary scene in Sydney in the 1920s and the post-punk alternative music scene in the same city more than half a century later – even down to identifiable inner-urban precincts, drinking places and domiciles. The second was the extent to which Kirkpatrick's writers crossed between quite exclusive small scenes around bohemian clubs and proto-avant-garde journals on the one hand and, on the other, popular commercial media, including newspapers, magazines, cinema and visual design. Again, this resonated with media and culture in Australia in the 1990s, notwithstanding the tendency at the time to see commercial crossover by serious artists as novel.

Bohemian Rhapsody sought to generalize the insights gained from observing these similarities, asking whether they might illuminate a larger historical canvas. It considered generations of bohemian groups in Australia beyond Kirkpatrick's literary cohort, including Melbourne's modernist avant-gardes of the 1930s and 1940s, the Sydney Libertarian Push of the 1950s and 1960s, and the radical countercultures of the late 1960s and 1970s. The documentary also visited the conflict around modernism in Australia from the 1920s to the 1940s, especially the attempts of major state-based galleries, artists' societies and publishers – largely controlled by artists identified with the late-nineteenth-century bohemias around impressionism in painting and realism in literature – to reject key forms of modernism as 'decadent', 'primitive' or lacking in accomplishment. This too struck a chord with the 1990s, when veterans of the mid-century avant-garde and countercultures of the 1960s and 1970s – most of whom were ensconced in key cultural institutions – sought to reject a new aesthetics associated with 'postmodernism'.

There are two points about this line of thinking that are relevant to the questions around the conceptualization of the fringe and mainstream that we have begun to raise above. The first is that small scenes or bohemias are understood as concrete historical formations. They are seen as having their own internal dynamic, organized around conversations between co-creators, feedback between artists and intimate audiences and particular relations to institutions and place. They might indeed be seen as little institutions themselves. While never entirely formalized, they have recognizable patterns that are reproduced over time, even as each generation has also made them their own. This makes it possible to consider fringe or bohemian formations as having their own *traditions*, an idea that Moore developed at length in the book that eventually followed from the ABC documentary, *Dancing with Empty Pockets: Australia's Bohemias Since 1860* (2012).

The perspective is one that contrasts strongly with some of the more abstract conceptualizations of the fringe that emerged from the counterculture, particularly those that took as a major point of reference the political upheavals of the late 1960s. For the latter, the fringe has tended to be set off not only against *dominant* institutions and traditions – those of the state, for example, or of major corporations – but against institutions and traditions *as such*. This opens onto the second point about the perspective. The historical approach has the effect of relativizing or normalizing the counterculture, framing it as an event in a series rather than a more extraordinary rupture after which everything must be seen anew. In doing so, it works to check the pretension that became associated with the cultural and intellectual legacy of the 1960s and 1970s, but in a different way from those who have sought more robustly to counter or extinguish that legacy. To normalize is only to establish a distance; it is not to frame as an adversary.

Kirkpatrick is by no means a solitary figure. We have foregrounded him here because of his place in the development of the book, but he belongs to a broader body of work in Australian cultural history. Other examples relevant to fringe formations and bohemias include Ann Galbally's (2002) biography of painter *Charles Conder: The Last Bohemian*, Richard Haese's (1981) *Rebels and Precursors* on the interwar modernists, Anne Coombs' (1996) *Sex and Anarchy: The Life and Death of the Sydney Push* and Clinton Walker's (1996) *Stranded: The Secret History of Australian Independent Music*. This work is all but invisible in attempts in Australia to think in general terms about the media and cultural industries. For international readers, it might also appear too local to be of general interest, leading only into obscure backwaters of Australian Studies. But concrete historical particularism can itself be considered in abstract terms, not just for the actual particulars that might be in the frame but also as a style of thinking. We suggest in *Fringe to Famous* that it has an essential contribution to make to fresh approaches to cultural industries and cultural policy.

After the creative industries

But historical particularism is not the only input to our analysis of relations between fringe and mainstream. Notwithstanding the reservations we have indicated above, we have also been drawn at times, both individually and collectively, to more abstract anti-romantic arguments. An important context, for Moore, was the generational conflict already mentioned with veterans of the mid-century avant-garde and the counterculture. Examples of the latter in Australia included the playwright David Williamson, painters Colin Lanceley and Albert Tucker, broadcaster Philip Adams and art critic Robert Hughes, who took aim in the 1990s at a new aesthetic of pastiche, parody, sampling, irreverence and especially the embrace by 'postmodern' artists and academics of commercial popular culture. The jeremiads against postmodernism implicitly claimed for the earlier fringe a certain purity, representing everything that followed as tainted or compromised. Similar ideas informed resistance to generational change in the ABC, a resistance reinforced by longstanding tendencies towards a pious anti-commercialism. Against this, a sharper cutting edge seemed to be required than could be found in Kirkpatrick or Australian cultural history.

This edge was found, for Moore, in three main sources. The first was the work of a younger group of Australian scholars in media and cultural studies – including McKenzie Wark, Catharine Lumby and Mark Davis – who had been influenced by Foucauldian arguments against ideas of a pure outside to relations of power. This intellectual formation enabled an acid response to claims to such purity on behalf of the counterculture. The second input was Bourdieu's (1993: 201) theorization of the avant-garde as an 'upside-down economy' in which symbolic profits are acquired through a renunciation of material rewards. The theorization is one that seemed to apply particularly well to countercultural figures of the 1960s and 1970s, for whom a youthful rejection of the mainstream paid off handsomely in positions they later acquired in the very institutions they had once opposed. The third source was economic analysis, which allowed material interests in the fringe to be traced in quite concrete ways. In *Dancing with Empty Pockets*, Moore offered a historical account of the economy of bohemia in Australia, tracing the involvement of figures from fringe locations in commercial and public cultural institutions, including in many cases mass markets.

These perspectives, which had also influenced others of us as authors on *Fringe to Famous*, brought the project into alignment initially with a more systematic and thoroughgoing anti-romantic formation of the early 2000s – the 'creative industries' agenda we have already mentioned, which was associated at the time with Queensland University of Technology (QUT). One of the leading figures of creative industries in Australia, Stuart Cunningham, was involved in early conversations about the possible shape of the project. Mark Gibson and Maura Edmond had both participated, independently, in projects framed by creative industries arguments and led by other key figures at QUT. Aside from these personal connections, the creative industries idea was attractive in that it seemed to build on critical responses to ideas of the purity of the fringe. In a loose sense then, *Fringe to Famous* could be described as having started out as a creative industries project. We even drew on the hard-edged economic rhetoric of the creative industries in proposing, in the funding application, to advance a National Research Priority specified by the ARC: 'Promoting an innovation culture and economy'.

Yet it is also our encounter with the creative industries agenda that has crystallized our reservations about anti-romantic arguments. In an early project meeting on whether we might sharpen our conceptualization of the fringe by framing it as a site of business innovation, we concluded that such a conceptualization would lead to economic reductionism. This is a move we could not make. One of us (McAuliffe) has been a director of an art museum, another (Moore) has been a television programme maker, a third (Edmond) has been a curator, programmer and writer in film and multimedia – and all have long-standing interests in the specifically cultural values to be found in music, art, film, literature, television and online media. Our conviction in the need to maintain a distinction between economic and cultural value has been deepened by conversations with creative practitioners in research for the project itself. The distinction is one that is strongly held by artists and not only, as the creative industries proponents liked to suggest, of the unreformed purist kind – those, as John Hartley (2005a: 19) once put it, who are 'miserable, self-loathing and critical'. Indeed, it is often articulated most clearly by buoyant personalities who have found commercial success at the heart of the cultural industries.

We are not the only ones for whom an encounter with the creative industries agenda has been a point of reversal. The best-known example in Australia is Justin O'Connor, who joined QUT from the UK in the late 2000s. O'Connor's earlier work had seemed aligned with the agenda, if not actively contributing to its formation, but on arrival in Australia he reacted strongly against it, becoming its fiercest critic (O'Connor 2009). Another is Kate Oakley, for whom QUT was also a point of reference in charting a change of course, although from the greater distance of a continuing base in the UK. Oakley had been co-author with Charles Leadbeater in the late 1990s of *The Independents: Britain's New Cultural Entrepreneurs* (Leadbeater & Oakley 1999), an important text in the development of creative industries arguments. From the mid-2000s, however, she followed a similar trajectory to O'Connor, becoming increasingly critical of the economic reductionism of their later permutations (Oakley 2009). A third figure worth mentioning is Toby Miller who, while less immediately engaged, moved from a one-time associate of anti-romantic formations in Australia to an uncompromising critic of the idea of the creative industries (Miller 2009).

We do not wish in *Fringe to Famous* to rake over the coals of arguments for or against the creative industries. Despite their heat in the late 2000s, they are arguments that have now largely gone cold. Our interest is rather in the kinds of relation between fringe cultural formations and mainstream institutions that might bring life to arts and culture in the 2020s and beyond. O'Connor (2016: 7) has written in a surprisingly regretful mode of a fading of the creative industries agenda from the mid-2010s: 'The rise of the creative industries ... articulated real aspirations and opportunities whose disappearance represents a significant loss, not only in themselves but to the larger sector of which they are a part.' While he is no less critical than he was in the late 2000s of their economic reductionism, he points now to what may be a greater concern: a vacuum that has been left behind 'after the creative industries'. It is a vacuum, for O'Connor, that reflects a more general malaise at the end of the cycle of neo-liberal reforms that have galvanized public policy thinking since the 1980s: 'Neo-liberalism, as an active reforming agenda may now be moribund but at present there is not much to replace it, and interregnums breed monsters' (O'Connor 2016: 51).

In *Fringe to Famous*, we have responded to the confused crosscurrents of this moment in two ways. The first is relatively modest. In the project meeting in which we confronted the limits of our tolerance for anti-romantic arguments, we agreed that a practical way forward would be to 'go to the empirical'. This has guided our approach to the interview research that provides the main evidence base in the chapters that follow. We avoided organizing the interviews around strongly theorized perspectives, whether they be those suggested by the creative industries advocates or their critical opponents. We decided, that is, to align ourselves neither with ideas such as 'innovation systems' (Cunningham et al. 2004) nor with themes such as the 'precarity' of creative work (Gill & Pratt 2008a). We approached the interviews in a way that was open and conversational, drawing artists, producers, commissioners and cultural activists to offer their own conceptualizations of relations between fringe and mainstream and their own ideas about the value that may or may not be derived from them.

It quickly became clear, on adopting this approach, that the field of creative practice is shaped by similar tensions to the field of scholarly debate. A striking example is the response of cultural activist, festival director and institutional innovator Marcus Westbury when we asked for his thoughts on the idea of the 'cultural entrepreneur', often invoked in attempts to bring together cultural and economic thinking. If the label applies to anyone, one would expect it to apply to Westbury. He is known, among other things, for having brokered access by artists to unused spaces in urban precincts, the 'Renew' initiative that has supported artists while also helping to revitalize run-down centres such as Newcastle on the central coast of New South Wales. Such initiatives draw on a strong anti-romantic strand in Westbury's orientation to culture and the arts. At the beginning of his television series *Not Quite Art*, he sits briefly in an art gallery, playing with the conventions of reverential aestheticism – 'Have you ever just sat in an art gallery and contemplated the work on the wall for hours?' – before shattering them – 'Nah, neither have I!' – and heading for the street. Yet for all his worldly economic nous, Westbury (2014) bristles at the idea of entrepreneurship: 'Whenever I see "entrepreneur" on someone's business card, I just want to punch them in the face.'

There is a certain value in simply documenting these tensions in the field of practice. Doing so confirms, at least, that scholarly debates around the creative industries have been more than academic spats or theoretical navel-gazing. They reflect problems and questions that are also felt in the fields that scholarship seeks to describe. We hope that our attempt in the book to 'think with' practitioners may help to improve the reception of academic analysis in fields of practice. This was a particular weakness of creative industries arguments, which often betrayed frustration at a lukewarm reception among those they were supposed to serve. As Cunningham (2008: 1) put it wistfully, those in the cultural sphere have been their 'own worst enemies in many ways'. To return to the example above, there is clearly a need for a way to recognize the role played by figures such as Westbury, a role that is critical to exchange between fringe and mainstream. But if the term 'entrepreneur' has now acquired such exclusively business connotations as to be disowned by those seeking to realize cultural values, it is no longer a term that can easily be used. In later chapters, therefore, we have preferred others, such as 'animateur'.

Our second response to O'Connor's interregnum has, however, been more ambitious: to attempt a reconceptualization of the relation between fringe and mainstream. In big picture terms, we suggest, the current moment might be seen as the denouement of a fifty-year cycle of thinking about fringe cultural formations since the late 1960s – a point at which both the romanticism of the counterculture and the anti-romantic reaction against it have reached a point of exhaustion. Yet there is also a sense in which current debates remain trapped within these antinomies and unable to move forward. The point might indeed be made of O'Connor himself. In rejecting what he sees as the pollyannaish view by creative industries of commercial processes, he has tended simply to invert it. In the essay cited above, he sets up a stark opposition between culture, represented as 'under immense threat', and a 'market-machine for the capture of "profit without production"', whose dominating logic is financialization and the battery of digitized metrics that goes along with it' (O'Connor 2016: 51–2). The opposition may succeed in reaffirming the distinction between culture and economy, but it is so severe and uncompromising that it becomes impossible to imagine how the two could ever meet.

We do not pretend that it is easy to avoid these antinomies but want to suggest a way they can be moderated. This is to historicize. The approach borrows from one developed by Raymond Williams (1977: 11) in addressing impasses in mid-twentieth-century debates about culture: 'When the most basic concepts ... are suddenly seen to be not concepts but problems ... there is no sense in listening to their sonorous summons or their resounding clashes. We have only, if we can, to recover the substance from which their forms were cast.' It also draws on previous work by Mark Gibson (2007), which adapted the approach to address similar impasses in the 1990s and early 2000s in debates around the concept of power. There are certain similarities between Williams' approach and Michel Foucault's (1977: 31) idea, now more often cited, of 'histories of the present'. The latter shares with Williams in drawing attention, as Ian Hacking (2004: 70) puts it, to 'how our present conceptions were made, how the conditions for their formation constrain our present ways of thinking'. Our only qualification in citing Foucault in this context is that we turn the approach on certain ideas associated with Foucault himself.

The argument we want to make, more specifically, is that the all too familiar positions that organize debates around the idea of the fringe have largely been abstracted from a specific historical experience: the experience of the counterculture of the late 1960s and 1970s – a moment, to state the obvious, that has now well and truly passed. If this is so then, to follow Williams, there is 'no sense in listening to their sonorous summons or resounding clashes'. A more constructive approach is to place them in their context so that it becomes possible to move on. The objective here is particularly to unburden the idea of the fringe from simplistic, reflex charges of romanticism. Without wanting to deny that these charges may have been apt in relation to ideas of the fringe that emerged from the counterculture, it is much less clear that they are so today. At this point, the argument joins with the 'Kirkpatrickan' or cultural history perspective outlined earlier. The two angles we have taken on the conceptualization of the fringe – one empirical, the other more theoretical – reinforce each other in suggesting a need for greater curiosity about fringe cultural phenomena, not merely as discursive constructs but as concrete historical formations.

The uses of history

The case studies we have chosen in *Fringe to Famous* are art forms, to use Bourdieu's (1993) terms, with robust 'fields of restricted production' but which also have impact in the 'field of large-scale production'. Like Frith and Horne in

Art into Pop, we have been interested in cultural forms with a clearly defined 'niche' or 'art' aspect, but which have also resonated in the wider popular culture and achieved commercial success. Rather than focusing on just one art form, medium or genre, we have considered five. Structurally, the book is based around chapters on each of the examples previously mentioned: Australian independent music scenes from the 1980s to the early 2000s; the transformation of local surf wear label Mambo into a successful consumer brand; the creation of a major cycle of Australian television comedy through outreach by public service media and innovation by artist-led independent production companies; the emergence of a network of Indigenous screen creatives as successful screen storytellers at home and abroad; and the development of an experimental and internationally oriented independent games community in Melbourne.

Addressing multiple cases clearly imposes limits on the depth that can be brought to each one, but it was important for us to take a comparative approach. One of the strengths of synoptic terms such as the 'creative industries', and before it the 'cultural industries', has been in raising issues to a level of abstraction that allows them to break through as policy objects, gaining the attention of governments, international bodies and the corporate sector. A further reason for working across artforms is that they are connected, particularly in smaller markets such as Australia. For example, bands such as The Boys Next Door, Sunnyboys, The Go-Betweens and The Triffids emerged from social worlds that intersected closely with those of adjacent fringe formations in art, fashion and journalism, benefitting from the talents of peers who created posters, wrote street press reviews, edited zines and produced records and video clips. Such networks amplify the significance of fringe formations around particular art forms, to the point in some cases that they assume the proportion of subcultures or even movements. Obvious examples since the 1980s would be Mod, Punk, New Romantic and Goth, which have had similar features to older cases such as the Angry Penguins modernist avant-garde of the 1940s.

There have been two major international moments in the period we are considering when accelerated exchange across artforms has occurred. The first was the period following the counterculture, in which aesthetic experimentation was rapidly mass-produced and consumed in popular youth culture. One important development was the breakout of counter-cultural music of the 1960s into the mainstream music industry (The Who, The Rolling Stones, The Kinks, Simon and Garfunkel, The Byrds, Bob Dylan). Another was Monty Python and much of British comedy with origins in university revue and avant-garde or

22 *Fringe to Famous*

countercultural aesthetics. Australian equivalents of this counterculture to pop culture crossover in the 1960s and 1970s included the Dada-esque comedy of Barry Humphries and the absurdist TV series *Aunty Jack*; cinematic translations by Tim Burstall of the Pram Factory's oeuvre to suburban drive-ins; and from the same 'Carlton bohemia', the carnivalesque counter-cultural chart-topping pop groups Daddy Cool and Skyhooks (Australia's Roxy Music) under the aegis of independent record label Mushroom.

The second major international acceleration began with the arrival of punk in the latter half of the 1970s. While best known for re-energizing and democratizing rock n roll music, punk was also much wider in its aesthetic ambition, synthesizing ideas from earlier avant-garde and countercultural movements, including anarchism, nihilism, dada, situationism, pop art and camp, and was a forerunner of the intellectual and aesthetic turn that became known as postmodernism. Punk's impact was felt immediately across fields including design (record covers, posters), screen (music videos, documentaries, feature films), fashion (from DIY subcultural style to Vivien Westwood), publishing and writing (fanzines like *Sniffin' Glue* to glossy magazine *The Face*), and politics (Rock against Racism and Red Wedge). As became clear from our interviews, punk was a major touchstone for the generation of alternative artists coming of age in Australia in the late 1970s and 1980s, much as expressionism and surrealism were for the Melbourne interwar modernist avant-garde.

While we bring the case studies up to the present, the approach we have adopted clearly has a strong historical emphasis. With the partial exception of Chapter 6 on games, we have relatively little to say about the implications of digital media and the challenges they have posed since the 1990s to the 'legacy' cultural industries. This might appear to give *Fringe to Famous* a certain 'retro' quality, particularly when seen together with our defence of the idea of the fringe. Respondents to early conference paper versions of following chapters have sometimes quizzed us on whether we are suggesting a return to subculture theory of the 1970s and 1980s. We have also encountered scepticism that there is anything today to compare with the hallowed fringe formations of the twentieth century. There was indeed a long conversation within the authorial team over whether the 'underground' of the 1970s and 1980s could any longer be said to exist. There is a danger here: if we accept that even the *idea* of the fringe belongs now in the past, then seeking to defend it could only lead to nostalgia.

An obvious general defence of a historical approach is that the past is the only evidence base we have of the factors contributing to cultural and economic value in the arts. It is an evidence base that is surprisingly underused. Even within the limited domain of arts policy, as veteran arts administrator Leigh Tabrett (2013) has pointed out, there is little serious analysis of the effectiveness of previous interventions. While programme evaluation is routine in most other policy domains, the arts are seen implicitly as exceptional, operating not so much on the basis of arguments and evidence as according to a principle of Medician largesse. The creative industries paradigm has gone some way to correcting this, resulting in what has now become a regular flow of well-researched reports on workforce trends, the size of different sectors, the relationship between the subsidized and non-subsidized areas and contributions to gross domestic product (e.g. Trembath & Fielding 2020). As we have remarked, however, the creative industries perspective has excluded factors that cannot be represented in economic terms. If we are to recover a distinction between cultural and economic value, therefore, there is a need for a different kind of analysis of evidence from the recent past.

On the more specific question of whether studying the fringe commits us to nostalgia, we will make three points here before leaving it to readers to judge for themselves. The first is to return to the insight captured in Williams' historicizing method – or, for those who prefer, in Foucault's 'history of the present'. To see new possibilities in the present is often only possible through a reimagining of the past. In current debates around culture and the arts, we appear to be suffering a condition that Ghassan Hage (2009: 101) has called 'stuckedness', 'a situation where a person suffers from both the absence of choices or alternatives to the situation one is in and an inability to grab such alternatives even if they present themselves'. The most obvious response to such situations is to scan the horizon for the 'new', but as Hage implies the problem may be as much in our capacity to *recognize* the new as in whether the new has presented itself. We visit the past in *Fringe to Famous* not to dwell there, but to reshape understandings in such a way that we can 'grab alternatives' that may be immediately in front of us. We return to this idea mostly directly in the conclusion, where we outline ways our arguments might contribute to revitalizing Australian cultural policy in the wake of the creative industries.

A second and related point is that digital media have not transformed the cultural industries as radically as was widely predicted until the 2010s. It has become increasingly clear over the last decade that hierarchical, centre-periphery structures are not the product only of broadcasting or the press but have survived the transition to network distribution. Indeed, the danger in the 2020s is that default assumptions may have swung to the opposite extreme, attributing to 'big tech' an overwhelming power over the field of cultural production. As Jean Burgess et al. (2022: 12) suggest, it is the latter idea that now needs to be tested: 'A potentially serious problem with some of these forms of critique is that they risk echoing, mirroring or amplifying – rather than debunking – the dominant myths about the power of technology.' While the details of these arguments may be specific to digital media, their general form is remarkably similar to mid-twentieth-century debates over the 'culture industry' or even of the nineteenth century in relation to industrial capitalism. This brings into question a common assumption of the 1990s and early 2000s that the emergence of the 'digital' somehow invalidates historical comparison.

Finally, we suggest that there is evidence there, for those who care to look, of contemporary fringe formations. In Chapter 2, for example, we consider the case of young musician Nic Warnock whose practice emerged from a social scene in Western Sydney in the late 2000s and early 2010s. As Warnock (2015) describes it, the scene was organized around the idea of 'more niche, more exciting music, not feeling like … we have to work within the constraints of the music industry and the music press was saying was the stuff we should have'. If we can get past the idea that such aspirations are somehow impossible, 'romantic', we might still fall back on a weaker argument that contemporary fringe formations lack the potency of those of the past. This would leave us looking backwards, even in engaging with the present, to earlier seminal moments when such potency could be found. To do so, however, would be to buy into what is perhaps the greatest conceit of those moments: that their potency belonged entirely to the fringe. Our argument in *Fringe to Famous* is that potency belongs to hybridity. The question for the present then is how to reconnect the fringe and mainstream.

1

Imagining hybridity: A history of the present

How does a focus on crossover and hybridization between fringe and mainstream cultural production place us in relation to others who have worked on independent, alternative or *avant-garde* cultures and practices? What ideas of the 'fringe' and the 'mainstream' do such a focus commit us to? We have begun, in the Introduction, to position our argument, but many questions remain. *Fringe to Famous* is clearly not the first book to address the broad set of issues we are canvassing. There are also histories of more applied thinking, particularly in cultural policy, in which these issues have been extensively engaged. In this chapter, therefore, we attempt to map the field in which the book is situated and which it seeks to address. In doing so, we hope also to provide some bridges between the Australian case studies discussed in following chapters and wider international discussions and debates.

An obvious starting point, as we have already indicated in the Introduction, would be to say that the focus on the crossover between fringe and mainstream puts us at odds with a certain kind of romanticism – a romanticism for which the fringe represents an 'authenticity' or 'purity' to be kept apart from the corrupting influence of mass distribution or the commercial cultural industries. Our interest in the book is precisely the opposite: in *hybridity* between fringe and mainstream, 'culture' and 'commerce'. Like many kinds of hybridity, the phenomenon often involves tensions and difficulties – strained relationships, moments of conflict, difference and dissonance. Our argument, however, is that it is a hybridity that is also enormously *productive*. In the Australian case, it has been the seedbed of many of the major cultural developments of the last forty years and has provided the basis for substantial cultural industries. It is questionable, in this context, whether attempts to isolate or quarantine the fringe are, in any way, desirable.

On this point, the position we are setting out may appear a familiar one. To take a distance from romanticism has indeed become something of an orthodoxy in media and cultural studies over the last thirty or forty years. Once upon a time, the line has run, there were attempts to claim a special status for small cultural circles – an insight or aesthetic sensibility that set them apart. Whether the base for these attempts was in Leavisite literary criticism, Frankfurt School critical theory, music subcultures or artistic avant-gardes, they have been tried and found wanting. They have been condemned, politically, for cultural elitism and, more theoretically, for dubious metaphysical ideas of transcendence. While one might sympathize with some of their aims, it is argued, the romantic tendency is one we must ultimately reject. It might only be expected, therefore, that our position draws to some extent from these general lines of argument.

What may be more surprising, however, is that we also take a distance in *Fringe to Famous* from certain kinds of *anti*-romanticism. This may appear, at first, contradictory, but there is a difference between *taking a distance* from romantic ideas of the fringe and more systematic attempts to eliminate or destroy them. The reasons for wanting to make this distinction will become clearer in what follows, but in summary we could say that the criticisms that have been ranged against romanticism often seem to us to have over-shot their original targets. They have gone well beyond questioning ideas of authenticity, sometimes bringing into question the very idea of the fringe. A scepticism of ideas of a radical 'outside' – a scepticism with which we broadly sympathize – has extended to a more programmatic suspicion of claims even to a cultivation of values that are, in a more ordinary sense, 'different', 'alternative', not widely shared.

The idea we wish to advance in *Fringe to Famous*, of a generative hybridity between the fringe and mainstream, requires that we recognize a difference to be hybridized. In the remainder of this chapter, therefore, we focus somewhat more on the dangers of a zealous anti-romanticism – one that seeks to close off such a recognition – than we do on the better-known pitfalls of romantic ideas of purity and authenticity.

The approach we adopt in the chapter is to offer a historical overview as a background to where we find ourselves today. We attempt, firstly, to trace the origins of anti-romantic tendencies in a reaction to the counterculture and radical movements of the 1960s and 1970s. Secondly, we consider a kind of compromise settlement between romantic and anti-romantic positions that developed during the 1980s and 1990s. In academic writing, this took the form of a broadly 'Foucauldian' formula (referencing the work of Michel Foucault, although the 'formula' might be considered as a broader phenomenon); in social democratic politics, it was developed through the idea of cultural policy. Thirdly, we review the disintegration of these formulae and the emergence of two divergent perspectives that have developed in response: one we have labelled the 'creative industries paradigm' and the other 'left culturalism'.

Finally, we suggest a basis on which one might now affirm a hybridity between the fringe and the mainstream. This basis is found in work that avoids both romantic and anti-romantic tendencies, drawing particularly from what might be called the 'cultural industries' moment of the 1980s – a key example being Simon Frith and Howard Horne's (1987) classic *Art Into Pop* – and, for a more theoretical articulation, from approaches drawn from the cultural sociology of Pierre Bourdieu.

Before proceeding, however, it may be worth reflecting briefly on Australia not only as a field from which we have chosen our empirical case studies, but as a location from which to think about these general issues. Since at least the 1980s, Australian work in media and cultural studies has shown particularly strong anti-romantic tendencies – to the point, at times, when an 'Australian' position in international debates has been identified in these terms (see, for example, Jameson 1993: 29–30). The figure who best exemplifies these tendencies is probably the cultural theorist and intellectual historian Ian Hunter (1992; 2001), whose influence has been more pervasive in Australian media and cultural studies than his international visibility in these fields might suggest. Perhaps better known are two broader Australian intellectual formations in which anti-romantic tendencies have been developed in systematic ways – the so-called 'cultural policy' position of the 1990s (Bennett 1992; Cunningham 1992; Bennett 1998) and the 'creative industries' arguments associated with the Centre for Creative Industries and Innovation in the mid-2000s (Cunningham 2002; Hartley 2005a; Flew 2012).

Fringe to Famous has been influenced by these formations and borrows from them in a variety of ways. But we would locate ourselves within a counter-tradition in Australia that has always also been present. This is a counter-tradition that was revealed most explicitly during the 'cultural policy' debates of the 1990s, in critical responses by figures such as Tom O'Regan (1992), Meaghan Morris (1992a) and McKenzie Wark (1992). These responses shared a certain Australian idiom – unsentimental, irreverent, suspicious of metropolitan pretension – but refused the tendency for a scepticism of romantic claims to harden into its own form of dogma. Many of the cultural forms discussed in the book could be seen as also belonging, to use Raymond Williams' great phrase, to this 'structure of feeling'. The art of Reg Mombassa might be taken as emblematic. It embraces the secular, the material, the profane; it adopts stylistic elements from commercial art and popular media; but there is always also a nod of recognition to something else, a difference that is not entirely explicable in these terms – the difference, that is, of the fringe.

The shadow of the counterculture

What could account for an animus against the idea of the fringe? What could explain a desire to exclude or deny it? It is often suggested that hostility towards the fringe can simply be attributed to social conservatism. There is clearly some basis for this. An example from Australia might be the Christian conservative and 'family values' crusader, the Reverend Fred Nile, who campaigned for decades against the Sydney Gay and Lesbian Mardi Gras. It is a mistake, however, to overstate the influence of this kind of conservative censure. While it may often have contributed to localized forms of repression, its political and cultural potency has proven, in the long term, limited. Nile was reduced in later years to praying for rain with a diminishing band of followers, while Mardi Gras swelled to become a major civic festival, broadcast on national television and reaching out to include families from the suburbs (Marsh & Galbraith 1995). Nile himself became a parodic figure, often appearing in effigy on Mardi Gras floats, alongside spangled semi-naked figures, mustachioed men in leather-clad embrace and the wonderfully named 'Dykes on Bikes'.

What has not been sufficiently recognized is that the more serious challenge to the idea of the fringe has come from *within* – from those who have themselves been closely associated with fringe cultural forms. A graphic example is provided by the Canadian scholars Joseph Heath and Andrew Potter (2004) in their book *Nation of Rebels*, which takes aim more specifically at the idea of the 'counterculture'. For Heath and Potter (2004: 31), the ultimate logic of this idea was captured in the gruesome 1994 suicide of Kurt Cobain: 'Cobain had taken a lethal overdose of heroin, but, for good measure, had decided to finish the job by blowing off the left side of his head with a Remington 20-gauge shotgun.' The important point here is that Heath and Potter strongly *identify* with Cobain. They see their criticisms as applying also to 'us punks' (15) – those who have loved the music and who shared a similar history. Yet the criticisms are also uncompromising. The suicide, they argue, was more than an individual act of despair: Cobain was the 'victim of a false idea – the idea of the counterculture' (13).

For Heath and Potter, the idea of the counterculture has been a prison-house. It has set impossible standards of what it is to exist outside the 'mainstream', leading people into positions that are literally unliveable. There are certain ironies to this critique. Heath and Potter reject the countercultural tendency to represent the mainstream as if it is a single, homogeneous entity: 'capitalism', 'the system', the 'dominant paradigm'. Yet the idea of the counterculture *itself* looms for them as an object of precisely this kind – one whose hold appears, if anything, to be even more tyrannical. It is an idea, they argue, that

> has become so deeply entrenched in our understanding of society that it influences every aspect of social and political life. Most importantly, it has become the conceptual template for all contemporary leftist politics … So if the counterculture is a myth, then it has misled an enormous number of people, with untold political consequences.
>
> (Heath & Potter 2004: 16)

This seems to us part of a wider pattern. The last thirty years have seen a sustained and wide-ranging effort by many of those who were touched by the counterculture to expose and cauterize the continuing influence of ideas associated with the fringe cultures of the 1960s and 1970s – to neutralize or reverse what are seen as problematic aspects of their cultural and political legacy.

To explore this phenomenon fully would require a history of the counterculture and its extraordinary persistence as a point of reference in debates around culture over what is now more than half a century. It is clearly not possible to offer such a history here. The important point, however, is that in the 1960s and 1970s fringe cultures became strongly associated with the idea of revolution. As Todd Gitlin puts in his book, *The Sixties*, as one who was himself involved in movements in the United States at the time:

> To invoke The Revolution was to claim title to the future; to see beyond the raids and trials and wiretaps and empire and war and guilt … *The* Revolution: The name of our desire became firm and precise … To speak of the Revolution was automatically to acquire a pedigree, heroes, martyrs, allies, texts, and therefore anchorage.
>
> (Gitlin 1987: 345–6)

There are three closely related developments that might be identified here. The first was the assumption by the fringe of an oracular status. The crisis of political and institutional legitimacy of the 1960s and 1970s – a crisis captured by Gitlin in the image of 'raids and trials and wiretaps and empire and war and guilt' – produced a vacuum that allowed the perspectives of fringe groups to gain a surprising currency. As the Establishment was discredited, the fringe came into view as a potential source of revelation or truth. The second development was an extraordinary conviction associated with this: 'the name of our desire became firm and precise'. The third was an intellectual audacity and aspiration to system-building. The idea of revolution supplied 'a pedigree, heroes, martyrs, allies, texts'. It offered, above all, 'anchorage' – a firm foundation on which to build.

Amongst all these strengths, however, and inseparable from them, are the problems identified by Heath and Potter. While the oracular status accorded to the fringe gave it a potency it would not otherwise have had, it also burdened it with expectations of purity and authenticity. While the conviction of the counterculture enabled a boldness and capacity for action, it also sowed the seeds of hubris. While the intellectual system-building associated with the idea of revolution offered a seductive power and reach, it also risked becoming a prison-house – an internally consistent labyrinth without windows onto other worlds. If ideas of the fringe since the 1960s have developed in the shadow of the counterculture, it is this dual aspect that we need to understand – the volatile *internal* relation between identification and rejection, hope and despair.

The Foucauldian formula

In academic writing, a major touchstone in working through this legacy has been the writing of Michel Foucault, which has come to represent a hinge or balance-point between keeping faith with and rejecting ideas of revolution that came out of the 1960s and 1970s. There is some basis for this in the life and work of the man himself. Foucault was, on the one hand, a romantic figure, with impeccable credentials as a radical thinker and 'outsider'. He was a French intellectual who spent a formative stage of his career immersed in the political and cultural turbulence following the events in Paris of May 1968. He was an activist for prisoners, dissidents, homosexuals and other marginal groups. And he participated, himself, in bohemian milieux – particularly gay underground scenes in Paris, Hamburg and San Francisco (Macey 1993). On the other hand, he can be seen as exemplary in his *rejection* of romanticism. He was a searching internal critic of the left, intensely conscious of the ways in which revolutionary and liberatory movements can produce their own orthodoxies and generate their own forms of authoritarianism. He was also an influential innovator in anti-romantic forms of analysis, representing human affairs in terms of 'technologies', 'apparatuses' and forms of 'governmentality'.

The context for Foucault's own thinking can be gauged most readily from his occasional political writings and particularly his interviews (Gordon 1980). In a 1971 interview with some Maoist militants, for example, he questions the idea of establishing 'people's courts' to try the police for violence during clashes with popular revolutionary movements. Such an idea, he suggests, risks recreating the political structure it seeks to oppose:

> Can we not see the embryonic, albeit fragile form of a state apparatus reappearing here? The possibility of class oppression? ... I am wondering whether the court is not a form of popular justice but rather its first deformation.
>
> (Foucault 1980: 2)

It is worth noting the *mildness* of Foucault's probing here. At no point does he question the desire for revolution as such and it would be fair to characterize the interview as a respectful conversation 'among comrades'. At the same time, he introduces a note of caution about where the idea of revolution might lead. He refers in the interview to the lessons of the French Revolution. Stalinism and the Soviet Union would almost certainly have also been somewhere in mind. Foucault had spent time in Warsaw in the 1950s and remained in contact throughout his life with political dissidents in Eastern Europe.

These concerns can also be seen as informing much of Foucault's theoretical and historical writing. His subjects were almost always of a kind that might be expected to incite ideas of revolution or liberation – prison systems, discipline, punishment, surveillance, sexual repression and regimes of power. It is also significant that the *possibility* of revolution is never categorically denied. Yet Foucault also sought consistently to question the ground for any simple or naïve revolutionary conviction.

The characteristic move here was to ask whether there is any pure 'outside' to the regimes or systems from which we seek liberation (Gibson 2007: 24–5). This was, in fact, the key point of contention in the interview cited above. For his Maoist interlocutors, 'the people' were an agent external to the system; if they were to take possession of the courts, they could therefore be trusted to bend them to the ends of the revolution. For Foucault, by contrast, the social relations to be found within the courts cannot be dissociated from the *form* of the court. Simply changing the identity of the agents will not change that form, so the social relations will remain intact. Many of Foucault's more influential ideas turn around a similar argument. The structure of panoptic surveillance systems, the implication of subject positions in discourses of power, the inseparability of ideas of sexual liberation from ideas of repression, the inherence of all political relations in forms of 'governmentality': in each case, Foucault introduces problems or challenges to the idea that there could be any simple or straightforward overthrow of 'the system'.

This dual character has made Foucault a multivalent figure who has been used to authorize widely divergent positions. In the mid-1990s he was being claimed, on the one hand, by David Halperin as a patron saint for the AIDS Coalition to Unleash Power (ACT UP) and queer political activism. For Halperin (1995: 3), Foucault was 'a gay man whose life and work have come to represent, especially since his death from AIDS in 1984, important sources of intellectual and political inspiration to many lesbians and gay men, as well as to a number of variously identified cultural radicals'. He was, decidedly, a figure of the fringe. Yet at the same time, Foucault was being invoked by Tony Bennett in *Culture: A Reformer's Science* as the very model of political sobriety. The value of Foucault for Bennett (1998: 70) lies in his rejection of 'heady' approaches to questions of power – his injunction to take account of 'the more mundane and technical means through which power is routinely exercised'. The anti-romantic aspect of the Foucauldian formula is heavily underlined. Foucault's perspective encourages us, Bennett suggests, 'to focus on the detailed routines and operating procedures of cultural institutions'; they 'allow us to see how cultural resources are always caught up in, and function as parts of, cultural technologies which ... play an important role in organising different fields of human conduct' (Bennett 1998: 82).

But this tension of the 1990s between the 'radical' and 'sober' Foucault, between Halperin and Bennett, has resolved over time very much in favour of the latter. Indeed, Foucault can now be seen in retrospect as something of a staging post, allowing an organized retreat from the counterculture and the revolutionary mood of the 1960s and 1970s. Bennett once admitted that his engagement with Foucault was, in part, a settling of accounts with his own 'erstwhile theoretical self' (quoted in O'Regan 1992: 419). It was a way of subduing the impulses associated with the cultural Marxism to which he, himself, had previously subscribed. Once this bridge was crossed, it was no longer strictly required.

While Bennett's trajectory in this has had its own specificity – moving on to Latour, Bourdieu and various other interests – it can also be seen as part of a wider movement towards a more technical, 'applied' focus in media and cultural studies. This movement is often attributed to external factors – demands from outside the academy that knowledge be 'useful', the need to engage with technical aspects of changes within media, the dominance of 'neoliberal' ideologies. But it is important, again, to recognize that there has also been an internal process at work. The invocation of 'detailed routines and operating procedures' has served quite a specific *rhetorical* function. It has been a counter-theme and riposte to figures of revolution and resistance; it has worked continually to neutralize or reverse any lingering influences of the counterculture.

A significant fallout from this has been increasing pressure on the very *idea* of the fringe. Taken seriously, the Foucauldian formula demands that there can be no recognition of an 'outside' to the dominant system. In fact – and as Foucault himself argued – the very idea of 'dominance' is brought into question. If there is nothing external to regimes of power, then there is nothing left for those regimes to dominate. Power needs to be thought of in entirely different terms. The implications for the idea of the fringe are clear. To the extent at least that the fringe is thought of as a sphere removed or set apart from the 'mainstream', there can be, strictly speaking, no fringe.

The 'cultural policy' formula

A similar line of development can be traced in progressive politics outside the academy. It can be seen particularly in the centre-left governments of the late 1980s and 1990s – the Hawke-Keating government in Australia, the Clinton Democrats in the United States and New Labour in Britain. These governments were, to varying degrees, porous to ideas that first emerged within fringe groups in the 1960s and 1970s, but also tempered them in significant ways.

They were resistant, in particular, to their more reflective ethical and aesthetic modes. As accounts such as Gitlin's make clear, the counterculture was a ferment of ideas about what might constitute a good society, with a bewildering array of comparative models in play: rural communes, nineteenth-century avant-gardes, Maoism, matriarchal societies, Indian mysticism, Black cultures of the American deep south and the cosmologies of Indigenous peoples. The centre-left governments of the 1980s and 1990s were marked, by contrast, by a much narrower consensus around values. The *ends* of progressive politics were taken largely as given – being defined, for the most part, by a pursuit, within a post-industrial market-based economy, of greater formal equality around gender, race and class. Debate was constrained to technical questions around *means*.

An important terrain for the negotiation of this tension has been cultural policy. By this, we mean policy that has taken culture as an explicit object, as distinct from an older state patronage of the arts. The origins of the idea of cultural policy in this sense are often traced to the Greater London Council in the early 1980s (Bianchini 1987; Garnham 1987; O'Connor 2009), but the major example at national level was Australia's *Creative Nation*. Launched in 1994 by Prime Minister Paul Keating, one-time manager of a rock band called the Ramrods, the policy made clear overtures to the counterculture. It borrowed some of its heroic quality, proclaiming itself 'the first cultural policy document in our history' and promising finally to drive a stake through the heart of the 'cultural cringe' – the colonial belief that 'nothing Australian should be considered of cultural value until it has been approved in London, or perhaps New York'. It also engaged openly in a reflection on values:

> To speak of Australian culture is to recognise our common heritage. It is to say that we share ideas, values, sentiments and traditions, and that we see in all the various manifestations of these what it means to be Australian ... We seek to preserve our culture because it is fundamental to our understanding of who we are. It is the name we go by, the house in which we live. Culture is that which gives us a sense of ourselves.
>
> (DCA 1994)

At the same time, influences associated with the counterculture were contained. The significance of their admission in *cultural* policy can only be understood alongside their exclusion elsewhere. Keating had little tolerance, in particular, for deviations from hard, 'expert' approaches to economic management, famously deriding advocates of alternatives as 'Balmain basket-weavers' (Morris 1992b; Bowen 2015).[1] While culture is honoured in *Creative Nation*, it is confined to the

---

[1] For non-Australian readers, Balmain is a suburb in Sydney that might be loosely compared with Islington in London or, perhaps, Haight-Ashbury in San Francisco. It has a strong working-class history and was the original site for the formation of the union movement in New South Wales. It gentrified rapidly in the post-war period, but retained a reputation – at least until the 1980s – as a site of political radicalism.

sphere of expression and identity. It is also tied to superordinate goals of national development and, more fatefully, economic growth:

> This cultural policy is also an economic policy. Culture creates wealth. Broadly defined, our cultural industries generate 13 billion dollars a year. Culture employs. Around 336,000 Australians are employed in culture-related industries. Culture adds value, it makes an essential contribution to innovation, marketing and design … It attracts tourists and students. It is essential to our economic success.
>
> (DCA 1994)

These tendencies were greatly amplified in the 'Creative Industries' platform of New Labour in Britain in the late 1990s and early 2000s. The latter still offered bridges to the counterculture. The theme of 'Cool Britannia' sought to revive the memory of Swinging London of the 1960s and was experienced within the arts and cultural sector at the time as the end of a state of siege – a welcome relief after the long years of repression under the conservative governments of Thatcher and Major (Greenhalgh 1998). As the name suggests, 'Cool Britannia' followed Australia's 'Creative Nation' in capturing these energies to nationalism. But there was also a significant departure in the completeness of their subordination to economic development. Unlike the Australian policy, 'Creative Industries' did not include a framing affirmation of the importance of 'ideas, values, sentiments and traditions'. Its centrepiece was a 'mapping document', assessing the contribution to the national economy of a number of industry sectors: advertising, antiques, architecture, crafts, design, fashion, film, leisure software, music, performing arts, publishing, software, TV and radio. The policy was bluntly presented and the language detailed and technical. The section on design, for example, opens without a preamble as follows:

> Fees earned by UK designers abroad have doubled in the past decade, amounting to £350m in 1995. Some 20% of design companies generate at least a quarter of their fee income from overseas sales. The largest consultancies are the most globally focussed and the most dependent on overseas markets.
>
> (DCMS 1998)

The programme can be read against the background of internal divisions in British Labour over how much to retain and how much to jettison of the radical language the party had absorbed during the period of the New Left and the counterculture (Panitch & Leys 1996). 'Creative Industries' was firmly on the side of jettisoning. While culture was admitted (or at least 'creativity'), it was only when subordinated to market discipline and a clear refusal of older revolutionary themes.

Social democratic thinking around cultural policy has followed a similar trajectory, therefore, to Foucauldian frameworks within the academy. Both formations were, in their development, relatively porous to ideas emerging from the fringe. But both formations have also offered mechanisms of containment – ways of restricting the influence of those ideas, particularly of any revolutionary implications that may have been associated with them. In both cases, these mechanisms have hardened to the point where they have become not so much mechanisms of containment as of expulsion or abjection. In both cases too, this turn is best described not as a conservative prohibition of the fringe, but as a progressive *inhibition*. It has come not in the form of external action, but an internal reaction – the determination of a movement to disavow the fringe cultures that were once the source of much of its energy.

The creative industries paradigm

It is in the fallout of these developments that we have sought, in *Fringe to Famous*, to examine the crossover between fringe and mainstream. If the compromise settlements sketched above have disintegrated, no longer able to manage their internal contradictions, how might we construct new kinds of relations? Where are the materials for doing so?

If we consider the state of play in academic writing, the situation does not at first appear promising. The dissolution of the Foucauldian formula has resulted in a separation and polarization between the two contradictory tendencies that the formula had held in tension. It has resulted in work, on the one hand, in which the anti-romantic tendency is taken to its logical extreme. A key example of this, for us, has been the Australian 'creative industries' paradigm mentioned at the beginning of the chapter – not to be simply identified, we should say, with the British New Labour *policy*. This has been a paradigm in which anything that might qualify as 'fringe' is represented as adhering to the values and logics of market relations: there is no longer any difference to be hybridized. On the other hand, there has emerged a kind of neo-romanticism – an effort to reinstate the difference of the fringe. In this case, an emphasis on conflict and contradiction appears to foreclose any prospect of crossover or hybridity.

We suggest in what follows that there are nevertheless grounds for optimism. Our argument throughout the book is that closer empirical engagement with actual fringe cultures can free us from some of the problems associated with the abstract *figure* of the fringe inherited from the contexts we have sketched above. Examples from our own research will follow in later chapters. In what remains here, however, we point to positive potentials emerging from the breakdown of the formations that have dominated thinking about the significance of the fringe since the 1960s and 1970s. In short, we do not see *Fringe to Famous* as cutting entirely against the grain of other work in the field. While there are points of difference, the book meets up with developments that are also appearing elsewhere.

If we turn first to the creative industries paradigm, initial appearances here seem particularly unpromising. At least in its programmatic manifestos (Cunningham 2002; Hartley & Cunningham 2002; Hartley 2005a), the paradigm has waged an uncompromising campaign against romantic tendencies in media and cultural studies. As a result, it has come to be seen by many as representing a nightmarish capitulation to the business school – a 'surrender of the field', as Graeme Turner (2011) colourfully put it, to a narrow economic instrumentalism. If there is still a place for the fringe in the creative industries paradigm, it would appear to be only in a neutered form – as an 'R&D incubator' for business development in the creative industries (Cunningham *et al* 2004). There is no space allowed within the paradigm for anything that does not belong within a single, continuous terrain defined by business interests and market relations. Everything takes its place as a functional element in what would once have been called the 'mainstream'.

In case there is any doubt here, and to reinforce what we have already stated in the Introduction, we do not subscribe to this kind of economic reductionism. We wonder, in fact, whether the principals in developing the perspective entirely believe it themselves: they have been accomplished exponents – indeed leaders – of cultural analysis at earlier stages in their own careers (Cunningham 1991; Hartley 1992; Hartley 1996). But there are other ways to consider the creative industries paradigm than in terms of its theoretical adequacy or 'truth'. The paradigm is perhaps more productively viewed as a kind of experiment or 'What if?': What if we push the Foucauldian formula beyond its breaking point? What do things look like on the other side?

The important point to note about the monistic perspective of the Creative Industries paradigm is that it normalizes relations between 'large' and 'small' scale cultural production – between the 'mainstream media' and those agents that have traditionally been labelled 'amateur', 'independent' or 'alternative'. Within the Foucauldian formula, such relations continue to be coded in terms of 'power' and 'resistance'. Foucauldians may point to nuance and complexity in how these terms are used, but the emphasis on antagonism remains. It is an emphasis that inhibits recognition of movement or crossover between 'large' and 'small', let alone fusion or hybridity. The radical *post*-Foucauldian character of the creative industries paradigm allows this inhibition to be removed.

A good example is a book by Stuart Cunningham on social media entertainment, co-authored with American television and media industries scholar, David Craig (Cunningham & Craig 2019). The book might be described not only as post-Foucauldian (even though, admittedly, Foucault is occasionally invoked as an authorizing point of reference), but in a certain sense also 'post creative industries'. While the work it presents is heavily conditioned by the creative industries agenda – an agenda for which Cunningham has been a tireless advocate – it is less concerned with prosecuting the case than with exploring the terrain that emerges if one accepts it as a point of view. The book examines a phenomenon that might classically be described as 'fringe'. It is a study of 'social media creators' – media practitioners who start as complete unknowns, gathering small followings on online platforms such as YouTube and Instagram and start to develop wider connections from there.

What is remarkable about the study, in terms of the issues we have been raising, is how straightforwardly it is able to represent movement and hybridity between 'small'- and 'large'-scale cultural production. Social media creators, as Cunningham and Craig describe them, range from rank amateurs – teenagers in the bedroom, with no media training, experimenting in front of the camera for a handful of friends – to major international franchises such as the Swedish YouTuber PewDiePie, who has received billions of page views and generates advertising revenue in the millions of dollars per annum. Between these two extremes, there is a spectrum involving various degrees of fusion between the DIY style of small online communities and professional practices borrowed from more established figures or the mainstream media. The framework is one that allows Cunningham and Craig to develop a detailed and sophisticated account of the way the phenomenon is being shaped by technologies, policies and business strategies.

The only thing that remains underdeveloped in this account, for us, is attention to the specifically cultural dimension. It is not that awareness of, or commitment to, this dimension is entirely absent. Cunningham and Craig's motivation is, in part, to validate young creators who are working to build communities in online spaces. There is often a poignancy to their account of the existential positions of these figures – a poignancy that is impressive given their generational distance from the figures themselves. Speaking at the Melbourne launch of the book, Julian Thomas suggested a parallel with E.P. Thompson's classic *The Making of the English Working Class*. It could be read as an attempt to trace bottom-up forms of organization around cultural expression in communities who lack access to established institutions. Yet the cultural dimension is also clouded by the intellectual formation of the project in the creative industries paradigm – a paradigm, as we have seen, that refuses the idea of an 'outside' to business structures and processes.

Cunningham and Craig come closest to departing from this perspective in a chapter on the cultural politics of social media entertainment. They point out that digital media forms are much more socially diverse than mainstream media – a fact that certainly deserves attention. Examples include the prominence of LGBTQ creators in social media entertainment and Asian Americans in the United States. These are discussed in the context of classical theories of the cultural politics of representation, such as George Gerbner and Larry Gross's argument that an absence of media representation for a social group involves a 'symbolic annihilation' (Cunningham & Craig 2019: 187). In practice, however, such groups are considered only as equity categories. The emphasis is on the mere fact of their presence in social media entertainment, not the cultures they may be developing on online platforms – or the differences between such cultures and the 'mainstream'. While a space is opened up for a recognition of cultural hybridity between the fringe and mainstream, this space remains unexplored.

In summary then, the creative industries paradigm is strong in its attention to *crossover* between the fringe and mainstream, but weak in its attention to *difference*. It is a weakness that might possibly be overcome. There are, indeed, positive signs in the work of younger scholars who, while associated with the paradigm, have been less involved in its formation. Some of this work has explored cultural differences in fringe social media formations in more substantial ways. But the weakness is also one that is more than accidental. The paradigm has been formed around a systematic anti-romanticism: the lack of attention to cultural difference is not simply an oversight; it is inherent in the way the paradigm has formed.

Left culturalism

The major attempt to address this weakness has been in the other, contrasting, response to the dissolution of the Foucauldian formula – what we will call 'left culturalism'. The term has been used in the past in relation to early British cultural studies (Milner 1994), but we will use it here to refer rather to a tendency that emerged from around the mid-2000s in response to a widespread displacement of cultural discourses by economic forms of analysis. Some of the sharpest formulations have been in criticisms of the idea of the creative industries – both the Australian paradigm discussed above and the policy approach originating with British New Labour (Oakley 2004; Schlesinger 2007; Banks & Hesmondhalgh 2009; O'Connor 2009), but these criticisms can also be seen as part of a more general front. Left culturalism, in the sense we are using it, has been particularly strong in the UK, through the work of figures such as Angela McRobbie, David Hesmondhalgh, Mark Banks, Kate Oakley, Andy Pratt, Philip Schlesinger and, although he now works in Australia, Justin O'Connor. It also meets up in various ways with critiques of 'neoliberalism' (Brown 2015; Davies 2015), although the latter have a much wider ambit.

Much of the recent work that has explicitly addressed questions of the 'fringe', 'alternative', 'independent' or 'avant-garde' has developed within this general formation. An example is James Bennett and Niki Strange's (2015) edited collection *Media Independence*. The interest of the book is signalled in the title. In his introduction, Bennett (2015: 1) sets the theme by quoting a definition from the *Oxford English Dictionary*:

> *Independence*: The condition or quality of being independent; the fact of not depending on another; exemption from external control or support; freedom from subjection, or from the influence of others; individual liberty of thought or action.

The agenda being set here could be seen as the opposite of that of the Creative Industries paradigm. It is to assert – or perhaps rather to *re*-assert – the possibility of genuine difference within media or cultural systems. It is to invite us to consider areas or practices as 'not depending' on the rationales or logics that govern wider economies.

This agenda suggests the kind of framework needed for a recognition of the specificity of the fringe. But it must also be noted that it has a defensive quality. Bennett wants to argue that the principle of independence is important: 'Media independence', he suggests, 'is central to the organization, make-up, working practices and output of media systems across the globe' (Bennett 2015: 1). But he is on guard, from the outset, against possible criticisms. In fact, he avoids committing himself to the idea that independence within the media is an actual reality, suggesting instead that it is a 'utopian ideal' (2) – something that is *aspired to* in the knowledge that it can never be achieved. Independence, in this perspective, is not a positive phenomenon but a discursive construct. It belongs, variously, to a set of ideas about liberal democracies, to industrial categories in the packaging of media and culture, to aesthetic codes and ideas of cultural value, or to moral or ethical ideas about working practices in the media.

A similar tendency to hedge the defence of the idea of independence can be found in other contributions to the collection. In a chapter on the concepts of the 'alternative' and 'independent' in popular music, for example, David Hesmondhalgh and Leslie Meier (2015) feel bound to acknowledge that these concepts are dubious. Music was given a special place in post-Enlightenment aesthetics, they admit, because of supposedly special links to subjectivity – links that were thought to be manifest in its power 'to express, arouse or instil emotion':

> Versions of that idea are often naïve and ill thought out, and are often dismissed by sniffy theorists as 'romantic'. But many versions hint at real contradictions and struggles over culture in societies where capitalism provides the main way economic life is conducted.
>
> (Hesmondhalgh & Meier 2015: 96)

The strategy taken here is common in many recent attempts to uphold the idea of the independent or the fringe: to concede the 'naivety' of the idea, but find ways of offering qualified affirmations nonetheless. Hesmondhalgh and Meier are clearly uncomfortable with the reflex responses of 'sniffy theorists' and they attempt to neutralize criticisms of romanticism by placing the word in scare quotes. Ultimately, however, they submit to the perspective they are wanting to push back against. A saving grace is found for the idea of independence only in the fact that it has meaning *for others* or that, despite its errors, it indirectly registers problems or tensions that *are* real.

Such defences of the idea of independence seem to us to concede too much to the anti-romantic arguments they are seeking to resist. Hesmondhalgh and Meier's characterizations of the idea of independence are characterizations that belong to quite specific ideas of the 'alternative' or the 'fringe'. They are ideas that can be traced most directly to the notion of the fringe as oracle – a notion, as we have seen, that was associated with the counterculture. While, for Hesmondhalgh and Meier, this notion must now be heavily qualified, held back from revealing itself in its 'naïve' form, it remains the notion that is presented for consideration. The perspective is one in which the independent and the mainstream continue to be represented as starkly opposed totalities ('freedom' vs 'capitalism'; 'subjectivity' vs 'instrumentalism') and an accent is placed on struggle and contradiction.

While left culturalism makes an essential contribution in affirming the possibility of values other than those of the market, therefore, it also leaves us with two problems. The first is an inhibition about recognizing those values in positive terms. This problem could also be seen to affect the work on independent cinema of scholars such as Geoff King (2005) and Alisa Perren (2012). This work is clearly motivated by a belief that the principle of independence is an important one. King (2005: ix) dedicates his book on American independent cinema to 'the many independent filmmakers [...] whose work continues to inspire' and it is obvious that he has deep knowledge of and respect for those who work in the field. Yet he is also compelled repeatedly to put the word 'independent' in inverted commas. Admittedly, this is often necessary as a way of highlighting the way it has been taken up as a category within marketing and promotional discourses – a phenomenon that is ironized in the title of Perren's book, *Indie, Inc.* But an intense self-consciousness of the discursive aspect is also corrosive of the idea that the word could *ever* describe actual qualities of cultural production – that independence from the institutions and values of the market is, indeed, possible.

A second problem has been a tendency to tie the recognition of independence to themes of conflict and opposition. For Hesmondhalgh and Meier, this recognition is introduced through reference to 'contradictions and struggles'. The theme of conflict is also central to the extensive literature on creative labour, which has increasingly reached back before Foucault to Marxist concepts of exploitation and class struggle. In an agenda-setting essay introducing a double issue of *Theory, Culture and Society*, for example, Rosalind Gill and Andy Pratt (2008b) suggest that we understand the position of fringe cultural workers through the work of Italian autonomist Marxists such as Antonio Negri and Maurizio Lazzarato. We should see such workers, that is, as belonging to a 'precariat' – a subaltern class defined by a structural antagonism to new forms of capitalism. The scholarship in this field is extensive and it is not possible to summarize it with any justice here. Suffice to say that it represents the fringe and the mainstream as radically opposed. It is inimical, in other words, to the themes we wish to develop of crossover and hybridity.

As in the case of the creative industries paradigm, however, other possibilities have emerged at the edges of this broad approach. An example here might be the work of Angela McRobbie. Indeed, McRobbie could be seen as something of a crossover figure between the two tendencies we have been discussing here. She has been quite strongly identified with the perspective we are calling left culturalism: she has never entirely broken from her early formation in the Birmingham Centre for Contemporary Cultural Studies in the 1970s and 1980s, she was an early critic of creative industries policy in the UK (McRobbie 2004), she has written extensively on creative labour (McRobbie 1999; 2002) and has been a significant figure in the debates referenced by Gill and Pratt. Yet she has also been at least somewhere within the orbit of perspectives associated with the creative industries idea. It is perhaps significant that hers is the only clearly identified 'critical' piece included in John Hartley's (2005b) edited collection on the creative industries (McGuigan 2006).

An important context for McRobbie's work has been her teaching practice, which has put her in continuous contact with young, aspiring creative practitioners. She opens her book *Be Creative* by describing her Wednesday afternoon consultations with Masters students at Goldsmiths College in London: 'What I have seen unfolding in front of my eyes during these supervisions is a microcosm of the new creative labour market' (McRobbie 2016: 1). The student cohort, which is largely international, has significant work experience – ranging from 'events management in Athens, to working behind the counter in a fashion chain like *Zara* in Madrid, to having an internship on a women's magazine, to working in a gallery in Istanbul' (2). It represents, in many ways, a front line in a globalizing interface between fringe cultures and the commercial cultural and creative industries.

McRobbie admits that she has, in the past, been suspicious of this interface. For many years, she stopped teaching subculture theory, realizing how easily the classical work of Birmingham figures such as Dick Hebdige could be turned to commercial ends:

> The pathway here could be traced through the idea of bricolage, 'cut ups' and the subversion of style, as theorized by Hebdige, finding its way out of the classroom or seminar room of the art school into the hands of the fashion designers, the graphic designers and communications graduates able to translate the ideas

of the street and of 'authentic' working-class culture or even of revolt into the
very stuff of collections, or for the 'edgy' visual image of global labels such as
Dior or YSL.

(McRobbie 2016: 7–8)

Over time, however, McRobbie has developed a more sympathetic view of this
ambiguous hybrid space. While she would clearly still prefer that there was a
clearer separation between culture and commerce, she recognizes the complexity
of the world to which her students belong and has softened her insistence that
they be kept apart. Just because something is of commercial value, she concedes,
does not mean that other values may not still be active: 'The commercial value
of what Sarah Thornton called "subcultural capital" cannot be under-estimated
but this does not mean its field of influence is totally depleted of political value'
(McRobbie 2016: 8). In contrast to the general emphasis of left culturalism on
conflict and contradiction, she sees room for compromise.

Imagining hybridity

If we were to position *Fringe to Famous* in relation to recent literature in media
and cultural studies, it might be at the point where McRobbie meets Cunningham
and Craig. We have suggested that the two positions have developed out
of different responses to the breakdown of the Foucauldian and 'cultural policy'
formulae – formulae that made it possible, from the 1980s to the early 2000s,
both to associate with the fringe *and* to claim a relation to the 'hard' disciplines
of governmental and economic thinking. They are responses that have been
strongly divergent – often indeed antagonistic – but the grounds for divergence
seem to us also be moderating. It is in this space that we see potential to define
new relations between the 'fringe' and 'mainstream'.

In the remainder of the chapter, we will indicate three ways in which we
have sought to strengthen this potential. The first has been to historicize the
idea of the fringe. Many of the problems we have considered above can be
traced to the capture of this idea by the intellectual and political paradigms
that developed around the counterculture – paradigms, as we have seen, in
which the fringe was associated with revolution. It is this theme that triggered
the internal reaction against the counterculture of figures such as Heath and
Potter, that spurred Tony Bennett and others of his generation to prosecute a
campaign against their 'erstwhile selves'. It is its continuing shadowy presence

that restrains Cunningham and Craig from opening up a difference between cultural and economic value. And it is the same presence that makes it difficult for McRobbie to see the fringe and mainstream as anything other than opposed.

If we take a longer view, however, the countercultural capture of the idea of the fringe recedes. As we outlined in the Introduction, the original conception for *Fringe to Famous* came out of historical work by Moore (2012) on Australian bohemias going back to the mid-nineteenth century. These groups qualify as 'fringe' in the sense that they have centred around small scenes strongly differentiated in tastes and values from the society at large, but most have not been, in any clear sense, revolutionary. Australia's first great bohemian figure, Marcus Clarke, could be seen as an Antipodean adaptation of the dandy. He came from an English upper-middle-class family and had received an elite public-school education. After arriving in Melbourne in the 1860s, he styled himself the 'peripatetic philosopher' and scandalized the colonial establishment with a flamboyant style and a disregard for class boundaries and other social proprieties. He cultivated a keen sense of difference, shared with a small circle of associates, but showed no clear intention of overturning the larger social order.

The perspective gained from such historical examples can be brought to the present. The creative practitioners we interviewed for this book have been, without exception, committed to a distinctive set of values around their art. Friction between these values and commercial imperatives seems to us a routine feature of the cultural and creative industries. It can be found even among those who have reached the peak of commercial success. In Chapter 4, we discuss the case of comedian Steve Vizard, who became in the 1990s one of the highest-earning creative talents in Australian television. When asked about his relationship with network executives at the time, Vizard (2014) described it as 'oscillating between fervent, creative dialogue and outright warfare'. There were constant fights, 'really quite real', over differences between artistic and commercial priorities. Yet such fights were not part of any revolutionary programme. Indeed, Vizard had been a partner in a conservative law firm and had connections, through business and social networks, not only with Labor but also with the Liberal Party (Tippet & Lawson 2005).

The post-Foucauldian positions we have been considering above have little to say about examples such as this. The creative industries paradigm would have us believe that the kind of friction described by Vizard does not exist. Creative practitioners are imagined as hard-wired for integration into circuits of capital,

Figure 6 Steve Blackburn, Steve Vizard, Michael Veitch, Jane Turner and Alan Pentland (L-R), shooting the very first sketch for *Fast Forward* at Werribee Mansion, *c.* 1989. Courtesy Steve Vizard.

springing from the womb with a spreadsheet and a business plan. Yet the left culturalist perspective also fails to resonate. It is unclear how Vizard's practice could be understood through the labourist perspective of autonomist Marxism. Behind both creative industries and left culturalist positions, we suggest, there continues to lurk the countercultural figure of the revolutionary fringe. It is this figure that needs now to be relativized – not denounced or destroyed, but simply contextualized.

The second approach we have taken has been to revisit the 'cultural industries' moment of the 1980s. This is the moment in the recent past when it seemed most possible to maintain a dual focus on cultural and economic discourses and processes. While it was also the moment in which the problems identified above were emerging, it left a rich archive to which we can still return. It is important to recognize that responses to the counterculture always covered a spectrum. For some, the theme of revolution was to be taken literally. Whether it was taken to heart or rejected, the social relations involved were understood almost mechanically, through concepts such as Louis Althusser's (1971) 'ideological state apparatuses'. For others, however, the theme was always more performative or metaphorical. To affiliate with the idea of revolution was not to join a grim cadre but to adopt a mode that was playful or performative.

This mode has often been associated with the cheap sell-out – the Che Guevara T-shirt worn merely as street fashion, in betrayal of the 'real' revolution. These are the kinds of examples that McRobbie and others have had in mind in expressing reservations about hybridity. Concerns in this area cannot be simply dismissed: there can be little doubt that ironic appropriations of revolutionary iconography in commercial contexts have often involved a glib disregard for serious articulations of difference. It cannot be assumed, however, that playful or performative invocations of revolution have always been of this kind. We might also note that there is a spectrum in the way revolutionary figures and rhetorics can be invoked, with subtle weightings as to the seriousness and kind of opposition or contradiction that is being suggested. In other words, performative uses of the idea of revolution do not always or necessarily imply a lack of respect for the differences that the idea has sought to capture.

As we have indicated, a particular inspiration for us has been Frith and Horne's (1987) *Art into Pop*. While the latter has quite a specific focus – the role of the art school in the development of British popular music in the 1960s and 1970s – it is also exemplary as a study of commercial-cultural hybridity. In establishing the ground for such a study, Frith and Horne explicitly seek to moderate revolutionary themes still very much current at the time. They are critical, for example, of the conceptual framework of Dick Hebdige's (1979) classic *Subculture: The Meaning of Style*. While Hebdige sought to reclaim a place within mass culture for creativity and self-expression, he also maintained a strong opposition between art and commerce. The mass consumer was allowed agency within the terms of this opposition, but only in a highly circumscribed form – that of 'expressive defiance', or symbolic revolt against the generalized institution of mass fashion.

Frith and Horne were prescient in recognizing that such conceptual schemas work ultimately to produce an appearance of endless sameness. They are schemas that project, as an opposite to revolutionary desire, an undifferentiated society and economy in which there is no relief. This sense of flatness was a key theme in writing of the late 1980s around the concept of 'postmodernism'. But, for Frith and Horne (1987: 8), the idea of a world reduced to a single principle too often 'assume[d] what is being asserted – the co-option of art by commerce, the superficial response of audiences, the inability of anyone (save a few, privileged critics) to grasp what is going on'. In making this point, they open the possibility of imagining hybridity. Fringe and mainstream, art and commerce, do not relate as monolithic abstract entities, but through an ongoing series of concrete encounters – of arguments, lines in the sand, performative expressions of difference, but also of cooperation and compromise.

Finally, and as discussed in the Introduction, an important point of reference for us has been the sociology of Pierre Bourdieu, particularly the perspective developed in *The Rules of Art* (1995). The latter offers what might be called an unromantic account of the specificity of art and culture – *un*romantic, that is, as distinct from *anti*-romantic. Bourdieu was of the same generation as Foucault and was engaged with similar problems in left intellectual circles in France during the 1960s and 1970s. He also shared with Foucault a suspicion of the idea, often associated with May 1968, that culture might represent a radical 'outside' to establishment structures or regimes of power. This suspicion was, admittedly, sometimes expressed in forms of anti-romanticism. In what is probably his best-known book, *Distinction* (1984), Bourdieu assigns culture a functional role in reproducing social hierarchy, stripping it of any serious claim to independence. Elsewhere, however, he departs from a simple anti-romantic perspective, entertaining an idea of artistic autonomy.

It is significant that Bourdieu develops this idea with reference to historical examples. *The Rules of Art* is a study of nineteenth-century cultural fields, in particular French literary modernism and the circles that formed in Paris around figures such as Baudelaire and Flaubert. These circles could be seen as classic claimants to the mantle of artistic autonomy and one might expect them, therefore, to be exposed to an anti-romantic critique. Bourdieu is certainly severe in his assessment of attempts to rest claims to autonomy on easy assumptions of the transcendence of the aesthetic domain. Such assumptions are dismissed as 'vapid' (Bourdieu 1995: xv). But this is not to reject the idea of autonomy as such; it is to suggest rather that autonomy be understood as a *social achievement*. The perspective, for Bourdieu, is the very opposite of a disrespect for art: 'It is to offer a vision more true and, ultimately, more reassuring, because less superhuman, of the highest achievements of the human enterprise' (xx).

There are obviously issues of adaptation in applying ideas developed in relation to literary culture in nineteenth-century Paris to twentieth- and twenty-first-century Australia. But the important question, in relation to the debates we have considered in this chapter, is really one of *possibility*. Over the last thirty years, it has become a hardened orthodoxy in many quarters that claims to independence or autonomy will always be bogus. It is an orthodoxy, as we have seen, to which many who would like to reject it have even succumbed. It is in this context that Bourdieu's defence of the possibility of autonomy is important. For us in *Fringe to Famous*, it also restores the possibility of recognizing hybridity.

2

Subverting the high ground: The hybridity of punk and post-punk music in Australia

On a Saturday night in 2015, punk band Royal Headache took to the stage at the Sydney Opera House as part of the state-sponsored Vivid LIVE festival. As the band launched into their back-to-basics indie anthem, 'Down the Lane', fans invaded the stage, inciting a rush of security and police, abruptly ending the concert. Suburban punk svengali Nic Warnock had programmed Royal Headache with other acts from his label, R.I.P Society, because he 'wanted our bands to occupy the high ground of Australian culture, and subvert it' (Warnock 2015). A viral YouTube video of a melee at a World Heritage-listed venue proved his point, demonstrating the continuing power of punk to shock, resist and provoke.

Royal Headache exemplifies distinctive patterns of the contemporary Australian musical fringe. Formed in 2008, the band built a passionate following playing to packed pubs and bars in inner-city Sydney and Melbourne. Their 2012 debut album *Royal Headache*, released by a label based in an outer-suburban record store, was lauded by online music bible *Pitchfork* as one of its highest rated garage punk albums of all time ranked at number 16, with the 2015 album *High* ranked 19th (Album of the Year 2023). Meanwhile, *New Musical Express* compared Royal Headache's energy and style to the Sex Pistols, The Jam and Oasis, declaring the track Garbage 'The Best Guitar Song of 2015' (Wilkinson 2015). Grounded in the DIY amateurism of punk, Royal Headache received critical acclaim for their refusal to be a 'proper' band or a 'product' (Scott 2015). At the same time, the band was 'in the curious position of being an underground act who write songs so great that they demand mainstream attention' (Wilkinson 2015). Using digital tools, online media, self-management strategies and indie networks, Royal Headache could attain the creative autonomy traditionally sought by bohemian and avant-garde artists while also enjoying global visibility and acclaim.

Figure 7 Nic Warnock, 2013. Photograph by Douglas Lance Gibson. Courtesy Douglas Lance Gibson.

Figure 8 Royal Headache [n.d.]. Photo by McLean Stephenson. Courtesy McLean Stephenson.

This crossover between fringe and mainstream has a long history in Australian music. Transgressive underground aesthetics and refusal of 'proper' status had been modelled forty years earlier by glam group Skyhooks. The band melded the values of the pub rock underground – 'raw, unpretentious, hardworking, gritty and very unlikely to be heard on radio' (Coupe 2015: 14) – with the sophisticated social observation and arch humour of fringe cabaret. Signed to Michael Gudinski's independent label Mushroom, Skyhooks parlayed carnivalesque performance and louche bohemianism into crossover success, with multi-platinum albums in 1974 and 1975. Their underground pedigree was affirmed in the banning from radio airplay of six of the ten songs on their first album. Yet signed to 'a fully operating monopoly' (Coupe 2015: 16) that integrated ownership of artists, venues, booking services, print media and record label, they also achieved great success within the structures of the conventional music industry.

By the 1980s, punk had aggressively redefined independence as a refusal of the normalized and monopolistic character of such a mainstreamed rock counterculture. However, autonomy was not pure or absolute, but understood in transactional terms. The relationship with the mainstream was negotiated through engagement with structural innovations (music video, college radio), attention to industry process (especially promotion and distribution), critical refinement of musical approaches (appealing to more diverse audiences), the cultivation of a growing fan base, hustle, politics and even legal action.

The term 'affiliated indie' emerged for bands with this hybridized tactical status. A good example was Hoodoo Gurus. Formed in Sydney in 1980, three of its members had made a mark in Perth's punk underground in the late 1970s. A few years into their career, the Hoodoo Gurus began to negotiate more mainstream channels – boutique subsidiaries of major labels, television pop shows, top-40 singles, music videos, big-name producers. The move was seen by some as capitulating to commercialism, but it could equally be seen as driven by a commitment to democratic participation. Refusing to be confined to inner city cliques, the band made challenging, changing and surprising pop art. Lead songwriter Dave Faulkner (2018) sees mainstream engagement as a widening and deepening of punk's egalitarian ethos of 'respecting the audience, no matter who they are'. In this context, the use of mainstream resources contributed, paradoxically, to artistic autonomy.

Affiliated indie saw a more general move by musicians to explore mainstream structures and practices. Especially in the critical areas of contracts, branding, promotion and production, the autonomy that had secured credibility with audiences in the underground could be preserved in the mass market through careful bargaining and continual vigilance. In the twenty-first century, a new articulation of autonomy has extended and elaborated on this meeting of fringe and mainstream. There is a complex continuum of middle-ground practices and vectors through which musicians engage with commerce, changing technologies and the cultural institutions of the state to increase and diversify their national and international audience reach, enhance their skills, generate a sustainable income as professionals and make a mark on popular culture.

In this chapter, we consider the terms of crossover between fringe and mainstream in Australian music from the 1980s to the 2010s. What has been the relationship between independent artists and mass markets over this period? What conditions have enabled a flourishing of alternative band scenes? What practices, infrastructure and policy settings have allowed their hybridization with commercial formations and popular success for some acts at a national or international level? In pursuing these questions, we look first at the potency of the fringe that emerged from punk, turning then to its mainstreaming as 'affiliated indie' in the 1980s and 1990s and then finally to the sustainable, self-managed indie of the twenty-first century. First, however, we return to the general questions of interpretative frameworks discussed in the last chapter, considering how they might be addressed in the case of music.

Rock romanticism and postmodern criticism

Notwithstanding examples such as those we have introduced above, music is probably the most challenging field of those we consider in the book in which to overcome obstacles to a recognition of hybridity between fringe and mainstream. As an art form, popular music – and rock in particular – is the case that was most captured by countercultural formations and in which romantic mythology around the fringe has been most heavily accreted. This has meant that music has also provoked a heavily armed anti-romantic backlash, a phenomenon that can be seen in the academic field in a widespread project of deconstructing the idea of the counterculture and puncturing claims to creative autonomy. Both positions make it difficult to stake out a space for recognizing the productive potential of crossover and hybridity.

Ideas of disjuncture and radical difference between fringe and mainstream have been a major theme in rock music from the outset, having roots in its black cultural origins in the United States. It was Black Americans who first developed the form on mainly independent record labels and via 'coloured' radio stations on the fringe of the white mainstream pop industry and later in the overtly radical underground of the late 1960s. For the white musicians who took rock into the mainstream, a key attraction was always its aura of social and cultural revolution. A fascination with Black performance and rhetoric was central to the formation of such popular groups as Jefferson Airplane, the Rolling Stones and MC5. American and British musicians engaged extensively with Black Power politics and African American music in the critical years of 1968 and 1969, establishing an enduring framework for understanding the form (Burke 2021).

The dominance of this framework can be seen in the fact that it has been reproduced even during moments where the 1960s legacy has been repudiated. The most notable example is punk, which sought in the late 1970s to distance itself from the legacy, acerbically rejecting the artistic pretension and rhetorical inflation of those who continued to follow in its mould. Even in doing so, however, punk paid tribute to the revolutionary aspirations of the counterculture, attempting to rejuvenate it in a more potent, self-reflexive and contemporary form (Marchetto 2001: 29). Two celebrated bands that transformed vague 1960s resistance into overt socialist politics in spirited post-punk critiques of Thatcher's Britain are The Jam and The Clash, with the former re-working the Mod sounds and styles of The Who, The Kinks and Black soul, while the latter integrated Jamaican ska and the Rude Boy pose.

A major body of writing on rock music has itself emerged from the countercultural moment or its punk and post-punk echoes. It has valourized the pure music fringe and criticized any pursuit of mass audiences as 'selling out'. A classic example is a 1969 article by Germaine Greer (1986: 15) in London's *Oz* magazine arguing that the Underground is 'where life is, before the Establishment forms as a crust on top, and changes vitality to money'. This position first developed in music journalism, but has also informed the work of scholars, filmmakers and other commentators. Notable examples include monographs by Julie Burchill and Tony Parsons (1978), Dick Hebdige (1979), Greil Marcus (1989), Michael Bracewell (1997), the BBC documentary history of rock music *Dancing in the Street* (1997), Barry Miles (2010) and most recently Mark Greif's (2016) *Against Everything*. In Australia, examples include the articles and books on fringe experimentation and resistance by Clinton Walker

(1982; 1996) – who coined the term 'the Inner City Sound' – Bob Blunt (2001), Andrew Stafford (2014) and Robert Forster (2017) and the documentaries on Melbourne's punk scene by Richard Lowenstein (*We're Living on Dog Food*, 2009; *Autoluminescent*, 2011).

We have already seen examples of the reaction against this tradition in the previous chapter. While our focus there was on the status of fringe or independent cultural production in general, it is worth noting that the sharpest differences on this question have generally emerged in relation to music. To return to Heath and Potter's (2004) assault on the 'myth of the counterculture', for example, it is no accident that a key example should be Kurt Cobain. While Heath and Potter's critique is a general one, it is music, above all, that exemplifies for them the liabilities associated with the counterculture. It is in music that the idea of a radical distinction from the mainstream has been most powerfully articulated; it is in music that the countercultural hubris associated with this idea can be most clearly observed, and it is in music that the idea has seemed most at risk of becoming a prison-house, allowing no relation to the wider world other than rejection or 'refusal'.

In academic writing, the case against romanticism in relation to music developed most clearly in the 1980s in the work of scholars such as Simon Frith. In a classic article 'Towards an Aesthetics of Popular Music', Frith (1987) pointed out that the concept of artistic independence is often associated with an ideal of creative production as completely autonomous from the society in which it takes form. Within the terms of this ideal: 'Serious music matters because it transcends social forces; popular music is aesthetically worthless because it is determined by them' (Frith 1987: 133). Yet for even the most celebrated examples, Frith argued, the idea of transcendence is impossible to sustain in the face of evidence: 'The reality is that rock, like all twentieth-century pop musics, is a commercial form, music produced as a commodity, for profit, distributed through mass media as mass culture' (136–7). The problem was not that an original purity of the underground or of punk had somehow been lost; it was that the idea of purity was always ill-conceived.

The argument, to this point, is essential for the kind of position we are wishing to develop in *Fringe to Famous*. It is only when we overcome the idea of a radical opposition between fringe and mainstream that we can begin to identify positive potentials in crossover or hybridity. Frith's own work with Howard Horne (1987) in *Art into Pop* is one of the best examples we have of this perspective and has been for us a major inspiration in developing it in the Australian context. For the sake of the perspective itself, however, it is also important now to identify the points where the critique of romanticism has hardened into a more systematic *anti*-romanticism, bringing into question the very possibility of the fringe.

A useful point of reference here is an essay of the mid-1990s by David Tetzlaff (1994), which identified just such a turn. Tetzlaff engages with Frith and is critical of many of his arguments, but his concern is not so much with Frith himself as with what he calls 'Frithism' (96). The latter was the form taken in music scholarship of a wider 'postmodern' movement in which the critique of romanticism became the ground for a sweeping countermovement within progressive politics and culture. A keystone of this development was a sustained attack on the idea of 'authenticity' that had been crucial in distinguishing the underground from the profit motive and artifice of the mainstream cultural industries. The full-blown postmodern critique sought not only to moderate the concept of authenticity; it sought to destroy it. Its target was not simply the absoluteness of the distinction between mainstream and fringe; it was the distinction itself.

In retrospect, the postmodern moment can be seen as having laid some of the groundwork for the 'creative industries' arguments of the 2000s. If music is simply a business, then the analysis of music can be reduced to business analysis. This conclusion was not drawn in the 1980s as the principle that there is no outside to the commercial mainstream was only selectively applied and its full implications had still to play out. As Tetzlaff points out, Frith was quick to dismiss claims to independence by musicians of the 1960s and 1970s, but implicitly exempted progressive art rock figures such as David Bowie and Bryan Ferry who were more aligned with postmodern sensibilities. While it is true that the latter engaged extensively with the mainstream commercial system, they did so through an artistic vision that had clearly been formed elsewhere. This was essential both to their self-understanding and reception: 'none of this serious artistry would have been possible without the development of the Rock ideology Frith describes' (Tetzlaff 1994: 104).

Tetzlaff draws a useful distinction between 'music that is *sold* as a commodity and music that is *created* as a commodity' (111). The important question, he suggests, is not the attitude of musicians to market *mechanisms* but their attitude to market *rationality* – whether they use the market 'to forge a unique individual statement, to speak to the passions of a subordinate community, or just to try to make as much money as possible' (111). This distinction was as important to the post-punk artists admired by Frith as it was to those associated with the counterculture, and it is a distinction that continued to rest on values forged in close peer interactions within small scenes. While these scenes became increasingly complex and fragmented through the 1980s, losing their alignment as a singular 'underground', they nevertheless remained critical: 'Bowie and Roxy were clearly of the progressive Rock scene of the mid '70s, still defined in opposition to Pop (epitomized by 'Seasons in the Sun' and 'Afternoon Delight') that was seen as witlessly commercial' (105).

If it is important to maintain a scepticism of rock romanticism, therefore, it is equally important to moderate tendencies that have developed in reaction against it. A useful reference point in maintaining this balancing act in the Australian context is a debate of the 1990s between McKenzie Wark and Marcus Breen in which Wark played the postmodern critic to Breen's rock romanticism. In an essay on crossover into the mainstream by progressive pub-rock band Midnight Oil – culminating in their signing with multinational record company CBS – Wark cites a classic articulation by Breen of the romantic position. However sound the songs may be in origin, for Breen (1986: 15), if they 'suffer a transformation and become an extension of the marketing nexus of the dominant cultural and social values, their meaning is changed'. This for Wark (1999: 109) is to criticize art for what it lacks, rather than identifying 'the potential it contains within itself for exceeding the conventions and limitations of the day'. In seeking to defend a lost purity, analysis becomes merely reactive, unable even to describe the realities of creative production in a complex market-oriented society, let alone recognize the positive possibilities they might hold.

Wark's rejection of romanticism opens up a fertile terrain of analysis similar to that explored by Frith and Horne. Taking the example of Midnight Oil, she is able to show how a hard-won credibility gained through close engagement with small audiences can provide a bargaining position over terms of access to larger ones:

> After money, credibility is the most precious commodity in circulation. As far as the majors are concerned, once you buy that the rest is easy. This is why the majors are prepared to deal with acts like Midnight Oil and cede a certain amount of business and artistic autonomy to them.
>
> (Wark 1999: 108)

The engagement of a band like Midnight Oil with a multi-national record company is therefore not so much a 'transformation' – implying loss – as a *negotiation*. It is not only the fringe formation that is altered but also the mainstream. The resulting hybrid needs to be assessed not according to abstract criteria but in terms of its specific qualities and effects.

There are also problems, however, in Wark's determination to consign rock romanticism to the dustbin of history. Like Frith, she clearly had strong sympathies with the specifically cultural values associated with small scenes. Yet her caustic dismissal of attempts to represent these scenes as outside of or opposed to the mainstream risks undercutting their claims to uniqueness. While Wark excels in demonstrating the positive *interaction* between fringe and mainstream, it is Breen who is more attentive to the dangers of a loss of distinction between them. His monograph *Rock Dogs* remains an important source in understanding the way punk in Australia 'created a sense that there was a space for opportunities' (Breen 1999: 71). He was also more alert than Wark to the problems of utilitarian music industry policies and programmes introduced by Labor governments in the 1980s and 1990s, and which might now be seen as forerunners of creative industries economism.

While avoiding a simple romanticism therefore, we have been careful in this chapter to recognize the importance of spaces in which alternatives to 'market rationality' in Tetzlaff's sense are able to take form. We have drawn, for example, on Frith and Horne's argument that public institutions such as Art Schools can be important incubators of aesthetic and political values that then hybridize with commercial markets in complex ways. An important reference here is also the more recent writing of Andy Bennett and Ian Rogers (2016) on the sites and places of collective participation in music scenes. In relation to specifically Australian contexts, we have built on Katherine Albury's (1999) analysis of the role of the ABC's youth network Triple J in producing subcultural capital among its listeners, Liz Giuffre's (2009) work on the ABC's music video programme *Rage* and David Nichols and Sophie Perillo's (2016) investigation of the gigging circuit in Melbourne.

A book that deserves particular mention is David Nichols' (2016) *Dig*, an encyclopaedic yet analytical history of Australian rock and pop from the 1960s to 1985. Nichols draws on a pre-academic career as a music journalist spanning fringe zines to the mass market *Smash Hits*, membership of cult band The Cannanes and a biography of post-punk band The Go-Betweens (1997). His work provides a nuanced, complex and granular history alive to the potential of artists and enablers from fringe scenes (a notable example being the bands that emerged from the Carlton performance scene in Melbourne) to transform music and popular audiences despite the tensions involved in the business of music. It resonates with the analysis by Tony Moore (2012), important in the genesis of *Fringe to Famous*, of a long tradition in Australia of counter cultural artists working between commercial and public sector cultural industries throughout the twentieth century.

The constitutive hybridity of punk in Australia

Punk in Australia was, almost from the beginning, a hybrid formation, involving fusions between 'bottom up' energies incubated in small inner-city scenes and 'top down' forms of patronage, particularly from public broadcasting. As a countercultural movement, it may have been brief (1975–79), but it helped shape the ethics, structures, attitudes and aesthetics of what ultimately came to be known as 'Indie' creative practice – a cultural movement stretching from the post-punk early 1980s through the 1990s and the first decade of the new century to the present. While centred on music, punk had a wider cultural impact on fashion, visual art and design, music video and cinema, arts journalism and comedy. These were integral to the music in any case, bonding its interlinked, urban bohemia through shared codes and rituals of production and consumption. At its outset, punk met most of Bourdieu's (1980: 285–90) criteria for new players shaking up and jostling with established artists in a cultural field working within the 'field of restricted production' – except that they took aim at established rock and pop operating in the 'field of large-scale production' as well as 1960s countercultural music grandees that had grown complacent.

In Australian cities in the 1970s, networks of young people were making similar demands and playing low fi, stripped down, spiky music. Pioneering Australian punk bands included Sydney's Radio Birdman, Melbourne's Boys Next Door (featuring a teenage Nick Cave), Perth's The Scientists and Brisbane's The Saints, who were part of small inner-city scenes structured around a gigging circuit of pubs, parties, student unions and pop-up venues. In accordance with Bourdieu's conceptualization of the avant-garde field of restricted production, the punk artists were the audience for their peers. Remembering his days in a punk band, Dave Faulkner (2018) recalls 'everyone who was in the punk scene ended up forming a band ... It was just one of these participating things: we were an audience for each other. The rest of the city of Perth didn't know who we were or didn't care, and we didn't either ... we found our own gigs, and often our parties became gigs.' Faulkner taught himself to play guitar and, with university and art school friends, briefly joined Perth's first punk band the Cheap Nasties, and then later formed The Victims, with fellow future Hoodoo Gurus member James Baker, and they became the top band in the 'scene that we created'.

Infused with a DIY ethic, punk made a virtue of a diversity of practices of production, distribution, promotion and recreation that carved out a measure of autonomy from the dominant popular music recording corporations and public relations machines. This origin helped to generate a mythology of radical difference that belies the scene's hybrid evolution. Followers of bands frequently contributed to its style and DIY business package. Musicians wanted a sensible, more intimate partnership with audiences who enhanced the bands' cultural value by publishing fanzines, producing community radio shows, writing reviews for the emerging music street press, directing video clips, designing record covers and posters and dutifully turning up to gigs.

To understand the structuring of the urban music fringe that emerged from punk in the early 1980s, it is important to go beyond the music industries and even music making. The 'alternative' music market was also created by a wider ensemble of small-scale cultural, media and business practices and institutions – intimate, raffish inner urban venues; independent record labels; self-published fanzines and street press; design studios within art colleges; 'op shops' and fashion boutiques; community FM radio stations; video and filmmaking facilities and art-house cinemas. All of these helped to produce an 'alternative' music field of restricted production in the 1980s and early 1990s, a field that has persisted to some extent until today.

Post-punk music countercultures emerged in down-at-heel inner city villages with cheap share house accommodation, often in nineteenth-century terrace houses or art deco apartments within walking distance of tertiary education, cafes and pubs. Peter O'Doherty, who joined his older brother's art school band Mental as Anything in 1977, described the importance of the surrounding urban precinct of Darlinghurst, a bohemian haunt since the 1920s, as a magnet due to its cheap lodgings and plethora of venues. He recalls the 'Mental's' first concerts in 'Darlo' attracted 'a really interesting audience of some art schoolers, some early punks, surfers … a really good mix' (2014). Moving to Sydney from Perth, Dave Faulkner (2018) joined the same alternative scene and recalls Hoodoo Gurus forming at a house party in the adjacent precinct of Paddington, on New Year's Eve 1980:

> We started writing songs … we were sharing a house, so we were working all the time. You get a couple of cheap flagons of wine, and it's going to be a fun day writing songs, and drinking and watching bad movies.

Steve Kilbey of The Church first encountered the counterculture on leaving Canberra for inner city Sydney, where he discovered the subcultural diversity of Paddington Market and an interconnected bohemia of shared house living – similar to that which was later vividly portrayed for the Melbourne punk scene in Richard Lowenstein film *Dogs in Space* (1986):

> I imagined it and I lived it in my own head and in the books I read and the films I tried to see … but I didn't have it until in 1979 I left the public service at 22, 23 and I moved to Sydney and I started selling t-shirts at Paddington Market and bang, there it was, baby … my house was full of people, fucking crazy people taking acid and everything … put your tape on, Steve and let's hear what Steve's doing with music.
>
> (Kilbey 2016)

Punk and the post-punk 'alternative' music valourized small-scale venues, in opposition to the stadiums and large concert halls where rock superstars and teen pop idols played. Sydney and Melbourne, though different in important ways, were both blessed with a plethora of small- to medium-size performance spaces, frequently pubs with a 'band room' or merely a stage in a corner, but also town halls and university union refectories. The intimacy and down-at-heel atmosphere of many of these spaces encouraged the ethic of audience participation. Faulkner (2018) stressed the importance of a loyal coterie of fans in getting a foothold and advancing in the inner-city scene: 'We had a hard core of fans. They dressed funny. We dressed weirdly too … We had a reputation around the city that when you booked us, you get an extra fifty punters through the door – the fans.' The ecosystem of multiple inner-city pub-based venues enabled bands to scrape together a living, hone their act and build sufficient credibility to move to the next stage.

Creative autonomy in the fringe in Australia was enabled both by ground-up community action and by public patronage. Both were the result of a synthesis of cultural politics and cultural entrepreneurship to access or build platforms, institutions and opportunities that enabled marginal groups and interests in preference to command and control of assets and people. Two outstanding examples are community radio and the ABC's Double J – the result of community agitation and enlightened federal government policy around the possibilities of a plurality of media that provided alternative spaces to the existing models of commercial and ABC radio, which were eagerly occupied by the new punk fringe.

Punk found a particularly sympathetic medium in community FM radio stations, an innovation of the social democratic Labor Government of Gough Whitlam, inaugurated in 1975 ahead of the punk disruption (Moore 2012). Stations such as 4ZZZ in Brisbane, 3RRR in Melbourne and 2SER and Skid Row in Sydney engaged countercultures and community groups, prioritizing new and diverse music by emerging local artists. In Melbourne and Brisbane, Community FM radio stations 3RRR and 4ZZZ each performed a similar promotional service for emerging punk scenes (Nichols 2016: 269–73) – playing their DIY demos, listing their shows and refining their fringe idealism, often bridging into ideas of resistance. For example, 4ZZZ channelled punk's anarchist politics and its energy into campaigns against the authoritarian National Party Government in Queensland, notorious for deploying draconian laws against assembly to suppress Brisbane's live music scene (Stafford 2014).

Sydney's live music and budding independent recording scene benefitted greatly from an experimental Contemporary Radio Unit auspiced within the ABC with the call sign on AM radio 2JJ. Also launched in 1975, Double Jay developed a symbiosis with the burgeoning community radio sector, and drew ideas and recruits from countercultural communities. It was required to prioritize Australian performers beyond the official radio quotas, with an emphasis on emerging talent, and embraced punk as the new alternative sound (Elder & Wales 1984; Matchett 2015). It began promoting emerging Australian acts and their local gigs in Sydney's inner-city warren of pubs and clubs, as well as its surfside and western suburbs beer barns, and organized outdoor concerts promoting bands such as Midnight Oil, Mental as Anything and Sunnyboys to larger audiences.

Double Jay is an excellent example of an established mainstream institution being transformed as it hybridized with the fringe. Its porosity to a diversity of countercultures, youth subcultures, radical groups and emerging social movements was predicated on an experimental collective management practice foreign to the hierarchical national broadcaster and an approach to programming in opposition to the commercial radio industry (Elder & Wales 1984: 6; Moore 2012: 274). Its openness to emerging and increasingly diverse music genres was explicit in its establishment, having been based on a report by researcher Glen A. Baker, who went on to co-author the influential monograph *The New Music* (1980), examining Australia's contribution to global punk and fragmenting music styles. Double Jay rejected the playlists and showbiz accents of Top 40 radio, allowing presenters to choose the music themselves. Its punk inflexion was strengthened by the infusion of a younger generation of staff from community radio, such as 4ZZZ's Stuart Matchett and, later after going FM, radical journalist Andy Nehl who had played in Brisbane's punk band The Black Assassins and saw the potential of DIY cultural politics to democratize and diversify the ABC.

Other forms of public patronage included the post-school education sector, where the three tiers of Universities, Institutes of Technical Education – where commercial art education often occurred – and local colleges of Technical and Further Education (TAFE) provided a trove of facilities and equipment which assisted post-punk music and media making. These included cosy venues for rehearsal and performance, design and printing facilities, video equipment, student newspapers for music review and the university-based FM stations, such as 2RSR at the University of Sydney and 2SER at the NSW Institute of Technology.

The importance of this context was clear in our interview with members of Mental as Anything, a band that first met and started jamming together at Sydney's premier 'art school', East Sydney Technical College. Chris O'Doherty (aka Reg Mombassa) spoke of 'art school' as an 'accidental' hot house for forming a band, recalling 'going to and playing at art school parties. Playing in houses mostly, playing to friends and fellow students and inner-city share-house types … People doing artistic, sort of, things' (Mombassa 2014). Mental as Anything's first single was shot at a gig in the 'Tin Sheds', Sydney University's silk screen workshop that also designed and printed band posters. Bands called on peers from university and art schools to produce innovative music videos on a shoestring. Peter O'Doherty (2014) recalls that 'lots of those filmmakers were hanging around and living in the same place as well. So, you know, we had people doing animated film clips for us'. When Stuart McDonald was asked to produce a short film for assessment at Melbourne's RMIT, he produced a clip on no budget at all that nevertheless remains iconic – of Nick Cave and The Boys Next Door, adorned in gothic attire, performing 'Shivers'.

By 1980, government was also seeding community-based experiments in public television, such as Sydney's Metro TV, which was where Hoodoo Gurus' first video clip was shot as part of a student project for their first single on Phantom. Dave Faulkner (2018) recalled that

[a]t this time music video was a cool thing. Everyone was making videos. It was a new art form. Metro TV … were doing a course on video making over a weekend … they said they needed a band for students to produce a video with. We get a free video clip out of it … We brought in a bunch of our fans who danced around.

Figure 9 Paul Worstead screen-printed poster for Mental as Anything upcoming gigs, 1980. Courtesy National Gallery of Australia.

Taken together, these public institutions enabled the Australian post-punk fringe in a manner analogous to Frith and Horne's post-war British art school, with the difference that the state's role was geared to youth creativity across media as well as an array of post-school educational options.

While government and community action did the heavy lifting, it is important to note that this post-punk version of the field of restricted production had its own very low-key commercial imperatives, evident in venues, a street press subsidized by niche ads and small-scale retailers of fashion items such as Sydney's Skin Deep, independent import record stores and especially labels. These interlinked enterprises composed what Walker (1982: 7) termed 'a minor industry … alternative to the Oz Rock establishment … providing for a small but hungry audience'. Straw (2015: 481, 483) has recently conceptualized this set of low-scale institutions as 'underground incubators', enabling scenes by making cultural activity visible and decipherable. They have an important function in shifting production and consumption from the private realm through public and collective 'sociability'.

Independent labels were the most important commercial entity for sidestepping the multinational record companies that dominated the local mass market through branch offices and affiliation deals. Notable labels include Au Go Go and Missing Link in Melbourne, and Regular, Red Eye, Phantom Records and Waterfront Records in Sydney, all of which emerged from within, or near to, the counterculture. Most of the key Australian artists emerging in the wake of punk started with these small-scale start-ups. Examples include Radio Birdman, The Boys Next Door, Mental as Anything, XL Capris, Sekret Sekret, Spy vs Spy and Sunnyboys.

While their budgets were always tight, the independents could access the cultural capital of a talented network who were peers in the scene to provide input for imaginative record sleeves, publicity and even merchandise such as T-shirts. For example, Phantom announced Sunnyboys with a cassette EP packaged in a flip top box-shaped-like cigarette packet, while Regular promoted Mental as Anything with lavish silk screen acrylic posters adorned with dadaesque images ironizing suburban iconography such as garden sprinklers and lawnmowers. 'We weren't deliberately trying to be arty', recalls Reg Mombassa (2014), 'but simply ended up doing our own posters and record covers, or getting our art school mates (like Paul Worstead) to do it. It was not contrived or anything. It was just that that was where we were. That was our world'. Similarly, Sunnyboys' Peter Oxley produced most of the band's iconic posters and T-shirts refining silk-screening skills honed printing surf shirts as a teenager and participating in Phantom's shift into street fashion.

For some of the artists we are concerned with here, such as Sunnyboys and Hoodoo Gurus on Phantom, the Indie label served first as an incubator within the fringe, and then as a stepping stone to deal with a bigger, more mainstream record company. Sunnyboys' singles and EPs attracted the attention of Mushroom, while Hoodoo Gurus' first single 'Leilani' sold close to a thousand on Phantom and was a calling card for larger-scale independent Big Time. However, while private sector cottage industries such as Phantom Records and Au Go Go needed to make a profit to be sustainable, they prioritized cultural value over economic value by being selective, keeping their scale and overheads low (Oxley 2018).

The distinction between the 'alternative' scene and the music 'industry' in Sydney in the 1980s was mapped by venues. According to Faulkner (2018), the industry hung out at the Manzil Room at Kings Cross, a louche 1970s club, from where they pushed 'mainstream' bands such as Divinyls and Moving Pictures and assembled acts with synthesizers trying to imitate new romantic music: 'They had disdain for Hoodoo Gurus and bands like us. We were not part of that. We were the Trade Union Club, the Southern Cross Hotel, but also going out to the suburbs and playing to the people.' While the post-punk fringe was clearly demarcated, it was not a citadel. As demonstrated by Nichols and Perillo (2016) in their archaeology of 1980s Melbourne gigs, the inner-city venue circuit encompassed the suburbs, meaning that from the start post-punk bands such as Mental as Anything, The Boys Next Door, Midnight Oil, Sunnyboys, The Church and Hoodoo Gurus were playing to audiences composed of blue-collar and office workers who were not part of a counterculture.

Similarly, the independent record labels hot-bedded the studios and equipment of the multinational recording industry after hours, drawing on the skills of technicians and wannabe producers who worked for the majors by day and played with the independents by night. The boundary between the two fields was distinct but permeable. The freedom afforded within the fringe made for a diverse, interesting, democratic and at times transgressive cultural experience, and for some bands who moved further into the field of large-scale production, the challenge was how to retain autonomy while making inevitable concessions.

Affiliated indie and negotiated autonomy

By the mid-1980s, a number of alumni of this punk counterculture were achieving critical and commercial success through crossovers into mainstream media, recording and touring platforms. Those 1980s post-punk bands that achieved larger audiences did so for a variety of reasons. Punk's mission to shake up popular culture by bringing more interesting and critical music to more people always held commercial potential. Many expressed the not unreasonable hope of building an economically sustainable career as artists. However, the commercial system was also embraced for its artistic possibilities. Dave Faulkner claims to have been motivated in part by a recoil from a snobbery in the alternative scene about playing to audiences outside the small inner-city coterie. Far from 'selling out', he sees the embrace of audiences from the suburbs as a widening and deepening of punk's respect for the audiences regardless of background: 'Punk rock was very egalitarian, and I feel the same way' (Faulkner 2018).

Likewise, Mental as Anything were motivated by a democratic impulse to engage with people in the suburbs, with whom they identified and who were the subject of their songs and much of their visual art. However, this orientation did not necessarily imply an abandonment of the fringe. For the bands we interviewed, it was rather about cycling between the two, retaining as much creative freedom as possible, while reaching larger audiences. This hybridity was, admittedly, a difficult balancing act. Faulkner, for example, acknowledged difficulties in meeting the expectations of peers from the inner-city scene, who sometimes cooled to the band as it became more popular. There was particular suspicion of the Gurus' diversification of styles, growing popularity, increasingly professional focus and the controversial sacking of the original drummer James Baker who disdained the band's expanding suburban audiences as unhip. The final parting of the ways occurred over Baker's reluctance to tour the United States, so 'we sacked him and it was considered [in the inner Sydney scene] to be the biggest heresy in the world, that showed what a sell-out [the band was]' (Faulkner 2018).

How did Australia's fringe music bands gain access to mainstream audiences in Bourdieu's field of large-scale production? There were a range of vectors available from the late 1970s that multiplied in the 1980s and 1990s. First a robust touring circuit established by cultural entrepreneurs who were savvy enough to link boutique inner city and outer suburban beer barn concerts. Second, broadcast media porosity with the post-punk fringe in the burgeoning music video genre, especially by public service broadcasters. Third, and most significantly, corporate recording industry outreach, coupled with the upscaling of successful indie labels that affiliated with offshore multinationals such as EMI – a model for the mainstreaming of 'Indie' that would gather pace through the 1990s.

'Affiliated Indie' was a relatively stabilized and semi-globalized field of restricted production, a key link in what Mathieson (2000) called the 'sell in' – the process by which major labels snapped up alternative Australian bands in the wake of Nirvana's success. It enabled bands to establish themselves within the fringe and domestic market, sign to larger local independent labels such as Regular Records, Big Time or Mushroom, that in turn enter into agreements with multinational companies that ensure overseas distribution, promotion, radio airplay (notably on US college radio) and touring, especially in the United States and Europe. Importantly for understanding the circulation from fringe to mainstream in Australia, media outreach to post-punk artists was largely a public sector intervention, while affiliated Indie was a private sector innovation.

It became an orthodoxy in the late 1980s and 1990s that mainstream media had ignored Australian music from the punk scene, but this idea stems mainly from the exclusion of some bands from AM radio. On the evidence of 'Top 40 Playlists' created by commercial AM teen stations, and the National Top 10 collated by ABC television's music programme *Countdown*, it is clear that Mental as Anything, The Church, Hoodoo Gurus and Paul Kelly and his bands broke through with some songs enjoying high rotation, and occupying positions in the Top 20 and even Top 10. The real radio game changer, however, was the migration in January 1980 of the ABC's Double Jay to the FM band as Triple J, and from 1989 its expansion beyond Sydney, first to the other capital cities, and then to regional centres through the early 1990s. This national expansion was the result of deft politics and lobbying by an alliance of local communities desirous of alternative music, ABC activist managers such as Andy Nehl and enthusiastic support from the youth chapters of both the left of centre Young Labor and the usually conservative Young Nationals.

As a 'national youth network', Triple J captured a new generation of Australian young people, a mass audience of suburbs and country towns while retaining the 'indie' cred it had helped to nurture and shape in Sydney (Albury 1999; Matchett 2015). Despite its scale, the new audience was diverse, local and many lived in rural and regional areas that had not previously enjoyed radio exposure to 'alternative' music. Matchett (2015) conceptualizes Triple J going national and regional as a broadening and democratization of the listening audience, 'challenging the station's ideas and consensus about what was good music ... JJJ is now mainstream, more successful than I ever imagined possible ... it's in the mainstream, and I think that's good'.

Television was also important in taking post-punk bands to a mass youth audience and building a cultural literacy through which 'alternative' music could be received. The major players were again public broadcasters – the ABC and SBS – but commercial television, notably the Seven network, was also sometimes involved. A survey by the authors of popular television rock music shows spanning different segments of the youth market demonstrates that emerging post-punk acts were obtaining mainstream air-time that dwarfed any on commercial AM radio and had a reach far exceeding Triple J. This discovery runs counter to the conventional account by music journalists and many musicians (see Walker 1982; 1996; *Long Way to the Top* 2001) that the Australian media ignored post-punk music until the advent of grunge and Nirvana in the United States. Music-specific TV programmes particularly interested in post-punk music were the ABC's *Flashez* (1976–7), *Rock Arena* (1982–9), *Beatbox* (1985–7), SBS's *Rock Around the World* (1981–4) and Channel Seven's *Night Moves* (1977–84).

'Top 40' music programmes also played a part in breaking some post-punk acts in the mass teen market. An example was Channel Seven's Saturday morning programme *Sounds* (1974–87), which profiled a number of post-punk bands with edgier fare featured on *After Dark* (1982–5), a late Saturday night programme with fresh-from-gigs inebriated studio drop-ins by artists. But the most influential programme was the ABC's *Countdown*, airing Sunday evening at 6 pm from 1974 to 1987 and comparable in impact to *American Bandstand* and the UK's *Top of the Pops*. *Countdown* was especially open to new international and Australian punk music from 1979 through to the mid-1980s, booking repeat appearances by The Saints, Mental as Anything, The Reels, The Riptides, The Church, Paul Kelly, Nick Cave, Sunnyboys, Models and Hoodoo Gurus.

Church front-man Steve Kilbey (2016) recalled the capacity of the ABC's *Countdown* to catapult an obscure band into the mainstream:

> Friday night, we played a gig in Sydney, The Governor's Pleasure, there were 10 people there. Monday night we played a gig in Melbourne after *Countdown*, there was 900 fucking people there and there were people trying to get in and there was a riot. It was overnight success except seeing I was ... started when I was sixteen, ten years had gone into it.

In recognition of *Countdown*'s influence, the ABC introduced the Countdown Music Awards in 1981 to 1987, effectively Australia's national music awards, credentialing and sanctifying excellence, popularity and impact. While mainstream 'industry' acts such as John Farnham, INXS and Cold Chisel dominated these awards, bands originating in the punk fringe were also recognized. Mental as Anything's *Cats and Dogs* was nominated for best album in 1981 and their *Fundamental* won best album in 1985; Midnight Oil won best single for 'Power and the Passion' in 1983; and Hoodoo Gurus won best debut album of 1984 for *Stoneage Romeos*.

A further important public service broadcasting initiative was the ABC's Antipodean nod to MTV, *Rage* premiering in 1987. Programmed from midnight to daylight on Friday and Saturday, *Rage* drew on an extensive and growing library of videos, including many from the punk and post-punk scenes. By the mid-1990s, it had helped to cement 'Indie' as a dominant music category in Australia. The original programmer Stephanie Lewis had emerged from the Sydney punk scene and had

ROADRUNNER

Vol. 5 No. 4, May '82 $1.00

THE CHURCH

XTC — Modern Folk
Orchestra Manoeuvres In The Dark
Lindsay Kemp
Gillian Armstrong On Starstruck
The Go-Betweens
Molly Meldrum
Soul People Special
Chic
B-52's

Is This The Taste of Victory?

Figure 10 *Roadrunner* magazine cover, May 1982, featuring The Church, and designed by Donald Robertson. Courtesy University of Wollongong Archives.

worked at Triple J. Producer Mark Fitzgerald recalled, 'I decided to make *Rage* as different as possible and emphasize the real differences it had: no compere, no commercials ... It would be wall-to-wall music. It would be unrelenting' (Williams 2017). The sheer length of the programme meant room to play the clips of even the most obscure bands and drove a hunger by programmers for new songs and a call-out to emerging bands to send in their homemade clips. '*Rage* is fantastic' argues Faulkner (2018) about its value back then and today, 'without *Rage* Australian music would be really in trouble. They play the stuff Triple J won't play. It's more important than Triple J for the edgy stuff'.

The normalization by *Rage* of Indie as a global and locally inflected aesthetic and relation to production and audiences was partly achieved through guest curation by local and international artists, who never failed to play a diverse Australian post-punk oeuvre in the context of global or Antipodean trends – gradually and retrospectively establishing an Indie canon giving pride of place to adamantly fringe bands, like The Triffids, The Birthday Party and The Go-Betweens, that neither sought nor received much mainstream coverage in the 1980s.

A crucial vector to larger audiences for many bands in the 1980s was collaboration with independent mid-level vertically integrated recording companies which had developed multinational affiliations. Offshore affiliation delivered the significant benefit of investment in production, promotion, distribution and touring. Of the 1980s artists we spoke with, The Church went straight to the multinational EMI, but Sunnyboys, Mental as Anything, Midnight Oil and Hoodoo Gurus took up the affiliation model. After first recording with Phantom Records, Sunnyboys were signed by Mushroom, the once countercultural *enfant terrible* that had earlier contracted, on the hastily conceived 'Suicide Records' sub-label, many young post-punk bands, including Paul Kelly and the Dots, Nick Cave and The Boys Next Door, Hunters and Collectors, Models and The Saints.

Faulkner (2018) recalls that Sunnyboys were the first of the bands from 'our world' to cross-over, with a 1981 breakthrough into the mass market, with Hoodoo Gurus following not far behind: 'They were bigger than us, earlier than us, but we kind of outgrew them.' The Gurus signed to Big Time, an Australian independent affiliated with offshore companies A&M and EMI. '[E]veryone in the industry laughed when we were signed up', Dave Faulkner recalled of Hoodoo Gurus' deal with Big Time: 'the prevailing wisdom was we were a bunch of losers ... Inner city ghetto music no one would listen to.' Released in the United States

Figure 11 Hoodoo Gurus, *Mars Needs Guitars!* album front cover (Big Time Records, 1985). Illustrated and designed by Richard Allan. Courtesy Hoodoo Gurus.

on A&M, their *Stoneage Romeos* was a hit on college radio, staying at number 1 on the alternative/college charts for seven weeks. When the second album *Mars Needs Guitars* was also picked up on this US alternative radio network, the band toured as support for The Bangles, then enjoying their first mainstream hit.

The affiliation deals negotiated by Midnight Oil, Hoodoo Gurus and The Church became early models of 'Global Indie', linking up niche fringe markets around the world to achieve a scale that was not possible within the domestic Australian market. As Faulkner (2018) explains,

we 'cracked' America but we didn't crack it in any mainstream way … we were as big in America as in Australia but in America that meant less [of potential market]. We got to number five in Australia but not top of the charts there … we were big in the underground.

Likewise, The Church's singles such as 'The Unguarded Moment' (1981) and albums such as *The Blurred Crusade* (1982) garnered loyal audiences for their literate neo-psychedelia in England, Sweden, Germany, Canada, Japan and college radio in the United States, which together represented a mass market for music sales and especially for touring. Kilbey (2016) believes they cut through internationally due to a unique sound: 'Well you know in 1982 … there was nothing really like us you know there was The Cure and The Psychedelic Furs and … and then there was us.'

There were areas of tension and sometimes serious conflict over economic and creative autonomy for the artists we interviewed, whether they were affiliated Independents or had made direct deals with multinationals. While there were opportunities associated with increased investment and distribution networks, there were also struggles over creative and financial control. In some cases, such as Midnight Oil's negotiated autonomy with CBS, a stable compromise was reached, paving the way for long-term success. In their early days Midnight Oil pursued a self-management strategy, refusing to work through booking agents and assuming the financial risk through bank loans (Wark 1999: 102). They took the bold step of starting their own independent label Powderworks and even ran their own DIY advertisement for their second album *Head Injuries* (1979). The low budget ad, which aired on late night commercial television in 1980, was so raw, raucous and physically confronting it had impact! Embarking on these initiatives, it helped that lead singer and spokesman, Peter Garrett, was a lawyer.

To break into the international market, however, Midnight Oil needed an affiliation with a major label and signed with CBS Records. With thirteen albums in the Australian Top 10, the band remains a model for how to negotiate a contract with a major without forfeiting autonomy. As Wark (1999: 103) argues, the approach of the Oils was to use its own hard-won 'credibility' and loyal audience as a 'bargaining chip', making a convincing case that authenticity stemming from creative control and keeping good faith with its fan base would drive financial success and promotion – an example of cultural value being the condition for economic value. This was achieved by settling for much less from the labels, modest overheads, recording albums cheaply and avoiding multi-record deals which, as band member Rob Hirst explained, 'tie you up, and put so much pressure on you have a mega-selling album, you still wouldn't recoup' (Wark 1999: 103).

For a number of Australian artists, the affiliation model worked well for a time, but eventually led to tensions between cultural and economic value and serious infringements of financial independence and creative autonomy. This resulted in bands breaking from affiliation arrangements (in the case of The Church and Mental as Anything), suing and ultimately acquiring the local label (Hoodoo Gurus) or submitting to control that diminished both commercial and artistic impact (Sunnyboys' experience of Mushroom and its US affiliate).

In the case of The Church, Steve Kilbey (2016) concedes that the EMI contract 'was a terrible deal' but maintains that they negotiated a significant degree of creative autonomy in the Australian production of the band's first two albums, which was predicated on Kilbey already having mastered the skills and knowledge of music production, and threatening to walk away:

> So when The Church went in to make their first album I knew how I wanted it to sound and I knew exactly … how it had to be … I was a complete prima donna … I'd go 'I want to do this' and they'd go 'no' and I go 'if you don't do this I'm walking out right now and you can stick your record deal up your arse' … I was going 'this is how it's going to be, this is going to be here, this is going to be there, you're going to sing this' … I had such a singularity of purpose and I was so sure and every time I insisted it always worked out that I got my own way.

Notwithstanding the band's Australian success, EMI head office judged their second album *The Blurred Crusade* – a chart topper in Australia – as unacceptable to the American market and refused to release it on the Capitol label. The impasse led to a parting of ways; the band eventually signed in 1987 with Arista internationally and Mushroom in Australia. Kilbey (2016) insists that through a series of record companies and managers, 'if anyone was trying to make my music … was trying to dumb it down or make it mainstream, I resisted that, yeah. I was resisting the zeitgeist'. He describes the negotiation as one of 'friction' that 'wore me out … Every time I wanted it my way I had to fight and rub up against all these mother fuckers who were trying to make The Church like whatever was … the latest things was that week. I'm going no'.

Despite generational differences, emerging bands often benefitted from cultural capital associated with the counterculture. A good example is Sunnyboys who, a few months after forming in 1979, attracted the attention of veteran 1960s rocker Lobby Loyde through an energetic live performance of all original songs penned by the eighteen-year-old lead singer Jeremy Oxley. Loyde was determinedly countercultural but well connected to industry players such as Michael Gudinski and had just kicked off the SCAM management agency in Sydney specializing in fringe bands such as The Triffids. He took on management of Sunnyboys, recorded their first EP with Phantom and brought them to Mushroom, producing the band's critically acclaimed first self-titled album in 1981 and its standout singles such as 'Happy Man' and 'Alone with You,' that catapulted them into a mainstream pop market Top 20 open to what was then termed the 'new wave'. For Peter Oxley (2018), '[M]ushroom gave us the opportunity to make an album; their connection with all the radio stations; and to get on *Countdown*. They were the biggest in Australia, and an Australian label'.

Sunnyboys' first album was a success. David Nichols (2016: 473, 475) describes it as 'perfect in almost every detail', 'firmly international' and the 'equals' of Buzzcocks, The Undertones and Blondie. However, it also raised the stakes, showing that a rapid ascent can often be short-lived. The relationship with Mushroom soured after a second album – *Individuals* (1982) – was hastily demanded to retain the assumed fickle enthusiasm of the bands' new legion of fans. A still exasperated Oxley (2018) recalls that '[i]t fell apart when Lobby took the album we recorded … to America and when it came back it was this complete shitty thing and we pleaded with Mushroom to let us remix it, and they said no and put it out. So we really lost a lot of faith in everything and that was the beginning of the horror'.

The band became frustrated with Mushroom's failure to negotiate appropriate affiliations in the UK and the United States with smaller labels plugged into audiences for 'alternative' music, and offshore impact eluded them. According to Peter Oxley (2018), Sunnyboys were comfortable performing to larger audiences 'a thousand people, maybe 800', but Mushroom could only envisage stadiums and the corporate A&M, missing the boutique labels who introduced The Go-Betweens, The Triffids and The Birthday Party in the UK. 'That was the thing about being signed to Mushroom', Oxley (2018) complains, 'you did lose a lot of control. You were told this is what was going to happen … They can do whatever they want, and it doesn't matter what we think'. There were also artists, however, who avoided this fate. Nick Cave and The Boys Next Door/The Birthday Party and Paul Kelly both left Mushroom to work with genuine independents at home (Missing Link in the case of Cave; White Label for Kelly) and abroad, asserting creative control over the next stage of their careers.

There were more genuine independent labels emerging from and crafted around the needs of this generation of alternative bands. An example was Regular Records, formed by Martin Fabinyi out of his enthusiasm and commitment to see his friends Mental as Anything out on vinyl. Frictions often remained, however, even in cases such as these. Chris and Peter O'Doherty lamented the treadmill of the band's success, where a run of hits led to the expectation and work pressure from record companies to keep producing more hits to the detriment of the art. Both agree 1982's *Cats and Dogs* was 'our most cohesive and strongest album' (Peter O'Doherty 2014), combining hit songs with creativity and attitude: 'We were still like a garage pop band' (Mombassa 2014). After that success, they felt the pressure to produce more hits, and subsequently their sound 'drifted to the centre' – partly as a consequence of record company pressure and partly a pragmatic inclination in the band: 'We were an easy going, sort of, egalitarian, democratic sort of band and whatever happened happened, and if someone's songs were popular you went with that. And that was how it went' (Mombassa 2014).

Tensions came to a head when Regular Records signed the band to Sony at the height of one of their most commercially successful hits 'Live It Up' (1985) which later featured in the film *Crocodile Dundee* (1986). As Reg Mombassa (2014) recalls, Sony 'didn't want any of the whacky art school stuff. They wanted the mainstream pop stuff. That was what they wanted. They didn't quite get that'. The follow-up album *Mouth to Mouth* (1987) was less successful, and Sony abruptly dropped them, cancelling a half million-dollar debt they owed the company. Despite Mental as Anything's fertile period as a critically acclaimed yet popular band, their mid-career commercial period has dimmed their earlier reputation as a subversive post-punk art band. 'The Mentals get pigeonholed for being what we were in 1986' laments Peter (2014), 'rather than what we were for those … dynamic five years before … All of our really interesting stuff'. '[W]e're not one of the critical canon of Australian bands that are loved by the critics and the uni students and the middle class intellectuals', conceded Chris (2014), 'We've been shut out of that.' This was the threat to cultural value in the affiliated Indie model of the late 1980s.

In the case of Hoodoo Gurus, tensions with Big Time arose over the production and marketing of their third album *Blow Your Cool* (1987), as well as over the non-payment of royalties. The band was also in disagreement with the American label over the single 'What's My Scene', a number 5 hit in Australia, which the Americans refused to release to commercial radio, reserving it for college radio. Faulkner (2018) explains that the American affiliate preferred to release an atypical song 'Good Times', particularly because The Bangles – who were popular at the time – did all the backing vocals on the track. 'We should have stood our ground then but didn't … you have to do what they say even though it's the wrong thing. It's not their fault ever.' The biggest problem stemmed from creative conflict with a big name producer appointed by Big Time records, an Australian who had worked with industry favourites, with whom the band felt they had little in common:

> That reminded us why we didn't want to be part of it – that world, that industry side of things … The classic rock star producer who thought he was shit hot and you were lucky to have him. He didn't understand our music, he was from the commercial straight world. Cold Chisel, Models … very mainstream … we had strayed too far.
>
> (Faulkner 2018)

The band sued Big Time at great expense on the issue of royalties. The band won and after the case the Hoodoo Gurus bought Big Time from the liquidators, who had few assets remaining other than the rights to their own record masters and those of other artists signed. As a result, the band gifted the rights to these masters to fellow Australian artists who had been with the label. The Hoodoo Gurus resolved that:

> [W]e will never get to that point again, where we're with a record label, they're not paying us, we're being marketed wrong, we have a producer who doesn't understand us … and it was a nightmare making that record.
>
> (Faulkner 2018)

In practice this meant negotiating contracts where they retained control, and this was the model going forward, leveraging their fan base and credibility for autonomy: '[W]e have produced every record ourselves since with a variety of labels, including Mushroom … "the lunatics running the asylum"' (Faulkner 2018).

The 'industry' experiences of The Church, Hoodoo Gurus and Mental as Anything were almost always difficult, fraught, conflictual, running strongly counter to the recent tendency, most evident in the 'creative industries' position discussed in the last chapter, to minimize differences between commerce and culture. In drawing attention to hybridity between the fringe and mainstream, the fields of 'restricted' and 'large-scale' production, we do not wish to minimize these tensions. Our position is rather that *despite* the antagonisms, fringe and mainstream often enter into complex hybrid formations that have benefits for both.

What is revealed then is the careful bargaining, persistent negotiation and vigilance required of artists who seek to preserve in the mass market some of the autonomy that had secured them credibility with audiences in the fringe and brought them to the attention of industry in the first place. Autonomy is always only *relative*. When autonomy is elevated to an absolute, cultural analysis succumbs to purist allegations of selling out that misses the specifics and context of each case, the degree of autonomy retained and how that independence is deployed beyond the fringe.

The Australian post-punk examples show how music countercultures nurture artists in a disposition to resistance and autonomy and are important for ensuring that at least part of the mainstream music offer pushes against what Wark (1999: 109) terms the 'conventions and limitations' of much mass culture. This process has persisted, albeit in different ways. The 1980s breakthrough bands were followed by an array of popular Australian Indie bands in the 1990s that in the wake of the mainstreaming of punk as 'grunge' in the United States represent an analogue prelude to the interconnected digital global Indie niche markets of today. For Faulkner (2018), still smarting about the accusations as the band crossed over in the 1980s, the 1990s breakout of Nirvana was a game changer, making it 'Okay to be successful because they were still underground. Even though you were the biggest band in the world you were not a sell-out. Just a good band'.

An indie for a new century: Sustainability and self-management

How are accommodations between fringe and mainstream negotiated today? In the early twenty-first century, they are often captured in the portmanteau term 'self-management', which melds notions of autonomy and accommodation, artistic and professional practice. The term has been associated with a shift in emphasis from rhetorics of resistance and negation to *negotiation*. Musicians work consciously to balance the tension between creative autonomy and popular scale, elitist and egalitarian approaches to audiences, precarity and remuneration, risk-taking and routine, the benefits of business planning and the constraints of corporate control. As young Melbourne musician Tejo D'Cruz (I Manage My Music 2020) puts it, 'It's cool to have a fuck-the-system attitude, but the system is so relevant now, and … you can use it in a way that is tailored to you and that can be a really powerful tool'. Autonomy and affiliation are now rarely experienced as a simple 'either/or'.

These developments are clearly related to structural changes in the industry. During the latter half of the 1980s and through the 1990s, the scale of the alternative scene grew to the degree that niche labels could establish international reach, indie bands achieved global profile through music video, and mainstream companies enjoyed major sales by accommodating upstart bands. Three factors in the formation of twenty-first-century indie in Australia have been critical in deepening the hybridization between practices previously marked as 'fringe' and 'mainstream': the fostering of strategic and business awareness among 'affiliated' musicians, the entrenching of popular music within state government creative industries policies (with direct support for professional practice through policy, funding and education) and the reinvention of the punk DIY sensibility within the digital disruption of the established corporate structures of the industry.

For young musicians today, a career is premised on extensive engagement with a global field of indie production, direct access to digital production and distribution tools, high-level training in artistic and professional practice in secondary – and tertiary-level education, opportunities for grants and industry subsidies, and the possibility of sustainable returns through a strategically crafted international profile. Teaching in a Bachelor degree programme in Music Industry, Caroline Kennedy-McCracken advises students to focus relentlessly on managing creative aspirations within industry formations:

> [W]hether or not you want to be aiming for … a Top 40 hit on the US Billboard charts, or whether you want a long-term career as a niche subcultural rock artist, you are making an art product, and you'd better know what you're making, and you'd better know where its context is, and you'd better know everything about selling that, and everything about not selling that. Inhabiting that context … you need to know what context to be in, and you need to know how to be in it.
>
> (Kennedy-McCracken 2015)

The advice condenses hard lessons learnt from the experience of affiliated indie. Kennedy-McCracken survived a decade as an indie, signing to Mushroom Records – The Plums (1992–5), Deadstar (1995–2001) – and witnessed first-hand the conflicts of art and commerce, as the now-mainstream label struggled to capitalize on the emerging grunge and alternative wave.

A pervasive theme in relation to the present has been of a collapse of earlier distinctions between fringe and mainstream. As Peter Chellew (2014), a thirty-year veteran of community radio, industry agencies and festivals, observes, the distinctions have 'flattened out' for musicians; there are now 'blurred lines' between the fringe and the mainstream. Another musician remarks that 'there's no proper way of doing it anymore' (RMIT Music Industry Students 2015) – no 'proper' mainstream and no 'proper' fringe – suggesting that the topography of difference and distance (outside versus inside, margin versus centre) has finally dissolved. The development has been widely associated with a further erosion of the idea of authenticity that was once seen to characterize the fringe. As critic Giles Fielke (2016) puts it, there is 'a sense of "inauthentic authenticity" to much alternative music being made in Australia'. The terms have become reversible, folding back on themselves.

It would be easy to conclude from this that the present is simply an extension of the postmodern moment of the 1980s and 1990s, deepening the conviction that there is no outside to the business logics that govern the mainstream industry. Such a perspective is often suggested by musicians themselves. Kylie Auldist, 'high priestess of Melbourne Soul', advises emerging musicians to 'treat music like a business' (RMIT Music Industry Students 2015). Many others speak of careful planning, hard-work and unrelenting focus: 'I know exactly what I'm doing every day for the next three months', says Josh Delaney, a musician producer and label owner (RMIT Music Industry Students 2015).

The redefinition of fringe practices in terms of business has been reinforced by the embrace of indie by industry bodies and government policy. There is now significant support for indie strategies of self-management within the mainstream music industry. The roll call of 'Australia's new generation of global stars' in Music Australia's 2016 industry plan consisted entirely of indie artists such as Courtney Barnett, Flume, Hiatus Kaiyote and Tame Impala (Music Australia 2016: 7). While Music Australia's goal was ultimately a commercial one – to 'take our rightful place as a top global music market' (Music Australia 2016: 4) – it was acknowledged that Australia's national, multi-billion dollar industry is 'almost exclusively made up of micro, small and medium businesses', with 99 per cent having an annual turnover of less than AU$2 million (Music Australia 2016: 5).

It would be a mistake, however, to see the new generation of self-managed musicians as having ceded the distinction between artistic and economic value. As in the era of affiliated indie, a pragmatic understanding of the business possibilities of art does not preclude an appreciation of the artistic possibilities enabled by business. Twenty-first-century indies have built on and transformed the negotiated autonomy models developed by post-punk artists of the 1980s and 1990s through a rolling series of mutually recognized accommodations between the two orientations. They continue to pursue artistic agency, supported now by informed and effectively equipped engagement with an industry radically reshaped by digital technologies. Treat music like a business, yes, but recognize the new opportunities emerging within a disrupted industry, take advantage of the training and funding schemes fostered by creative industries policy, ride the vectors of digital culture towards low-cost, high-quality production, simplified distribution and global profile.

A paradigmatic example is the Melbourne musician Courtney Barnett, who we were regularly directed to in the course of interviews as a model of contemporary independent practice. Barnett's background shares in many ways with the artists of the 1980s and 1990s we have discussed above. She studied briefly at art school, apprenticed in grunge bands (2010–11), releasing DIY recordings on cassette and CD. In 2012, she formed her own label, Milk! Records, with fellow musician Jen Cloher, releasing EPs of her solo work in 2012 and 2013. The new registers of critical acclaim and professional profile followed: buzz on *Pitchfork*, a listing on the Triple J annual 'Hottest 100'. The 2015 release of her first LP (on Australian, UK and US labels) secured eight Australian Recording Industry Awards (ARIA) nominations (with four wins) and a Best New Artist nomination at The Grammys. After that, it was a Brit nomination for Best International Female Artist and the Australian Music Award (both 2016), international tours, appearance on *Saturday Night Live* and *Jimmy Kimmel Live*, side projects with Kurt Vile, and a two-page review in the *New Yorker*.

Barnett's is a story of a very local performer (reflecting on Melbourne's inner-city in an Australian accent) establishing a workable and sustainable self-managed career (encompassing music, merchandise, social media, business interests, performing, high-end industry networks) while simultaneously securing powerful reputational status as an innovative artist with character and integrity. Foundational to that narrative is an enactment of the dual identity of indie artist and self-managed professional. Barnett is independent of conventional industry structures and yet astutely engaged with them. She is differentiated from the mainstream industry yet nominated for its highest accolades. What is particularly distinctive (to the point of serving as her brand) is an astute meta-narrative that constitutes a particular voice and mode of practice.

Barnett's work is grounded in a grunge tradition and scene but coloured by an observational, laconic voice. She speaks, in both music and media, in understated terms of vulnerability, locality and generational experience. Her songs are emotional and relatable but link with larger issues. These are projected as an affective ethics: 'Just having an opinion is a form of being political. It's

Figure 12 Courtney Barnett, photographed by Ian Laidlaw [n.d.]. Courtesy Ian Laidlaw.

my thoughts and my life, what I see and how I see it. All of that is political' (quoted in Piris 2016). Her gestures and conversations return, as they so often do among contemporary musicians, to subtle negotiations of integrity within a global industry. Barnett sells merchandise on her website: records, T-shirts, tote bags, even socks. She admits to being 'a huge merch nerd ... I've always been influenced by visual stuff. My dad worked at a printing factory and I love logos' (quoted in Piris 2016). Merchandise is a significant revenue stream for indie artists, but Barnett aligns herself with the consumer; sure, she sells it, but she likes it too. It's a generational marker, a wry confession that's half-way to becoming a song; pragmatism, self-management, self-deprecation, ethos and brand are interwoven.

Another example is the Sydney-based musicians associated with the independent label R.I.P Society, who couple self-management with a 'politics of ourselves' (Rae 2020: 118). Royal Headache guitarist Lawrence Hall (2015) explains that the band eschews heavy PR or management, following instead the self-management model of Washington, DC. DIY guru Ian Mackaye of Indie band Fugazi: 'You're keeping it within the family. There's no Mr 10% here. There's no anything else. We do it on our terms.' This politics is cast as a matter of ethics reminiscent of Foucault's 'care of the self' in which 'rules of conduct' (quoted in Rae 2020: 121) take shape as musicians 'open themselves to different practices to determine, for themselves, what works for them in that (socially embedded) moment and, indeed, what they are willing to do to create themselves in each moment' (Rae 2020: 131). It is in self-managed professional activity, in the artist's negotiation of the uncertain territories of the contemporary music industry, that this ethic is developed. In the case of contemporary indie, such ethics register in the abandonment of the old rules of the underground (autonomy, separatism, no sell-out) in favour of a practical openness of engagement with industry, media, audiences and markets.

This engagement is purposeful, analytical and critical; musicians consistently speak of the need to understand systems, their positions within them and the repercussions of decisions. Royal Headache drummer Chris Shortt (2015) articulates their determination to avoid the traps that ensnared previous generations:

> You hear about the music industry ... all the horror stories over the last probably thirty years of artists being picked up and then dropped, and having some ridiculous contract that has them basically as slaves to a label, and through the punk thing I never wanted anything to do with that. So once we got to a band that now is mildly successful, we want to maintain that independence and that control over our own thing, and never have to do something we don't want to do.

Warnock (2015) explains the transformation of independent labels like R.I.P as a response to a generational shift to part time bands or 'hobby bands with day jobs' (like Royal Headache) 'that weren't aiming for global domination', but for a sustainable artistic practice utilizing new, more accessible technologies:

> ... this system fostered their ability to be able to take these opportunities without having to give everything else up and put it all on the line. It was kind of like a more moderate approach to playing music from a fiscal point of view ... There's no advances, there's no huge recording budgets ... it's not go for broke, you know, it's just let's make this and throw it out through these avenues and play shows and do our best to have people hear our music but not bank on it.

Engagement is tempered by constant gestures of containment, deferral and refusal; side projects fragment conventional cycles of production and promotion, collaborations privilege communities of practice over the singular brand of the rock star, intermittent outputs and creative gap years resist the juggernaut momentum of success. In this, engagement is articulated as both participation and resistance. Self-management is emphatically about the care of the self. As indie musician Georgia Maq puts it, 'We stay true to ourselves by being self-managed' (I Manage My Music 2019).

As the example of R.I.P Society makes clear, the quest for independence remains, very much, a *social* practice. The stable of bands derives their ethic and aesthetic from a scene of peers that maps onto Bourdieu's field of restricted production. As Nic Warnock (2015) puts it of the musicians associated with R.I.P:

> I consider them all my peers, a part of my community ... They're all friends and they are all around the same way I'm around, a lot of the time. A mutual respect for the creative stuff that we make or facilitate but also in the way you operate.

The young emerging bands of R.I.P also point to the continuing importance of oppositional identities, overturning any idea that such identities died with the counterculture. They explicitly define themselves against what they perceive as the mainstream music industry. Royal Headache drummer Chris Shortt recalls having his world transformed through exposure as a teenager to a grassroots hard core scene. It is there that he met the future lead singer Tim 'Shogun' Wall through DIY performances at suburban police citizens youth clubs – a space that traditionally sought to direct youthful energy from delinquency to positive action.

Royal Headache speaks to the persistent importance of small scenes – formed, in their case, around a twenty-first-century reimagining of punk – in occupying and subverting mainstream media and cultural platforms. Their first label R.I.P is on the one hand an exemplar of the self-management model, but this ethic of subsidiarity and creativity autonomy is nourished by a commitment to what Warnock (2015) calls a 'a greater social dialogue' drawing on punk and the DIY principle, 'a collective or a continuation of some kind of music counterculture'. Beyond the all-important ethos, Warnock's social goal was to 'create these relationships between people and communities and artists and labels. Even complete scenes of music that weren't represented elsewhere'.

A further example is contemporary Sydney indie power pop band Bloods, which emerged in the 2010s, building on an extensive streaming presence and US tour with a coveted signing with Sub Pop Publishing, the Seattle label that broke Nirvana. The band shares with the R.I.P bands a punk inspiration, but has emerged from a different social scene. Lead singer Marihuzka Cornelius, who arrived in Australia as a child refugee from Panama, was exposed to post-punk subcultures while working on her father's leathercrafts stall at Sydney's Paddington markets, an equivalent to London's Portobello Road market and a magnet for inner city subcultures, queer fashion, music and art cultures. She credits her success – confirmed in 2020, when her image adorned the banners of the Festival of Sydney – with punk's rule-breaking attitude: 'I think on a personal level, having listened to so much punk music and that punk attitude has helped me get to where I want and that attitude of like there really aren't rules' (Cornelius 2015).

Figure 13 Bloods, *Work It Out* (Tiny Galaxy Records, 2014), album front cover. Courtesy Bloods.

Importantly for Cornelius, her oppositional stance is also bound up with being a woman of colour in a white male-dominated industry. Likewise, Barnett herself arose from and remains part of the hip alternative music scene of Melbourne's inner north, where she cut her teeth playing and writing songs in bands ranging from garage grunge to psych country. As recently noted by Homan et al. (2022), in an era where digital tools of production and distribution are nebulous, Barnett participates in a subculture that enacts its practice of independence socially in the physical spaces of live venues, cafes, pubs and recording studios, what Straw (2015: 483) calls the 'public contexts of sociability, conviviality and interaction'.

Royal Headache's critical success, between 2011 and 2015, as a back-to-basics indie band owes much to a globalized enthusiasm for a disruptive underground, but also to the actual attainment – thanks to Do It Yourself digital tools, online media, indie label R.I.P Society, creating their own label Distant and Vague Records – of the creative autonomy traditionally sought by bohemian and avant-garde artists. This freedom is articulated in the classic underground tactic of refusal – Royal Headache's avoidance of becoming a 'proper' band or a 'product' (Scott 2015) – but is reinforced by hybridizing self-management practices such as relationship-based business deals, modest production costs, and spasmodic, self-funded touring arrangements. Perversely, but also understandably, the band's ultimate declaration of autonomy was their decision in 2015 to break up rather than continue in acrimony.

In conclusion then, we might point to significant continuities in the relation between fringe and mainstream music in Australia over the last fifty years. It would be a mistake to believe that the twenty-first century has seen an evaporation of the tensions we have explored above. As we have seen, the extent of these tensions in earlier periods has always been somewhat exaggerated. From the counterculture to punk – and even in post-punk and affiliated indie – there has been a tendency to represent 'fringe' and 'mainstream' as radically opposed, such that any assertion by one must necessarily be at the expense of the other. There has never been a moment, however, when they have not also entered into complex hybrid formations. It certainly needs to be recognized that relations within these formations have generally been fraught, involving friction between different values, institutional imperatives and personality types. But it equally needs to be recognized that these frictions have also been productive, in both cultural and economic terms.

If the tendency in the late twentieth century was to overstate the antagonism between fringe and mainstream, it has become today more the reverse. The loss of the idea of a singular underground has been widely taken as evidence that the values associated with it have somehow evaporated. In an age of globalization and digital media, we are led to believe, the topography of cultural production has flattened, drawing all players into a single consistent terrain. It is certainly the case that organizational and spatial distinctions between fringe and mainstream have in many ways blurred. As we have argued, however, self-managed artists have built on twentieth-century legacies through a rolling series of accommodations between cultural and economic value. The former continue to emerge from small scenes of peer interactions. While more fragmented and dispersed, these scenes remain vital to the cultural economy.

3

Subcultural design: Wearing our art on our sleeve

The fringe maps its world on an intimate scale: an indie album is recorded in the bedroom, a comedian performs in a half-empty pub lounge, a designer stitches together an outfit at a kitchen table. And with that intimacy comes a determined understatement of ambition. Dare Jennings, founder of the global streetwear label Mambo, insisted, in the face of massive market success, that 'we're all here because some blokes started making things because they needed some things to go surfing with' (O'Neil 1996: 13). In 1974, Jennings had started making things – silk-screened T-shirts featuring the cult comic book hero, the Phantom – in a Sydney garage (there's that indie intimacy again). In 1978, he opened the Phantom record store, followed in 1980 by the Phantom Records label (home to Sunnyboys and Hoodoo Gurus, among others). And in 1984, he launched Mambo Designs, which made all sorts of things: loud Hawaiian-style shirts, posters, streetwear and uniforms for the 2000 Australian Olympic team. Along the way intimacy gave way to the global, and the garage was supplanted by the art gallery. Jennings' humble account of Mambo's origins was elbowed aside by market and institutional rhetoric. For the National Gallery of Victoria, publicizing a major retrospective exhibition, Mambo Designs was 'a purveyor of fashion, philosophy, art and design' (National Gallery of Victoria 2014). For Saban Brands, which purchased Mambo in 2015, the company was a 'unique, art-driven' label to be added to their portfolio of 'exceptional fashion and lifestyle properties' ('Saban buys Aussie fashion label' 2018).

Charting the relationship of alternative and mainstream cultures invites territorial analogies. There are insiders and outsiders, centres and peripheries, royal roads and obscure alleys. The mainstream occupies the pervasive terrain of cultural production, while alternative cultures figure as marginal enclaves, lying low on the fringe. Ideally, as a secret or resistant culture, the underground evades the cartographic eye altogether. Within academic studies, mapping can have a qualitative and vectoral tone. The entrenched mainstream is normative and stable; the underground is atypical and volatile. The mainstream holds and extends its ground while a deterritorialized underground seeks to evade incorporation and recuperation.

Our case studies demonstrate that such geographies, redolent of the romantic figure of combat between culture czar and creative underclass, are no longer adequate to the practices of either margin or mainstream. In the case of design, it is evident that both corporate culture and bohemia meet in contemporary street fashion, a common territory shaped by reinvented subcultural tropes and mobile retail tropes. Over the past forty years, the retail explosion of streetwear has hybridized territories and values alike. Underground style founded in the counterculture of the 1960s has become a globally ubiquitous fashion while the business structures of main street retail propel the performance of subcultural identities. Now a multi-billion-dollar global industry, streetwear emerged from underground fashions associated with alternative, marginalized and even, in the old sociological parlance, deviant subcultures. Initially improvised by amateurs, then formalized by designers into retail styles, streetwear outfitted youth cultures – surfing, skateboarding, snowboarding, rock, punk, hip hop and rap – before becoming a staple of the mainstream clothing market, where it is now referred to variously as 'urban wear', 'athleisure' and 'action sports' wear. This transformation, as English style guru Ted Polhemus has noted, reverses the usual 'trickle down' of high fashion to mass market in favour of 'bubble up': 'Instead of the bottom end of the market emulating the top, precisely the reverse' (Polhemus 1994: 10).

Streetwear: From kitchen table to mass market

Streetwear began as an underground market – 'a cultural revolution' according to pioneering American brand Vision (Vision Street Wear 2018a) – grounded in restricted production, subcultural display and micro-capitalist structures. The origins of streetwear lie in the late 1960s and early 1970s when surf wear expanded from a countercultural constituency into a widespread youth market. Small-scale production (often at a kitchen table and garage workshop level) in highly localized territories (surf coast towns in East Coast Australia and California) sold at a micro-capitalist level (street markets, workshop outlets) has since massified into a global, brand-driven business serving an intergenerational market ranging from teen to middle-age, valued at upwards of US$60 billion per year.

Studies of the commodification of surf culture lament the appropriation of a countercultural aesthetic and its redeployment as a general branding component within mainstream youth and leisure marketing. Surfing is characterized as 'the surfing culture industry'; a 'multi-billion-dollar concern … incorporated into the mainstream through the use of its style and image' (Lanagan 2011; Stranger 2011: 2). More recently, an anti-romantic perspective has questioned the very notion of an autonomous or resistant underground, casting it as an ideal as elusive as the surfer's perfect wave. But as streetwear emerged as an urban style in the late 1970s and early 1980s, classical claims for alternative and resistant style were reinvented by new, younger players emerging through different subcultures, even as the entrenchment of their designs in the retail sector deepened. The material and design histories shaping this field – hybridized at the levels of aesthetics, marketing and consumption – reveal the ways in which alternative and indie approaches meld with more conventional branding, business and retail practices to propel a passage from margin to mainstream.

While streetwear designers systematically relocated urban underground style into mainstream markets, their aesthetic – drawing on surf wear, rock'n'roll, punk and political graphics – used postmodern tactics of bricolage, irony and retro/camp to develop a disruptive voice within the rag trade, ratifying their claims that an underground ethos had not been abandoned. In this they echoed strategies of critique, founded in rhythms of engagement and dissociation, that emerged across early postmodern aesthetic practices. In the 1980s, Umberto Eco remarked upon the tendency to frame affect within ironizing pop cultural references, enabling speakers to simultaneously deploy and disclaim speaking positions (Eco 1985: 67). The tactic was so pervasive within cultural undergrounds that a 'vaguely ironic, slightly sarcastic response to the world' risked becoming itself a convention (Lawson 1985: 155). Theorists such as Linda Hutcheon and Fredric Jameson placed parody and pastiche at the heart of postmodern practice (Hutcheon 1989; Jameson 1991). Irony, mimicry, parody, pastiche; each allowed for, if it did not directly endorse, the idea that the underground had set aside its traditional fear of selling out and instead chose to buy in. Tactically, then, streetwear designers modified a central trope of classical subcultural theory: resistance through ritual became resistance through retail. The marginal was positioned within the mainstream as a disruptive agent rather than beyond as a territorially contained outlier.

In Australia, the emergence of a retailed underground was manifested in the creation, in the 1970s, of what were to become global surf wear brands. Quiksilver, Rip Curl and Billabong grew into the country's largest clothing manufacturers, all the while claiming that the countercultural ethos of surfing had not been subsumed by mercantile concerns. In the 1980s and 1990s, successful Australian labels associated with urban streetwear, such as Mambo, developed retail aesthetics that incorporated self-conscious, parodic meta-narratives around the transition from street to store, margin to mainstream. Others, such as Mooks, adopted a conventional corporate approach, systematically monetizing subcultural style and expanding into global enterprises. The contradictions that were to preoccupy the music scene in the 1990s – mainstreamed 'alt', mass market 'indie' – were acted out by streetwear designers in the 1980s. They played a double game, rooted in Polhemus's equation; street-style and subcultural authenticity were persistently invoked, both rhetorically and aesthetically, while the streetwear brand itself was self-evidently sustained by orthodox retail practices.

Mambo's aesthetic, along with its business tactics and commercial success, makes it a significant model for this distinctive transition from polarized territories (margin/mainstream) to a space of generative hybridity characterized by its participants' claims for indie infiltration and a subversive buy-in rather than pragmatic sell out. This was a transition already being played out in post-punk music, with which Mambo directly engaged in the operation of the Phantom Records store in Sydney, the employment of artist-musicians as designers and the sponsorship of live music gigs. Mambo made the double game of resistance through retail central to its brand, signalling the contradictions of a commodified underground in design, marketing and even in-store promotional material. This chapter will examine the contradictions with which Mambo grappled, and the tactics developed in negotiating underground attitude and main street retail. These included a negative aesthetic (retailing a critique of the commodification of the underground), appropriations of corporate agency (business structures allowing for a kind of guerrilla capitalism), and the canny development of modes of resistance in design (especially parody, pastiche, humour and irony). Mambo's tactics are related to those evident in others of our case studies; the enactment of an indie 'ethos' as a counterbalance to participation in mainstream markets, humour as a means of pivoting between resistance and assimilation, and a strategic operational status – the 'affiliated independent' – that staged independent practice within a mercantile territory.

Streetwear is a global fashion market rooted in the mainstreaming of subcultural style associated with sports, music and urban youth. The design and marketing innovations propelling streetwear, which date to the 1980s, were themselves an extension of earlier formations around subcultures and social movements in the 1960s and 1970s (Lewis 1976), such as surfing, punk and new wave. In 1982, Californian surfboard maker Shawn Stüssy transferred his company logo (his signature, executed in the manner of a graffiti tag) from surfboards to everyday clothing such as baseball caps and T-shirts. In this, he was doing what numerous workshop-based surfboard manufacturers had already done in the 1970s (among them Australian brands such as Quiksilver, Billabong and Trigger). The original small-scale production and informal retailing of the loose-fitting surf-oriented clothing preferred by surfers and skateboarders was amplified into general retail distribution; first through street markets and local surf-coast boutiques, then through distribution contracts with main street metropolitan clothing chains. This was typically followed by licensing deals driving international manufacture and distribution, retailing partnerships with major clothing outlets and department stores, and buy-outs and stock market floats assimilating what was once limited and localized workshop production into global consortiums.

Stylistically, street clothing was a cultural mash-up, combining elements of sports clothing (sneakers, loose fitting shorts and T-shirts) and branded major league basketball and football uniforms (with prominent, affiliation-declaring logos). Aesthetically, streetwear brought together elements of existing surf style (bright colours, intricate patterning emulating Oceanic cultures), punk graphics (collaged images, expressionist typography) and urban hip hop (repurposing of major league sportswear). This new design subgenre was popularized when US skateboard maker Vision, founded in 1976, named their Vision Street Wear brand in the early 1980s. Using prominent skateboard champions and emerging post-punk musicians as paid brand ambassadors, Vision occupy what they dub 'the sweet spot between music and action sports' (Vision Street Wear 2018a), establishing a hybridity within subcultural style that acts as a ready point of leverage into mainstream markets.

Through the 1990s, streetwear grew rapidly into a global youth fashion market with retail revenue now estimated at anywhere between US$60 and $290 billion per annum. In Australia, the largest fashion companies include surf wear companies crossing over into streetwear, such as Billabong (annual revenue AU$1.1 billion) and Ripcurl (annual revenue AU$431 million) (Fashion United

2018). This market has a deep history linked to long-standing assumptions connecting Australian costume to national mythology. In her study of the characteristics of a distinctive Australian dress, Jennifer Craik remarks on 'the centrality of swimwear and surfwear in iconic representations of the outdoors and casual Australian way of life as well as a central motif of generations of Australian fashion' (Craik 2009: 411). This centrality is rooted in the historical association in Australia of outdoor living, and especially beach culture, with health, liberty and egalitarianism. The sustained success of Australian surfers in international competition in the 1960s and 1970s consolidated surf wear as representative of both counter- and national culture.

Streetwear now encompasses all the features of the conventional clothing industry: aggregated brand portfolios, offshore manufacture, regional licensing, stock market floats and private equity investment. It maintains strong sponsorship and ambassadorial partnerships with prominent athletes and musicians, positioning streetwear as emblematic of 'a lifestyle that fused the world of music, art, fashion, and skateboarding' (Vision Street Wear 2018b). Today, major international streetwear brands, such as Supreme, mimic the tactics of luxury brands by fostering scarcity, fetishism, collecting and resale. In short, what Vision dubbed a 'cultural revolution' is now, in many of its business operations and brand tactics, indistinguishable from a mainstream or luxury product.

Streetwear and the calculus of cool

Clothing retail is a risky business and prominent Australian surf and streetwear brands have suffered from over-expansion, declining sales and failed stock market floats. In recent years, a retail downturn and unsuccessful floats have seen major players suffer public humiliations: in 2017, Billabong (incorporating the Von Zipper, RVCA, Xcel and Kustom labels) posted a loss of A\$77.1 million (Chau 2017); Globe International Ltd, owner of a portfolio of twelve skateboard and streetwear brands (including Mooks), declared the value of its trademark to be zero in 2014 (Inside Retail Australia 2014).

But the streetwear trade also faces a unique risk, inherent to the mercurial calculus of cool. Streetwear brands remain anchored in the invocation of the underground; this is the romanticism that remains the core of its appeal. Historical, stylistic and attitudinal roots in alternative and transgressive subcultures are claimed. Often an origin narrative is recounted as the underpinning of a brand's ethos, associating style and value with a place (a beach, an urban neighbourhood), a person (a skateboard or surfing champion) or a musical genre (rap, punk) – all of which are collated as an ethos of outsiderism, difference and resistance. When style circulates on a mass scale, the power of this mythos is diluted and underground status lost. Massification is both the goal and the Achilles' heel of the streetwear industry. Market ubiquity and a broad customer base deliver profit but put paid to claims for edgy, underground style. Time and again, streetwear entrepreneurs speak of market success as a threat to the integrity of the brand. Scale corrodes the defining obscurity and minority of the underground mythos; as Mambo's founder Dare Jennings put it, '[w]e don't want to go in and flood the market, especially the cult market. As soon as you lose the mystique you'll kill the market very quickly' (quoted in Chesterfield-Evans 1987).

A broadening market is seen as weakening a brand's defining association with youth; as one industry insider observed, '[i]t's the kiss of death if a 23-year-old, or 25-year-old, starts wearing it' (Askew 2003). The retailer's assumption that cool, marginality and resistance are the exclusive preserve of youth subcultures replicates a similar trope in first-wave subcultural studies associated with the Birmingham Centre for Cultural Studies. But both are at odds with the demonstrated capacity of the clothing industry to rebrand youth wear as adult apparel, as was the case in the establishment of jeans as high-fashion adult clothing in the 1980s (Sullivan 2006: 158–63). The hybridity of contemporary mass-market streetwear confuses both retailer and analyst alike. Contradicting its own claims that vitalism and rebellion are unique to the young, the streetwear industry successfully persuades the mature customer to invest in them. Determined to preserve the notion of bohemian resistance, subcultural theory sets aside a long history of the mainstreaming of youth style into adult markets.

What is really at stake in this lionization of youth and demonization of the adult consumer is brand management. The cross-generational embrace of street style – its normalization in the embrace of the adult consumer – significantly extends and expands the market. That is the retail goal. However, a brand built on the mythos of a resistant subcultural must deny that embrace even as it invites it. Reflecting on the decline in the reputation of Australia's Mambo streetwear in the late 1990s, then-CEO Angus Kingsmill observed that 'big corporations fell in love with them as did overweight, middle-aged tourists. So, the shirts were being seen on all the, if you like, wrong people for the demographic to whom

Mambo appeals' (Niesche 2014: 34). Or as Peter Oxley, Mambo employee and member of postpunk band Sunnyboys observed, 'we knew when Mambo's time was up when your uncle comes to the BBQ in a Mambo shirt and all the young ones are going, aw god ... dad wear' (Oxley 2018). Likewise, massification introduced class and gender signifiers at odds with claims to alternative status. 'Little girls from [elite private school] Pymble Ladies' College [PLC] wear Mambo and Stüssy', advertising agency director Mike Bowden remarked in the early 1990s, 'When it penetrates the hierarchy of PLC you've got to believe it's commercial. It sure isn't innovative and radical' (Cameron 1992). There is more to this than a putatively underground brand struggling with its own success. What it also suggests is the complexity of an historical moment in which what Raymond Williams dubbed 'residual and emergent' cultural tropes co-existed in seemingly unresolvable contradiction (Williams 1977: 122). The invocation of streetwear's authentic roots in subcultural resistance, articulated as a critique of its retail success by the very architects of that mainstreaming, is a residual romanticism voiced by the agents of an emerging hybridizing of margin and mainstream.

As the intersection of subcultural style and market structures grew in the early 1990s, both streetwear and alternative music were the locus of concerns at the mainstreaming of the underground. The breakout success, in the American market, of Nirvana and other American grunge bands in 1991–2 narrowed the distance between radical and normal, along with the time in which the gap was traversed. Gina Arnold, an astute chronicler of the US punk scene, remarked that by the mid-1990s, punk fans were no longer an underground but rather 'the perfect target market for anything' (Arnold 1997: 60). Grunge, observed Mambo's Dare Jennings, became 'a trendy fashion industry term' and street style just 'another term now in the mainstream' (Drugay 1994). There is something in Jennings' judgement that speaks of the difficulty that cultural agents themselves had in managing the residual and emergent, or perhaps of the centrality of a positional rhetoric in the management of hybridity. Jennings points to symptoms of inauthenticity – trends, industry, mainstream – with the intimation that grunge is a commercial, mass-market confection distinct from his product, rooted more in a locally inflected ethos.

Such reflections on margin and mainstream, and the corruption of the former by the latter, echoed then-current theoretical readings of underground and mass market style. Dick Hebdige's classic analysis, *Subculture: The Meaning of Style*, anchored authentic street style in 'a genuinely secret subculture of working-class youngsters' (Hebdige 1979: 25). In his centripetal model, a core of 'originals' coined subcultural style, while the 'hangers-on' who took it up threatened its value (Hebdige 1979: 93). Entry into the market further diminished authenticity. In Hebdige's formulation any centrifugal trajectory – 'the conversion of subcultural signs (dress, music, etc) into mass-produced objects (i.e. the commodity form)' – heralded the end of resistance (Hebdige 1979: 93). The social-semiotic value of style, its capacity for resistance, rested on secrecy, scarcity and specialization:

> Thus, as soon as the original innovations which signify 'subculture' are translated into commodities and made generally available, they become 'frozen.' Once removed from their private contexts by the small entrepreneurs and big fashion interests who produce them on a mass scale, they become codified, made comprehensible, rendered at once public property and profitable merchandise.
>
> (Hebdige 1979: 96)

As the concerns expressed by streetwear merchants in the early 1990s suggest, Hebdige's law – 'diffusion' equalled 'defusion' (Hebdige 1979: 93) – had become a commonplace. The simple spatial figure of high-value fringe and low-value mainstream held, even as brand management, sales analysis and marketing became more sophisticated in their segmentation and extensive in reach.

Hebdige's narrative, written around English punk, could equally be applied to the rise of streetwear in Australia. Between 1969 and 1976, all the major players in the surf wear industry were established: Rip Curl and Quiksilver in 1969 at Torquay, on Victoria's surf coast; Billabong in 1973, on Queensland's Gold Coast; Piping Hot and Trigger in Torquay (1975 and 1976, respectively). These companies began as kitchen-table enterprises and grew into major players in the casual clothing market. Along the way, design and branding elements – primarily a countercultural aesthetic combining spiritualism, ethno-exoticism and environmentalism – displaced the original, more directly functional characteristics of their products. Distribution through metropolitan clothing chains (themselves a mainstreaming of the 1970s 'head shop') made surf wear into general rather than subcultural apparel. This 'commodification of the sublime' as Mark Stranger dubbed it in the title of study of surfing (Stranger 2011) was the first formation of the cycle of subcultural mainstreaming that Hebdige lamented. If punk and new wave style represented a fourth-generation assimilation of underground to mainstream (the first being jazz, the second being hippy counterculture, the third surf wear), the fifth emerged in the mid-1980s, with the foundation of companies such as Globe International, which built its business out of a monetized subculture, parlaying a small distributorship of skateboards into a major portfolio Australian and international brands, entering the twenty-first century as the country's largest youth wear supplier (Huntington 2001).

Mambo and the subversive buy-in

The Mambo story begins, as so many fringe to famous narratives do, in small-scale, do-it-yourself (DIY) production. In 1974, Dare Jennings, a surfer and university drop out, set up a business screen printing T-shirts in a backyard shed in suburban Sydney. The enterprise – Phantom T-shirts – produced shirts featuring rock bands and cult comic characters (such as the eponymous Phantom) and was one of the many small-scale, craft and design ventures that emerged around urban youth subcultures in the late 1960s and early 1970s. Soon after its foundation, Jennings' backyard enterprise grew into Phantom Textile Printers and enjoyed a substantial annual turnover of AU$1 million (Power 1996).

Arguably, Jennings's T-shirt printery was an exercise in restricted production, opportunistic commerce with only a peripheral (if not instrumental) engagement with underground style. But in 1984, when Jennings founded Mambo Designs, he hired designers and printers with links to Sydney's extensive activist graphic arts scene. Design collectives such as Earthworks Poster Collective (active 1972–9), Lucifoil Posters (1980–3), Tin Sheds Posters (1983–90) and Redback Graphix (active 1979–94) produced dozens of posters annually, promoting rock gigs and benefit concerts alongside political campaigns addressing nuclear power, gay and lesbian rights, racism, Indigenous land rights, social housing and environmental issues. Many of them used intense colours, Andy Warhol-style stencilling and political satire based on re-purposing clichéd media imagery. While this aesthetic may have had its roots in modernist art movements such as Dada and Pop, it resonated strongly with the emerging collage and mash-up techniques of punk, new wave and retro styles. This direct affiliation with an underground aesthetic, and Jennings's foregrounding of its values as the ethos of Mambo, indicates the conscious management of the brand's status as a subversive infiltrator of the market, rather than a sell-out. In Hebdige's terms, Mambo's mainstreaming was staged as a self-conscious 'struggle for the possession of the sign' (Hebdige 1979: 17).

And yet there was no question that Jennings was in the business of selling apparel. Within two years of starting up, Mambo had increased production tenfold. By the end of 1987, the company was supplying 400 East Coast accounts in Australia, with major retail chains like General Pants ordering 360,000 units (Chesterfield-Evans 1987). Turnover was AU$5 million nationally and AU$1.2 million internationally (Chesterfield-Evans 1987). Fifteen years after its founding, Mambo's annual turnover approached AU$30 million (O'Neil 1996). But from the outset Jennings crafted a resistant, negative aesthetic, not only in Mambo's designs but in its business structure and his own public pronouncements on what was ironically dubbed the 'Mambo philosophy'.

Mambo entered an established market, openly declaring its scepticism towards the branding and marketed ethos of surf wear itself. Surf wear's entrenched 'endless summer' aesthetic – exotic beaches and crystal waters framed by idyllic tropical forests – was declared a marketing myth. As noted with punk, this declaration accords with Bourdieu's observation of the game of position playing in the cultural field, where emerging players seek to discredit the former avant-garde grown into an establishment as inauthentic (Bourdieu). The big surf wear companies, Jennings complained, 'have always sold surfing as a religion and it's a pretty easy thing to sell to teenage kids … From our point of view, I find that sort of stuff very cynical and unpleasant' (Collins 1997). As Reg Mombassa saw it, Jennings' concept was 'surf art is crap, I'm going to do some good stuff' (Mombassa 2014).

In 1985, Mambo sponsored a wave sailing competition at Merimbula, on the New South Wales coast. The poster for the event was designed by Paul Worstead, already a veteran of the Sydney poster collective and activist art movement, within which the aesthetics of Parisian May 1968 street posters melded with fluorescent Pop graphics. The dark, jaggedly drawn poster depicted a three-legged dog vomiting onto a beach littered with used condoms. This blunt rebuttal of the Edenic aesthetic of established surf wear manufacturers used raw, even repellent, branding to address the degradation of the environment and, by implication, the corruption of surf culture itself. Mambo's tactics were established early; they would participate in the youth wear market as snotty-upstart, court jester and forthright critic. A rude and raucous aesthetic, combining parody, mimicry and abjection, was pitted against the mainstream's fantasy vision of paradise.

This ethos was coupled with an agile, ironic voice – a negative aesthetic – that suggested that Mambo was in, but not of, the streetwear business. Jennings' successive ventures – T-shirts, a post-punk/alternative record store (Phantom Records discussed in Chapter Two) and Mambo itself – made for a brand that he could justifiably describe as 'a three-way split between graphics, a record

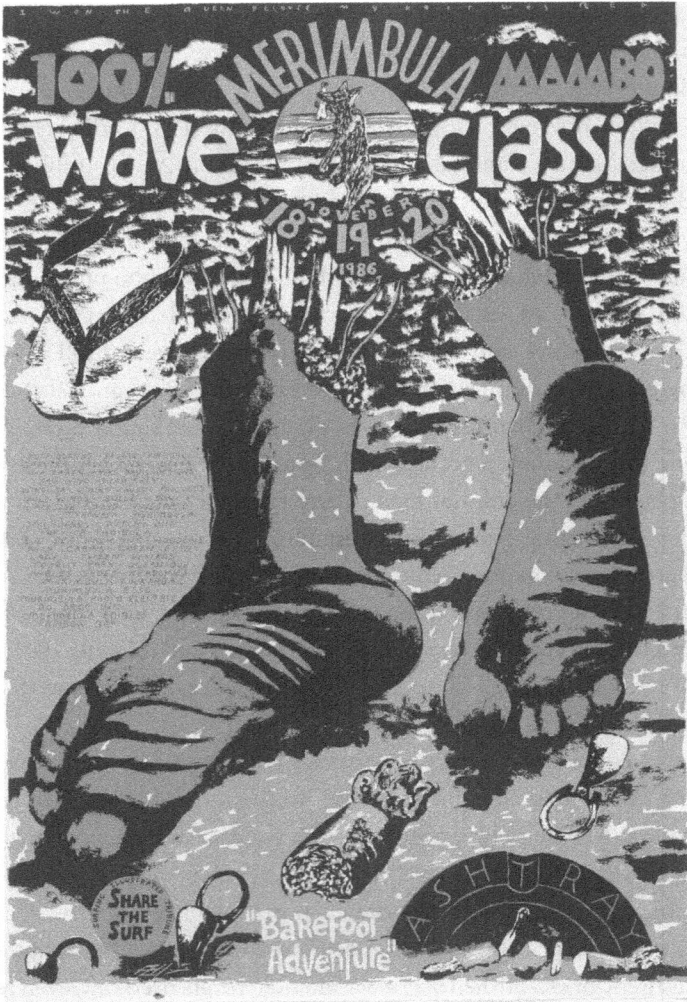

Figure 14 '100% Mambo Merimbula wave classic' poster, designed by Paul Worstead, 1986. Courtesy National Gallery of Australia.

label and the imagery of surfing' (Chesterfield-Evans 1987). He responded to the mainstreaming of surf culture with a powerful hybridization of its own mythic foundations in surfing, youth culture and rock'n'roll. He spoke with a tough-minded perspective, informed by the sceptical consciousness of 1970s political activism and ironic semiosis of the post-punk, new wave scene. Gerry Wedd's 1988 fabric design for Mambo, *Credibility Strip*, invoked the golden age of surf culture (the woody wagon, long boards and Beach Boys's tunes) but layered it with a dystopian vision of explosions, collapsing buildings, litter and hypodermic needles. Jan and Dean's paean to the endless summer, 'Surf City', was recast as Iggy Pop's 'Kill City'.

What gave Mambo its edge was a distinctive version of cultural politics, neatly meshing surfing subculture, inner-city leftist politics and iconoclastic Australian humour. The Mambo aesthetic was an astute hybrid of 1960s Pop art and 1970s political graphics. Its key designers – Richard Allan, Mental as Anything's Chris O'Doherty (aka Reg Mombassa), Paul Worstead, Gerry Wedd – were trained, exhibiting artists who revelled in the corruption of high culture by low and did not shy away from social commentary. Mambo's hallmark vulgarity was an offshoot from a distinctive genre of Australian comedy – so-called Ocker humour – which celebrated crass, vernacular and frequently carnivalesque humour as the authentic Aussie voice (Moore 2005). This mix connected populist humour with a resistant, activist style, effectively migrating the style of 1970s street posters and punk graphics into mainstream clothing retail. As Mambo's best-known designer, Reg Mombassa put it, 'Mambo celebrates Australian popular culture but it also makes fun of it and it's quite critical at times of certain political institutions and figures' (Poyner 2002).

All of this was propelled by a kind of knowing, critical consciousness suggestive of street-level semiotics. Mambo's version of retro made avant-garde and kitsch – once the defining antitheses in the struggle of high and low culture – into mutually reinforcing strategies. Mombassa (2014) observed the paradox that Mambo

> was like an art movement. It was a commercial art movement … And it was pretty organic … a collection of artists that Dare Jennings liked and got them to do stuff about Australian popular culture and politics and history and what have you. And dick and bum humour, too, which is always good.

Mambo designs were nostalgic, but biting, evocations of the colourful geometry and biomorphic patterns of mid-twentieth-century atomic age modernity. Retro was a meta-ironic, trans-temporal camp, combining the dated with the contemporary, the sincere and tongue-in-cheek celebration. Gerry Wedd updated the Tiki bar exoticism of long-lost beachside cocktail bars, recasting it as post-apocalyptic décor. A revivalist sensibility renewed historical sources with ironic and topical twists. Mombassa's targets included the masculinist tradition of the 'Ocker' Australian male (in an Hawaiian shirt patterned with meat pies

Figure 15 Mambo 'Safe Surf … just say no!' antinuclear T-shirt, designed by Gerry Wedd, 1990. Photograph: Michal Kluvanek. Courtesy Wakefield Press.

and beer bottles), and French nuclear testing in the Pacific (in a T-shirt featuring a beret-wearing troll farting a mushroom cloud).

Mambo's 'philosophy' was part of this ironic performance; a jibe at Hugh Hefner's 'Playboy philosophy' and claims by Australian surf wear manufacturers such as Grant Forbes (Rip Curl product manager) that they represented 'more of a philosophy than a business' (Loucas 1997). But rather than papering claims for a philosophy over what was essentially a large-scale corporate enterprise, Jennings structured Mambo so that his design aesthetic was the principal driver of the business. The Mambo studio was deliberately quarantined from the more instrumental elements of retail and manufacture, avoiding operating its own production facilities and shops, and streamlining international expansion through licensing deals rather than setting up manufacturing and retail infrastructure in new territories. This was an astute barrier against the common business peril of over-expansion but above all structuring the label as a studio that subcontracted production, distribution and retail made design the centre of the Mambo universe. This model was continued after Jennings sold Mambo to an investment consortium in 2008; business practices based in an indie ethos were recognized by the new owners as a means of growing volume while managing risk (Niesche 2014: 32). Artists were given remarkable latitude; as many testified, they were given no brief and no restrictions, Jennings simply selected what he liked from whatever proposals they presented to him. The artists saw the process as complementing and enhancing their art rather than diminishing it. The original cohort – Allan, Worstead, Wedd, Mombassa – saw Mambo clothing through the lens of 1970s activist graphics; a critical populism that took art and politics to the street. Far from mere commercial art, Mombassa (who exhibited his own art at Sydney's renowned Watters Gallery) thinks of Mambo as a force for cultural egalitarianism:

> I've still got a bee in my bonnet about art. Like top end fine art, there's all this stuff about the purity of it and the credibility of it and if you're selling fucking $50,000 paintings to rich people, what's so credible about that? ... It's still commercial ... I like the idea that normal people can appreciate art if they're given the opportunity. And t-shirts and posters and prints and cheaper ways of buying art or looking at it should be available.
>
> (Mombassa 2014)

Even when Mambo's new ownership gave the company a more mainstream character, it remained small and artist-oriented; in 2014, Mambo had a staff of fifteen, of whom eight were artists (Niesche 2014: 34).

In Hebdige's formulation, the commodification of a subculture's original innovation freezes its capacity for resistance. Mambo's tactics militated against that ossification. An open studio structure kept artists at a distance from the business. They were encouraged to persist with, and maintain the topicality of, a critical voice; branding was often characterized as intervention rather than assimilation or accommodation. Irony and parody were used to continually mobilize and destabilize the product/consumer nexus. Certainly these tactics could be contained, and, with new ownership of Mambo in 2008, this became the goal. As Jennings' successor, Angus Kingsmill, put it, '[o]ne of the bigger challenges has been balancing the irreverent art of the brand with the core values and customer expectations of our major retail partners' (quoted in Niesche 2014: 34).

Although a cult brand is shaped around fringe values, the primary encounter between brand and consumer – the point of sale – is conventional and takes place in an undisguised mainstream context. The skill lies in injecting a degree of dissonance into the transaction, one that uses irony to allow the customer to enact Mambo's own double consciousness. Colourful labels on Mambo clothing items mocked marketing hyperbole ('Makes you brainy') before undercutting the pitch ('Durability you can throw out next year'). Others reminded the purchaser of their own compulsion to buy: 'Your symbol of paying too much.' Alternatively, Mambo simply threw a spanner in the works. One fabric care label instructed the purchaser to '[w]ash bright colours with some very expensive white silk shirts'.

Australian streetwear: Global industry and national costume

At the same time, the growth of the streetwear industry in Australia represented the consolidation of the mainstreaming of the margins. Mooks was an Australian clothing label founded as the emerging streetwear or 'youth-urban' market took on more orthodox management and retail structures, expanding into multi-label corporations with listed-company status. Key figures in the establishment of the brand had existing track records in clothing manufacture and retail, combining both fringe and conventional experience. As such Mooks, while claiming roots in skateboarding subculture and street aesthetics, represented a conscious and large-scale mainstreaming of alternative style.

Mooks was one of a suite of brands umbrellaed within Globe International, a company founded by skateboard riders Peter and Stephen Hill. In 1984, while still teenagers, the brothers established Hardcore, a Melbourne-based company importing and distributing skateboard hardware (Huntington 2001). Through a combination of start-ups, licensing and corporate take-overs, the company grew into Globe International, a stock-market-listed company owning streetwear labels (M-One-11, Sista, Mooks), the Australian licensing to international streetwear labels (Ecko, Mossimo, Stüssy, Gallaz, Girl Star), and, through corporate acquisitions, 20 per cent of the global skateboard equipment market (Downie 2002). In 2001, Globe International was described as Australia's biggest youth supplier, with national chain General Pants carrying seventeen of the company's owned or licensed brands (Huntington 2001). Their products were retailed globally in thirty-four countries, with an anticipated value of sales of just under US$42 million (Huntington 2001).

Sean Cosgrove, co-founder of Mooks, began in wholesale, selling blank T-shirts to printers in the mid-1980s (Womersley 2006). After working in mainstream men's fashion in Melbourne, he teamed up with the Hill brothers in 1993 to become co-owner of a raft of streetwear outlets: Mooks, M-One-11 and Stüssy stores (Hoyer 2006). Cosgrove's observation that '[i]t was a move away from traditional clothing into the uncharted waters of streetwear' (Cosgrove 2006) is perhaps an overstatement; by the early 1990s new streetwear brands were building on robust foundations established by youth clothing retailers over the preceding two decades. Certainly there was an element of ambition, and risk, in Mooks' positioning within the retail landscape. The first Mooks store was opened on Chapel Street, Melbourne's major fashion retail strip, populated with emerging and high-end fashion label outlets. This gesture explicitly declared streetwear as a player in mainstream, fashion-forward clothing. The shop fit-out was designed by Marc Newson, who would go on to become an internationally

Figure 16 Richard Allan, *Farting Dog/Call of the Wild* design, 1987. Courtesy Caprice Australia Pty Ltd.

acclaimed designer, with clients that included Qantas, Louis Vuitton, Pentax and Samsonite. By 2001, Mooks shops were located across Australia and in Japan, New Zealand, Taiwan, Indonesia, the UK and the United States ('Junior Beat' 2001).

Richard Allan, one of Mambo's inaugural designers and producer of its iconic 'farting dog' motif, was Mooks' principal designer. In keeping with other emerging streetwear brands, such as Stüssy, Mooks designs were structured around the application of variants of brand name and logo to garments, as opposed to the elaborate pictorial graphics and custom fabric designs of Mambo. Simple retail strategies, such as Peter Hill's recognition that 'Surfwear was inappropriate for city life' (Buchanan 1994), propelled a simplification of design into branding essentials (especially logo) applied to uncomplicated, casual garments. Allan's logo for Mooks was a deceptively simple linear motif – a light bulb whose curved outline was interrupted by two discreet devil horns at its peak, with the wire filament replaced by a devil's trident. The effect was a sly invocation of energy, inspiration and mischief – a whiff of heavy metal Satanism, an allusion to youthful vitality and inventiveness. Stripped back and purposeful, Mooks' graphics focused on the branding task, in marked contrast to the wordy misinformation of Mambo's swing tags and labels, not to speak of their increasingly Baroque fabrics. At the same time, Allan maintained the scepticism towards mass marketing that had characterized Mambo during his time there. 'Street wear is a cynical marketing term that people apply to clothes for young people,' he observed. 'There is a lot of attitude involved but they are all just middle-class white kids who want to look like gangsters' (Buchanan 1994).

As a business, what distinguished Mooks from Mambo was the absence of maverick rhetoric, aesthetic provocation and social intervention. The Hill brothers ran Globe International in a way that the conventional clothing industry recognized and respected. As one peer observed, 'Stephen and Peter were always going to be in business. They had the means to do it, they were good at it' (Chessell 2003). In contrast to Mambo's model of small-scale design hub, Global International was described by one employee as 'quite a corporate set-up' adding, in a damning aside, 'I never saw the brothers skate the year I was there' (Chessell 2003).

Globe International's engagement with corporate structures in the clothing retail industry was the reverse of Mambo's. Where Mambo was positioned as an independent studio, licensing to larger producer-distributors, Globe was structured as an aggregated label portfolio, comprising its own proprietary brands and licensed product. Mambo steered clear of flagship retail outlets while

Mooks owned shops in seven countries. More significantly, unlike Mambo's Dare Jennings, the Hill brothers declined to act as brand figureheads, studiously avoiding media appearances; Globe International was no soapbox for the CEOs, nor was it a platform for political agency.

In a volatile and competitive market, Globe International's 2002 stock market float was regarded as a misfire, with downgraded earnings forecasts, dramatically declining share price and very low market capitalization (Askew 2003). Setting aside the poorly executed float, Globe and Mooks with it suffered from a syndrome common to the mainstreamed underground. 'The attraction of action sportswear turns on its being revolutionary, alternative, counter culture and rare,' one commentator observed, '[a]chieving mass popularity at least in the eyes of its key market can render the gear undesirable' (Askew 2003). As one industry insider observed, this was the persistent paradox of threatening mass-marketed alternative fashion, 'you've got to be anti' (Askew 2003).

Such pleas for resistance were made, perhaps not coincidentally, at a time when Australian streetwear was elevated to the status of national costume. The design commission for the Australian team for the Sydney 2000 Olympic Games was awarded by the organizing committee to Mambo, and its best-known artist, Reg Mombassa. The Sydney 2000 Olympics were seen by many – tourism agencies, cultural analysts, newspaper editorialists – as an opportunity to brand Australia on an international stage. The now-commonplace televisual spectacle of opening and closing ceremonies – replete with parades, pyrotechnics and pageantry – framed this brand, but within it the uniform of the Australian national team was considered a significant element, subject to intensive media scrutiny (Berry 2013). Rejecting a long design tradition of pocket-crested blazers and neat casual slacks, Mambo's proposal for the closing ceremony uniform featured cargo pants and one of Mombassa's signature loud Hawaiian shirts in his 'Suburbia' fabric. The combination of streetwear styling and Mombassa's ironic, cartoon-like images of 'Godzone' suburbia was lauded as an energizing injection of larrikin humour into the national brand. Four years later, at the Athens Olympics, the Australian uniform was again created by a designer with roots in streetwear: Richard Allan, one of Mambo's original team and a principal of the Mooks label. Streetwear, the uniform of feckless youth since the 1980s, was now centre stage in a national branding narrative. The irreverent, iconoclastic and outright scatological humour of Mombassa's and Allan's designs was now mainstream, endorsed by government agencies and embraced by the tourist market. Was this the moment of the underground's triumph – the subversive style infiltration of a national patriotic festival – or of its defeat by mainstream co-option and commodification?

The roots of streetwear have been associated with deviant subculture, with underground music, with the subaltern voices of suburbia. Street style is presented as authentic, resistant and empowering. Streetwear design has occasionally been a platform for political dissent and social effrontery. But as a business its passage has been from limited, backyard production towards a market of a global scale.

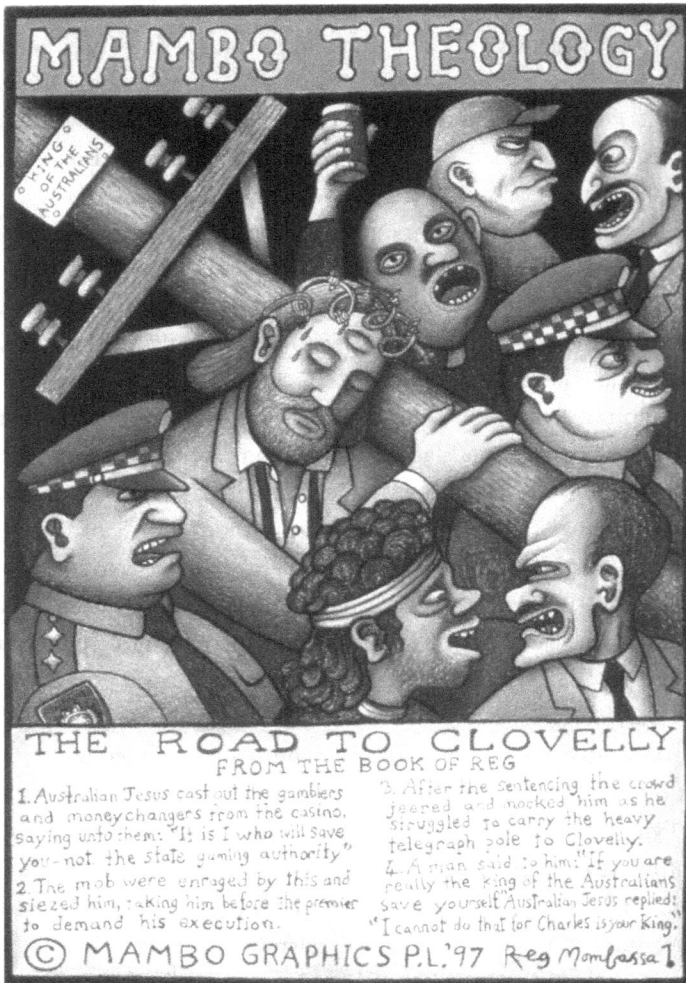

Figure 17 *Mambo Theology: The Road to Clovelly* by Reg Mombassa, 1997. Courtesy Reg Mombassa.

As such, it has never been able to avoid accusations that it cashes in on cool and sells out subcultural resistance. Contemporary street fashion remains positioned across both margin and mainstream, often in fluid and ambiguous contexts. As is the case with independent music, streetwear labels must attend to both symbolic and material economies. Street style is priced and promoted for retail consumption but it must also be managed as a form of rhetoric or cultural semiosis. The contradictory status of 'alt' and 'indie' as both underground and mainstream is propelled by the performance of a cultural status that shuttles between the two. The classical formation of that performance is staged by cultural institutions that frame design within the terms of the historical avant-garde and the structures of high culture. When the National Gallery of Victoria staged exhibition *Thirty Years of Shelf Indulgence* in 2014 (National Gallery of Victoria 2014), Mambo designs was characterized as ground-breaking, subversive, controversial and intensely political – in short, as representative of vanguard culture deserving of a place within official cultural histories.

Where once vanguard and mainstream were antithetical, each defining itself in its opposition to the other, mobilization across both spaces now appears to be normalized. When Melbourne-independent designers Perks and Mini (also referred to as P.A.M.) were included in the Frankfurt museum exhibition *Trading Style: Weltmode im Dialog* in 2013, they were located within an independent aesthetic that 'emancipates itself from the Haute Couture of Paris, London, Milan or New York yet competes on an equal footing when it comes to style and sensibility' (Hemmings 2013: 86). With a design aesthetic that registered 'their distaste for conventional methods of mass production and mass consumption of fashion' (Hemmings 2013: 86) and roots in street style, P.A.M. consolidated key strategies bridging margin and mainstream that had emerged in the 1990s. These included positioning as affiliated indie, the declaration of an ethos-based style and evocation of the traditions of the artistic avant-garde.

P.A.M. launched in Melbourne in 2000, as a design partnership between Misha Hollenbach and Shauna Toohey. With a background in street graffiti, skate wear and formal design studies, the partners have consistently straddled both art and couture, harking back to a modernist tradition including Paul Poiret and Elsa Schiaparelli without losing a connection with street attitudes. A collaboration with American grunge sculptor Mike Kelly in 2007 sits alongside an earlier affiliation with Paris-based emporium Collete, and exhibitions as artists in New York and Melbourne galleries. An enthusiastic endorsement of their designs by a Tate gallery curator in 2013 sealed their artistic credentials. Aesthetic diversification is also a key factor in affirming forms of creative autonomy in conjunction with relatively conventional retail practices; P.A.M.'s production of books, music and exhibitions registers as a commitment to art projects rather than the production of retail catalogue. As one of the team put it, 'We wanted an outlet to collaborate with other artists whose work we really admire' (Wilson 2001: 28).

All of these positional signifiers seemed to click into place with the opening of a flagship shop in Melbourne in 2015. Described by a reporter as 'so-cool-it's-frozen', the space was one where 'fashion and high art collide' with projections, white floors and vinyl records making it 'more like a gallery than a fashion store' (Harry 2015). Still designated as an underground label, P.A.M.'s endorsement by the Tate gallery was complementary rather than contradictory. What is striking in both trade and general media reporting on P.A.M. is the normalization of a 'mainstreamed underground' narrative. There is certainly no cynical strategy underpinning the label (on the contrary, it seems driven by sheer enthusiasm) and yet there is a recognizable, even typological form to it. There are the skate and graffiti roots of the designers, positioning their enterprise within an established retail genre. (In the United States, P.A.M. is referred to as a skate label.) There is the retro style of their early designs, allowing ready association with a wider 1980s revival trend as well as with the redolent referential nostalgia of contemporary youth culture. And there is the designers' direct participation in the experience economy of the contemporary art world, combining project, practice and performance in art constituted as a succession of events.

In design, a passage from fringe to famous is now structured around, and recognized through, genealogical elements (street and youth culture roots), strategic mainstream affiliation (fashion festivals, major retailer partnership, fashion media profile), maintenance and repeated assertion of indie ethos (anti-corporate rhetoric, emphasis on aestheticized values), and enactment of art world procedures and vanguard gestures (experimental projects, artistic collaborations, museum exhibitions). The notion of sell-out appears to be almost redundant, partly because the Warholian edict that 'business is the best art' is now a commonplace, and partly because young creatives have learned (from artists) that brand and credibility can be staged in mutually reinforcing ways within a mobilized, project-oriented practice.

4

From fringe theatre to prime time:
The case of comedy

In the late 1980s and 1990s, the television sketch comedy shows *Fast Forward* and *Full Frontal* were among the leading commercial properties in the Australian media. They were consistent prime-time ratings winners, drawing more than 30 per cent of the viewing audience. They won multiple awards and launched the careers of some of Australia's best-known screen talents – including Jane Turner, Magda Szubanski, Ernie Dingo, Gina Riley, Glenn Robbins, Eric Bana, Julia Zemiro and Shaun Micallef. In 1991, creator and producer of the shows, Steve Vizard, scooped the pool at the 33rd *TV Week* awards. Vizard himself took out the Gold Logie for Australia's most popular television personality, while *Fast Forward* was voted the most popular light entertainment/comedy programme. By the end of the 1990s, Vizard and creative partner Andrew Knight had sold interests in their production company, Artist Services, for more than $30 million (Lunn 1998).

Yet a significant inspiration for the shows had been a very different milieu – the 'small theatre' scene of the inner Melbourne suburbs of Carlton, Fitzroy and Collingwood in the 1970s and 1980s. This scene might appear the very antithesis of the glossy world of commercial television. It is best known from accounts of institutions such as La Mama and the Australian Performing Group collective at the Pram Factory in Carlton, which self-consciously defined themselves against the mainstream. Peter Cummins, an actor from the time, once described the performances as 'very uncouth theatre': 'Someone called us "the dirty jeans set". Our hair was long. We didn't wear make-up … Often we'd just do open improvisation'. It was, Cummins admits, an 'excruciating thing to watch' (Wolf 2008: 15). La Mama had been established in the late 1960s on the model of New York's radical fringe theatre by theatre director and cultural activist Betty Burstall. The scene was influenced by Antonin Artaud's 'theatre of cruelty', aspiring to 'engage in a primal experience and confront uncomfortable truths about the human condition' (Wolf 2008: 13).

There were points, however, where these hot houses of experimental or avant-garde theatre reached out to wider audiences. The best-known examples are hit plays such as David Williamson's *Don's Party*, which went on to become a box office success as a film directed by Bruce Beresford, who would later win Best Picture academy award for *Driving Miss Daisy*. A cycle of everyman working-class sex comedies in the first half of the 1970s such as *Alvin Purple* and *Petersen* also translated La Mama's sense of carnival and bawdy celebration of the body to the mass market, taking advantage of a relaxation in Australian cinema censorship and emerging distribution into suburban cinemas to reach new audiences. But for television comedy, the important sites of crossover were theatre restaurants that acted as popular outlets for the styles of performance of the dedicated small theatres – places such as The Last Laugh, The Flying Trapeze, Foibles and Comedy Café. These were generally very modest establishments. By Vizard's (2014) account:

> The main places ... were just little shop fronts that people had set up with a tiny little stage and a curtain. And they might take forty people and put on a crap dinner, you know. And they'd serve chocolate ripple cake. It was shithouse, but you paid virtually no money for it, and you got a show thrown in.

The low-stakes nature of these encounters was important, however, for the crossover that occurred. The performances in the theatre restaurants were often 'cutting edge': 'There was a real connectivity between both people who worked in those things, the people at the Uni who'd come and see them, and other performing arts groups.' But the audience was largely 'people from the suburbs driving in for a night out'. It was an audience who would have been unlikely to commit to serious theatre, but who were happy to try something different for a 'bit of fun'. They could always tell themselves that if the show was no good, they had still had a meal: 'You know, we've had ripple cake – it hasn't been all bad' (Vizard 2014).

It is this hybridization between the avant-garde and the ordinary, the experimental and the mainstream, that Vizard, Knight and their collaborators carried over into popular commercial television. The format of *Fast Forward* was ideally suited to modulating the relations between them. It was a fast-paced sketch comedy show, with segments ranging from political satire and send-ups of media personalities, other television shows or advertisements to musical parodies. It was classified as 'light entertainment' and drew on many of the techniques of popular comedy traditions such as vaudeville and variety, offering viewers a regular, predictable format that put them at ease. At the same time, it was punctuated by moments of surrealism, shock and absurdity, more usually associated with the experimental, fringe or avant-garde.

The dialogue between the two fields delivered innovation to a sketch comedy format that had become tired and routine. *Fast Forward* developed a self-reflexivity that broke with earlier television conventions. It placed the Australian media in the foreground as an object to be examined, as distinct from the politicians and national 'types' that had dominated 1970s satire, such as the *Naked Vicar Show* and *Paul Hogan Show*. Stylistically, it used the disjunctive format of commercial broadcasting – what Raymond Williams (1974) called 'flow' – to insert moments of irrationalism and surprise. It exuded a comfortable familiarity anchored in everyday suburban experience – transitions between sketches mimicked channel surfing and the show made frequent use of domestic video recording – while also opening spaces for subversion.

As the example suggests, television comedy is a particularly promising site for identifying hybrid formations between 'fringe' and 'mainstream'. In this chapter, we consider these formations drawing on interviews with key figures from a number of Australian examples. Comedy might be seen, in some ways, as an 'anchor' case for our argument in *Fringe to Famous* – one in which hybridity is intrinsic to the cultural form. It is also a useful case in refining ideas of the 'mainstream', particularly as they pertain to the media.

Comedy and the fringe

The analysis of relations between the mainstream and fringe has longer lineages in relation to comedy than probably any other cultural form, going back as far as the ancients (Hokenson 2006: 24–31). This has made comedy somewhat less prone than other fields to the countercultural capture of the idea of the fringe identified in Chapter 1. An important bridge between classical perspectives on comedy and more recent thinking has been Mikhail Bakhtin's concept of 'carnival', which was itself inspired by the French Renaissance writings of Rabelais. As Peter Stallybrass and Allon White (1986: 7) point out in their 1980s classic, *The Politics and Poetics of Transgression*, the concept allows a generous historical vision: '[T]he main importance of [Bahktin's] study is its broad development of the "carnivalesque" into a potent, populist, critical inversion of *all* official words and hierarchies in a way that has implications far beyond the specific realm of Rabelais studies.' The perspective is one in which the fringe never quite acquires the aura of revolution but is seen as belonging to ongoing traditions of public performance in which cultural differences and political tensions are played out. Perhaps also because comedy is by its nature unserious, it has been less prone to romantic pretension and, therefore, also to anti-romantic reaction. It has allowed more space for considering the fringe as material and historical.

This relative normalization of exchange between fringe and mainstream can also be seen in work, more specifically, on film and television comedy, where the fringe is often identified not so much as a particular position within the field as an influence and loadstar to be found, to varying degrees, throughout. As Steve Neale and Frank Krutnik (2006: 3–4) put it, for example, in their widely used text on the subject:

> comedy necessarily trades upon the surprising, the improper, the unlikely, and the transgressive in order to make us laugh … It is hardly surprising that comedy so regularly involves the representation of what the ruling and 'respectable' elements in society might regard as 'deviant' classes and their lives, since the attitudes, speech and behaviour associated with such classes can be used to motivate the representation of all kinds of impropriety.

It is true that the idea of a more specific 'alternative comedy' has some currency. The term was used, for example, in relation to edgy forms of political humour in Thatcher's Britain (Schaffer 2016), particularly by the group associated with *The Young Ones* and *The Comic Strip Presents* … , including figures such as Ben Elton, Jennifer Saunders, Adrian Edmondson, Dawn French, Alexei Sayle and Rik Mayall. But it is also common to identify the alternative *in* comedy, even when the comedy in question might be considered mainstream. An example would be Monty Python's *Life of Brian* which in 1979 had alternative and disruptive elements despite mass cinema release.

Screen comedy appears, then, as fertile ground for establishing the significance of hybridity between fringe and mainstream. Indeed, there is work in television studies that has already gone some way towards mapping out this terrain. An example is Doyle Greene's (2008) study of what he is bold enough to call 'avant-garde American television comedy'. The idea is deliberately provocative. In setting out his argument, Greene (2008: 3) is conscious of collapsing what are generally regarded as opposite extremes:

> On the one hand, American television exemplifies the working of the Culture Industry as defined by Theodor W. Adorno ... [It] can not only be seen as a collection of highly uninspired, and uninspiring, situation-comedies and comedy-variety shows, but a history of cultural commodities disseminating dominant ideology. Nevertheless, in certain instances, American television comedy has attained avant-garde and subversive moments.

In a series of brilliant readings, Greene identifies homologies between techniques used in certain strands of American television comedy and those of the avant-garde. He focuses particularly on figures such as Ernie Kovacs, Soupy Sales and Andy Kaufman who might be considered at the edge of the field. However, Greene draws attention also to avant-garde elements in more mainstream formats, from the 'rural comedies' of the 1960s – *Petticoat Junction*, *The Beverly Hillbillies*, *Green Acres*, where the theatre of the absurd met the heartland – to the 1990s–2000s animations *The Simpsons* and *South Park*.

It would be a mistake, however, to conclude that work on comedy has been entirely free of problems we have considered in *Fringe to Famous* in relation to other fields. Even as he questions an unthinking application to television comedy of Adorno's analysis of the 'culture industry', Greene does not fundamentally question the analysis itself. The avant-garde moments he identifies are presented almost as miraculous irruptions within a terrain that is assumed, indeed, to conform to a Frankfurt School picture of cultural production – as organized, that is, around standardization, neutralization of critique and subordination to the profit motive. This assumption directs attention from television institutions and economies, assumed merely to represent 'dominant ideologies', to the textual forms that resist or subvert them. The novelty of Greene's argument is to suggest that, in certain cases at least, resistance comes from *within* the mainstream cultural industries themselves. Even here, the assumption of a basic structural antagonism implies a risk that it might be expelled – as Kaufman was, eventually, from his regular spot on *Saturday Night Live*. The avant-garde, for Greene, is not so much hybridized with the mainstream as occasionally admitted as a fugitive presence.

Similar problems can be found in work on the carnivalesque. As noted above, the concept of carnival has clear strengths from the point of view of imagining hybridity, normalizing the tension between mainstream and fringe. It might also be distinguished from perspectives such as Greene's in that it brings the focus not to an exceptional avant-garde but to folk traditions of protest and revolt with a much broader social base. As the concept has been applied to popular media, however, its potential has often been lost, as the theme of dialogic tension has been displaced by that of structural antagonism. An example of this development was Terry Eagleton's complaint in the 1980s against the concept of carnival: that carnival was a 'licensed affair' or 'permissible rupture of hegemony' posing no real threat to those in power (Eagleton 1981: 148). That this point was, for Eagleton, 'almost too obvious to make' reflects the dominance in the wake of the counterculture of assumptions of a strict 'either/or': *either* the fringe represents a radical rejection of the mainstream, *or* it is functionally subordinated. No other possibility appeared imaginable.

These assumptions have been widely internalized even by defenders of the concept of the carnivalesque. The latter have been distinguished not so much by their analysis of the general form of relations between the cultural industries and the fringe as their assessment of the balance of power between the two. In an essay of the late 1980s, for example, John Docker (1988) suggests that the carnivalesque is far more potent than 'left pessimists' would have us believe. The foil for his argument, as for Doyle, is the Frankfurt School, but he goes much further in seeking to reverse its account of the dominance of the culture industry. The carnivalesque, for Docker, is a rampant, irrepressible force, consigning institutional and financial controls over cultural production almost to irrelevance. The article is a *tour de force* and has particular interest in relation to Australian television comedy-variety, which Docker interprets as the inheritor of a 'robust history of music hall, vaudeville and revue' (91). It has little to offer, however, in conceptualizing relations between mainstream and fringe. Anything associated with the former term is simply sidelined. The *industrial* dimension of television, where production is organized around formats, business models and employment relations, is seen as no more than matchsticks before the unstoppable tsunami of the carnivalesque.

The concept of carnival has receded in cultural studies over the past twenty years, never quite realizing the promise that it appeared to hold in the 1980s and 1990s. The work associated with it has been beset by reservations that were perhaps most influentially expressed in relation to closely aligned positions by Meaghan Morris (1990) in 'Banality in Cultural Studies'. The celebration of the popular, for Morris, often succeeded only in inverting the Frankfurt School pessimism it was seeking to contest, 'offering us the sanitized world of a deodorant commercial where there's always a way to redemption' (26). Relatively few in the 2000s and 2010s have followed Docker in amplifying the significance of the carnivalesque (although see Moore 2005). As noted in Chapter 1, there has been for the most part a contrary tendency to deny or exclude the fringe. It is true that one of the leading protagonists in this – the creative industries initiative – could be seen, in certain ways, as an heir to popular cultural studies of the 1980s and 1990s. It has shared the determination of the latter to fight free of critical pessimism in relation to the cultural industries. It has done so, however, not by insisting on the potency of the fringe but by dismissing as romantic any idea of an 'outside' to the mainstream, removing any ground from which the latter might be held to account.

A more general turn to industry-focused forms of analysis has seen a certain decentring of interest in comedy. There has been significant work from a creative industries perspective on *entertainment* (McKee, Collis & Hamley 2012) – work that has done much to correct the absence in popular cultural studies of attention to institutions, economies and technologies. The rubric includes comedy but has rarely brought a focus to comedy specifically. It has particularly avoided the themes of resistance, subversion and negation associated with the idea of the fringe – whether of the avant-garde or carnivalesque variety. Yet this absence has not been substantially addressed by the critical 'other' to the creative industries approach – the 'left culturalism' we considered at the end of Chapter 1. The latter has sought to reassert a critical distance from the creative industries, but it has done so mostly by focusing on labour relations. Again, comedy is comprehended under the framework – comedy actors, scriptwriters and producers can be seen as subject to exploitation and precarious employment along with others – but again, the perspective does not bring attention to comedy specifically.

There are signs, however, that this pattern may be shifting. An example is Brett Mills' (2017) book, with Erica Horton, *Creativity in the British Comedy Industry*. The book makes original contributions to the questions we have been canvassing, but in ways that are not immediately apparent. In an introductory chapter, Mills nods to the perspectives noted above – the Frankfurt School critique of the culture industry, creative industries approaches, left culturalist arguments, studies of creative labour – noting differences between them but remaining somewhat aloof on where he stands himself. The book appears to fit most clearly within a creative labour paradigm. Mills cites arguments by Andrew Ross, Richard Maxwell, Toby Miller, Kate Oakley and others about the need to foreground labour in the creative industries and his research is based on interviews with writers, directors, editors and producers about their work. But the labourist perspective is little more than a loose organizing framework and its associated arguments are rarely followed through. In moving to conclusions, Mills undercuts the critical themes of exploitation and precarity by pointing to the *rewards* that flow to comedy writers, editors and producers from their involvement in the industry: '[N]otwithstanding the ... structural issues apparent within the industry, if this book is to attempt to capture what those who work within it expressed most often about their day-to-day activities, it was pleasure' (Mills 2017: 165).

The ambiguity of Mills' position might easily be attributed to theoretical weakness, but we suggest that it is better seen as marking a subtle disengagement from a governing assumption of most debates in the field: that to recognize a distinction between mainstream and fringe is necessarily to imply a structural opposition. Drawing on Howard Becker's (1982) concept of 'art worlds', Mills (2017: 11) develops a view of creativity as diffused across 'cooperative networks', extending well beyond those we might conventionally designate as artists or creatives. An example is the network involved when comedians move from stand-up to television:

> While a stand-up comedian can write and tour a show with relatively little interference from others ... if that comedian moves into television production then suddenly large numbers of people – and a mass of industry norms – come into play. That the channels of distribution remain limited for television shapes its production processes and therefore the kinds of creativity that take place within it. But it also affects what constitutes creative labour as creativity becomes institutionalised as an aspect of television production.
>
> (Mills 2017: 155)

A crucial point here is that creative networks include those in *management* roles – not only editors and producers, but even those responsible for finance or production schedules (153). As Mills points out, such people often feel compelled to disavow creative input, as the artist is always the promotional vehicle, but this should not distract us from the fact that they can be critical to the realization of creative outcomes. In an important sense, they are 'artists' themselves.

This perspective is the closest of those we have considered to the one we will adopt in the remainder of the chapter. The removal of the assumption of structural opposition between fringe and mainstream makes it possible to recognize hybrid formations. This is not to lose sight of the fact that there is often antagonism. Mills rejects the suggestion of Richard Florida and others that creative work is organized only by the muse, somehow escaping the hierarchical, regulated world of industrialized production. To make comedy for a public service broadcaster, for example, is often to contend with deeply conservative institutions and to 'carry out work embedded in decades worth of policy' (155). In the commercial sector, the organization around profit often *does* lead to standardization and aversion to risk. If we are talking only of tendencies, the Frankfurt School analysis is not entirely wrong. The important point, however, is to recognize that they are *only* tendencies. In crossing from fringe to mainstream, comedians do not encounter abstractions such as 'bureaucracy' or 'capital', but specific individuals and institutions each with their own histories, their own receptiveness or otherwise to aesthetics or practices emerging from the fringe.

Cultural ecologies: A tale of two cities

A condition for hybridization between the fringe and mainstream is a porosity of social and institutional spaces of the kind that Vizard discovered in Melbourne's theatre restaurants, such that encounters between the two can occur. As the example suggests, a key area to consider here is the nature of urban cultural ecologies. In this section, we reflect on some features in the 1980s and 1990s of Australia's two largest cities, Melbourne and Sydney, that are relevant to the case of comedy. This is not to suggest that they are the only sites one might consider in the recent formation of Australian comedy, only that they are important ones, particularly in connection with large media institutions. The comparison is also useful in bringing to light some implications for creative production of the historical formation of cities.

An insight into the Melbourne case can be gained from a series of television workshops convened in 1985 by the Australian Film Commission (AFC), the federal government's screen funding and policy agency, bringing together the toast of the city's emerging comedy writers and performers. Assembled into groups to come up with fresh comedy ideas, the entrants were to compete for the prize of producing a television pilot for a commercial television network. The hopefuls, in their early twenties, were unknown to national media audiences at the time, but already veterans of university student revues and an inner Melbourne performance patchwork of boho cabaret haunts, kinetic comedy clubs and the theatre restaurants already mentioned above. Vizard (2014) describes a 'spider web' of places in inner Melbourne that nurtured emerging talent: 'Not only could you watch other acts, you could readily imagine that you could be one of those other acts; it was a really short step, and there wasn't just one channel.' It speaks volumes for this urban ecology that, within two years, participants in the AFC workshops – including Vizard himself, Glenn Robbins, Mark Mitchell, Peter Moon, Mary-Anne Fahey, Jane Turner, Gina Riley, Magda Szubanski, Rob Sitch, Santo Chilauro, Jane Kennedy and Michael Veitch – had created three highly successful sketch comedy series on competing television networks: *The Comedy Company* on Channel Ten, *Fast Forward* on Channel Seven and *The D-Generation* on the ABC.

These programmes represented a generational changing of the guard, and their circulating personnel would feature disproportionately in a succession of innovative, critical comedy over the next thirty years, winning popular audiences for commercial and public television networks and becoming the talk

Figure 18 Cast photo of a University of Melbourne Law Revue production, directed by Alan Pentland and featuring Tom Gleisner, Alan Pentland, Magda Szubanski, Costas Kilias and Libbi Gorr, *c.* 1984. Courtesy Steve Vizard.

of school yard bubblers and office water-coolers. The important point is that there were already hybrid spaces in Melbourne linking experimental comedy and suburban audiences, making the translation to the mass market feasible and scalable. As described again by Vizard (2014), these spaces generated a number of interconnected scenes:

> There were physical spaces, like [student] union theatres that were operational and that you could turn up to and do things. There was also a buzzing café scene, Lygon Street, the Pram Factory, a music scene and a theatre scene ... And then on top of that there was a theatre restaurant scene that was happening around that.

At one end of the spectrum was avant-garde dramatic theatre, which regularly deployed the 'larrikin carnivalesque' (Moore 2015) to interrogate Australian public life during a time of rapid change. Towards the middle was a web of inner-city comedy clubs, cabaret venues and theatre restaurants that had been established in the 1970s. The latter provided comedy practitioners with regular work and the understanding of audiences needed to become comedy professionals. It offered a substantial halfway house between the alternative comedy scene and the other end of the spectrum – the mainstream entertainment industries.

Consistent with Mills' analysis of British television comedy, the fringe in Melbourne gained its vitality not only from the front stage talents, but also from institution-builders who orchestrated the surrounding 'art worlds'. In a pattern that is found repeatedly, many of these people had been artists themselves. Most of the small comedy venues were the product of institution-building by counter-cultural dramatists of the previous decade, who provided community and media infrastructure occupied by the new generation. As Vizard (2014) explained, 'You didn't have to invent them [venues, cafes, theatre-restaurants], they were sort of hovering around.' A key figure in the Melbourne scene was Pram Factory alumnus John Pinder, who provided a model of how to move between the roles of fringe performer and impresario. Pinder's establishment, the Last Laugh, was the largest and best known of the venues, with a particular focus on emerging talent through its upstairs room, Le Joke.

A further major source of institutional support was found in the universities. Many emerging comedians first gained experience in student revues, honing their skills in writing, performing, directing, stage management, set design, publicity and production. The revues offered a low stakes environment for experimentation. Vizard (2014) recalls that

> everyone would have a crack. It was just a chance for people to participate. And that was actually the value, I thought, of Uni in those days. That your course was less onerous, and where you were going to end up was probably more achievable ... There was compulsory [student] unionism, so there were actual minimal facilities that were available. For a hundred reasons, there was space to experiment.

The vitality of the university performance environment in the 1980s and 1990s was enabled by an absence of tuition fees, credential pressure and vocationalism. The intangible free space between school and career implicit in full-time undergraduate studies allowed people 'to imagine, and to dream ... about things that society can be ... You were encouraged to imagine anything was kind of possible'. Students gained 'a sense of entitlement in the best sense of that word – the agency to do things and assume you can do things and have an impact by so doing' (Vizard 2014).

The theatre restaurants and other venues were, by Vizard's (2014) account, 'completely porous' to fringe formations emerging in the universities. There was indeed a significant exchange of people between them:

> Some of the owners of those places – the people who established them – were not themselves long out of Uni. They were staffed by people – as waiters and waitresses – by people who were at Uni. They were located, generally around Carlton, Collingwood, Fitzroy – all those inner suburbs that sort of spiralled around the Uni.

Comedy talents emerging within the university scene were often scouted by venues offering work opportunities. On the strength of a performance in the Architecture Revue, for example, Vizard and associates were invited by the Flying Trapeze in nearby Fitzroy to write and perform a paid show, thus initiating a professional comedy career. Having made this shift, Vizard met more established performers such as Wendy Harmer and wrote material for her – a process he refers to as 'cross-filtering' which meant 'we all started to work in each other's shows' (Vizard 2014).

As we have suggested, a further key value of small venues and theatre restaurants was in familiarizing comedians from fringe backgrounds with mainstream audiences. The theatre restaurants provided 'mediated spaces' between fringe arts practices and suburban audiences, providing an opportunity for artists to develop comedy that would resonate beyond their peers and comedy cognoscenti. The small size of Melbourne's middle-tier comedy venues meant they were intimate spaces, enabling genuine interaction between performers. Vizard (2014) recalls that

> you had this fantastic interface between mainstream audiences and kind of risk-taking, edgy first-timers who were testing stuff out. And it worked both ways, because ... from a creator's point of view, you're working out what to do. What's going to get a laugh? What's actually going to keep people's attention?

This encapsulates how a larger suburban audience, more representative than the elite audience for student revues, facilitates a more democratic comedy that can impact on mass popular culture. The ability to play to such an audience was a skill that performers took with them to larger institutions such as broadcasters.

How did Sydney compare with the Melbourne scene? A common element was a comedy fringe that developed out of university revues, but Sydney lacked the diversity and mixed audiences of small and middle tier venues. Its 'network of spaces' was therefore different, linking into student and cottage industry print journalism, community radio, niche pub-based theatre sports and even live music venues.

Sydney has a strong carnivalesque tradition developing out of a larrikin subversion of authority, levelling working-class slang, Dionysian, hedonistic sexuality and left-libertarianism – running as a thread from the light verse of *Smith's Weekly* and Tivoli vaudeville of Roy Rene in the interwar period to the *Philip Street Revue* and the media and theatre practice of the Sydney Push bohemia of the 1950s and 1960s. The latter phase merged with the counterculture of the 1960s and 1970s, first on university campuses and then in downtown subcultures, scenes and collectives associated with writer-directors such as Albie Thoms, Bruce Beresford, Mike Thornhill and Bob Ellis. Highlights included the satirical *Oz* magazine; the National Black Theatre based in Redfern, arising out of Indigenous activism and featuring Gary Foley; and an alternative 'camp' performance cycle, including Jim Sharman's *Shirley Thompson Versus the Aliens* (1972) and *The Rocky Horror Show* (1973–) which fed into the Gay and Lesbian Mardi Gras.

Sydney's university revues and the dramatic societies of large regional tertiary institutions played a similar nurturing role to those in Melbourne, gathering and hot-housing young comedians in low-stakes spaces that were tolerant of risk. Alumni of the University of Sydney revues include Germaine Greer, Clive James and Bob Ellis in the 1960s, and Grahame Bond, Rory O'Donoghue and Garry McDonald who developed *The Aunty Jack Show* for the ABC (Australia's early 1970s answer to Monty Python). The genre of choice at the University of Sydney in the early 1980s was camp comedic musical theatre. The standout example was Dennis Watkins, who posed as the fictional theatrical impresario Lamont Cranston, who 'presented' and starred in narrative revues in the tradition of Mel Brooks' *The Producers*. Watkins created a cycle of comedies parodying pop cultural history and contemporary issues – *Stalin the Musical, Dingo Girl, The Iceberg Cometh* and *Beach Blanket Tempest*, which in production standards and original music significantly exceeded the usual ambition of university revues. He went on to become head of ABC Television Comedy in the 1990s.

Why did Sydney lack the small-scale comedy and cabaret venues of Melbourne? A major factor was the dominance in New South Wales of large, licensed Leagues clubs in the suburbs and regions, subsidized by poker machine gambling. These establishments had sufficient resources to import international comedians to entertain mass audiences at low prices with discounted alcohol, rather than running the risk that unknown acts may empty seats. As Vizard (2014) put it,

> it was licensing laws … The Leagues Clubs, in essence, provided free entertainment. They were subsidized, so basically pokies provided free entertainment, and, virtually, a free prawn cocktail. How could a one-man band compete with that?

Victoria's wealth of home-grown comedy owes much, paradoxically, to its history of Protestant 'wowserism'. The tendency, surviving in the form of strong moral resistance to gambling, created the conditions in which the small venues could thrive.

While lacking Melbourne's subterranean warren of venues, Sydney did have a pub in the harbourside suburb of Glebe, next to the Harold Park paceway that specialized in fringe comedy nights. As well as stand-up and cabaret shows (often on tour from Melbourne), the Harold Park Hotel featured weekly Theatresports bouts, run by Dennis Watkins. These were especially popular with students and emerging comedians, who competed in the frantic art of improvisation. As the audience grew, Theatresports upgraded to a permanent home at the edgy Belvoir Street Theatre, located in the scruffy bohemia of Surry Hills. A celebrated theatresports champion of the mid-1980s was the nerdy, bespectacled Andrew Denton, a Woody Allenesque media graduate of the regional Mitchell College of Advanced Education where he had excelled in extracurricular drama, student radio and campus stunts. Moving to Sydney, Denton wrote freelance book reviews for the *Sydney Morning Herald* and ABC's Radio National. He described the Theatresports fringe as

> one of those great little creative circles that you dream of. And I did totally stumble into it; I'd never heard of it ... It was a social scene, so after the performance ... we'd go back to people's places. It was that classic thing of a group of young people who were all struggling, and trying to make it, feeding off each other once a week in this fixed place, in front of an audience which was very excited and very loyal.

(Denton 2014)

This social group of supportive yet competitive peers shared resources, opportunities and networks, offered constructive criticism and mentoring and provided opportunities to develop teamwork skills. Like the Melbourne comedians, Denton developed a strong sense of audience, rapid fire timing and a talent for off-the-cuff one-liners. He relished the fact that 'it was anarchic by nature', the performers were encouraged to 'muck about with it ... to play' (Denton 2014).

What Sydney lacked in small venues it also made up for in the density of media organizations, allowing graduates of the comedy fringe to finesse their acts in print and broadcast. Denton obtained a freelance gig, through fellow Theatresporter Gretel Killeen, writing comedy sketches for the ABC's youth radio station Triple J. He then moved to the commercial station Triple M, writing for, and sparring with popular presenter Doug Mulray. Denton found a particular value in radio as a staging post from the fringe to mainstream media: '[I]n radio, you go through more ideas in a week than you do in a year of television ... you do build your muscles' (Denton 2014). The media conveyor belt in Sydney built on small-scale practices of the 1970s, when student comedy makers such as the Aunty Jack group balanced unpaid gigs on community radio with work in downtown dramatic theatre or as freelance writers and dogsbodies at the ABC's radio division. Newcastle University drama graduate John Doyle, for example, found work at Triple J while teaching and juggling acting roles in plays at Sydney's Belvoir and Nimrod Theatres. Doyle later became best-known for his collaboration with Melbourne fringe theatre alumnus Greig Pickhaver, as one half of their sports comedy duo 'Rampaging' Roy Slaven and H.G. Nelson.

Media were also the vector from the fringe to mainstream for one of Sydney's other major comedy breakouts, The Chaser. Members of the group first attracted attention at the University of Sydney in the mid-1990s, where they participated in revues, edited the student paper *Honi Soit* and engaged in pranking of earnest political processes such as elections for the Student Representative Council. This subversive energy gained a focus in a satirical faux newspaper, *The Chaser*, launched in 1999 by Julian Morrow, Charles Firth, Dominic Knight and Craig Reucassel, who were later joined by Andrew Hansen, Chas Licciardello and Chris Taylor. Like many emerging student projects, the tyro editorial team exploited the advantages of university-connected fringe scenes. One of these was an abundance of free labour: according to Morrow (2015), they 'were willing to do shitloads of work for no pay because it was fun'. A second was a tolerance for risk: Craig Reucassel (2015) recalled that 'part of the freedom – because it was a highly defamatory publication – was that we had no assets or anything … we did odd jobs, were students, and did this on the side'. A third advantage was the opportunity to share resources through peer networks. The Chaser team drew on these networks for their initial investments in floating the newspaper. When they failed to raise the necessary revenue through retail distribution or subscription, they funded production by selling tickets to parties for friends, colleagues and a growing cohort of hard-core readers. Playing to comedy's carnivalesque participation, these crowd-funding parties became highly anticipated 'cool' events on the fringe calendar, enhancing the paper's profile.

The Chaser found something of a media distribution counterpart to Melbourne's performance venues in a network of small independent bookshops, such as Gleebooks, Elizabeths and Better Read Than Dead, which had similarities to 'indie' record stores. These outlets took a risk on stocking fringe or underground periodicals, allowing the group to gain a wider audience. This led on to book length Annuals, initially self-published and then in partnership with the independent publishing house Text, and eventually a break into broadcasting. A decade after Denton and Doyle's radio days, the underground profile of The Chaser masthead led to a late night radio spot on Sydney commercial radio station Triple M. In contrast to the Melbourne comedians who had emerged through live performance, The Chaser confess that producing a satirical newspaper gave them very little sense of their audience. In pre-social media days, there was no immediate feedback. Despite mass-producing a weekly periodical, their contact was largely with peers through quite elite events. For The Chaser, a sense of audience was developed only through electronic media, first in late night shift gigs on Triple M and then on ABC Television, assisted by experienced producers.

Institutional outreach: Festivals and public service broadcasting

Two other contexts deserve mention as important sites in Australia for crossover between fringe comedy and mainstream audiences: festivals and public service broadcasting. Participation in overseas Fringe Comedy Festivals, particularly the Edinburgh Fringe, has been a significant rite of passage for emerging Australian comedy performers, providing, in Bourdieu's (1993: 50–2) terms, a 'consecration' that establishes their credibility with peers back home and with wider international audiences. Notable examples include anarchic punk Canberra cabaret act the Doug Anthony All Stars, Hamish and Andy and Hannah Gadsby, all of whom have used success at international festivals to attract the attention of larger venues and mass media.

In Australia itself, the Melbourne International Comedy Festival (MICF) and the Adelaide Fringe have performed a similar role, due to their national and increasingly international profile. MICF has origins in Melbourne's fringe comedy scene of the early 1980s, and remains strongly connected to this community, demonstrated in a commitment to emerging talent, styles of comedy and practitioners from marginal communities. Like the Edinburgh Festival, it has itself become mainstream as a popular event on the Melbourne calendar, featuring commercially successful national and international acts and attracting mass audiences from across Victoria and Australia. Yet under long-time director Susan Provan, MICF retains many characteristics of a fringe start-up and still draws on public funding from the state government's Creative Victoria as well as sponsors and patrons. Diversity and outreach are structured into the festival. For example, through its Deadly Comedy initiative, MICF holds comedy competitions in Indigenous communities across Australia, bringing the festival to the local talent. The winners then compete on the main stage of the festival in Melbourne for a tent pole event.

An additional function of MICF and the Adelaide Fringe is to provide an accessible, one-stop shop for talent scouting by commissioning editors and independent producers who work in mainstream media, especially the public service broadcasters. In interviews for *Fringe to Famous*, former commissioners Courtney Gibson (2014) and Richard Fidler (2016) described how the ABC encouraged outreach to the festivals to identify emerging comic talent. The festivals also collaborate with the ABC Comedy channel and Foxtel's subscription-based The Comedy Channel (inaugurated by Steve Vizard's Artist Services) to record, broadcast and stream portions of their programmes, delivering performances by fringe comedians to much larger audiences.

Another piece of the festival ecology in Australia has been the short film showcase Tropfest, which first gave prominence to Paul Fenech (*Pizza Man*, 1995) and Jason Gann and Adam Zwar (*Wilfred*, 2002). Beginning in 1993 as a small event at the Tropicana café in Sydney's Kings Cross, Tropfest had grown by the early twenty-first century into a mass media awards nights and international franchise, which ran as a major event until 2019 when financial problems and then COVID-19 disruption put it into hiatus. In 1995, when Fenech entered, it was still, as he describes it, a 'very trendy little festival' (Fenech 2014). It was just beginning to increase in scale to a middle tier event, gaining attention at a time when 'film festivals had become a buzz thing'. Fenech (2014) acknowledges the festival as having given him a major opportunity: 'I owe my career to that first Tropfest. I think I came in third that year … Nicole Kidman gave me the award, and there were a couple of big players there.'

Fenech's breakthrough at Tropfest is particularly significant as it gave exposure to quite a different fringe from the university revue scene and inner-city performance venues. Fenech comes from a multicultural working-class background – one he described to us as 'very tough'. Before working in film and television, he had been a 'shitkicker', serving a stint in the army rather than pursuing higher education. He never had the opportunity, as he puts it, of 'being arty farty for the sake of it'. The community in which he grew up 'wasn't an intellectual environment', but one where one 'always had to work very hard at everything'. A result has been that he has taken a 'work ethic' approach to production, rather than the middle-class film school attitude of 'I've got a magic idea and it's going to be the best thing in the universe' (Fenech 2014).

The public service broadcasters have also been a major catalyst for crossover with the mainstream. As in the case of 'indie' music, the ABC and SBS have consistently undertaken initiatives to tap into emerging comedy talent in fringe scenes. They have been ambitious, often risky, commissioners of unknown comedians as well as new genres and formats, from *The D-Generation* and *Summer Heights High* to *Kath and Kim* and *Wilfred*. This is not to deny that commercial television has also done a share of heavy lifting. When it embarked on *Fast Forward* with Vizard and team, Channel Seven was building on a track record stretching back to the ground-breaking 1960s sketch series *The Mavis Bramston Show* and the working-class situation comedy *My Name's McGooley*,

What's Yours? Channel Ten led the charge in engaging alumni of the university revue scene when it commissioned Ian McFadyen, Mary-Anne Fahey, Mark Mitchell and Glen Robbins to create the hit prime time sketch series *The Comedy Company*.

The public service broadcasters have played a unique role, however, in offering dedicated programmes to facilitate exchange between fringe comedy performers and mainstream media. A recent example has been ABC's 'Fresh Blood', a call out to emerging comedy makers who are finessing their acts and

Figure 19 *Black Comedy* promotional poster, 2014. Courtesy Scarlett Pictures/ABC.

building audiences in live venues or online streaming platforms. In a similar way to the AFC competition in Melbourne in the mid-1980s, Fresh Blood invited contestants to produce a pilot episode for the national broadcaster's streaming platform ABC iView. In the programme's first year, the ensemble Fancy Boy was chosen to produce a full-fledged series for the ABC. The model draws on a tradition of outreach initiatives across a number of art forms at the ABC, including the music talent discovery initiatives *Demo Show* and *Unearthed* at Triple J (discussed in Chapter 2) and the short documentary competition *Race around the World*, which in the late 1990s broke the dadaesque talents of comedian John Safran.

The ABC and SBS have also played a significant role in outreach to under-represented or marginalized communities. An important case has been the recruitment from the late 1980s of Indigenous media practitioners and performers to ABC Television's Indigenous Programs Unit. The Unit has provided opportunities for Indigenous people to acquire production skills and gain experience in multiple televisual formats and genres, including comedy. It has encouraged risk-taking, experimentation and autonomy, drawing on cultural connection to Aboriginal activists and artists and the collaborative work practices of Indigenous communities. A notable alumna has been Rachel Perkins, director of Australia's first Aboriginal cinematic musical comedy *Bran Nue Dae* (2009). Comedy-specific Indigenous outreach continues at the ABC, with a callout in 2014 to First Nations communities across Australia, enabling an ensemble of performers and production staff to produce the successful series *Black Comedy* (2014–21).

Another who got a start through the ABC's Indigenous Programs Unit is Paul Fenech, just mentioned in relation to Tropfest. He was a trainee in the unit in the early 1990s while also working for the ABC as a dogsbody, literally sweeping floors. While this apprenticeship gave him skills in making film and television, it also sharpened his sense of difference: 'I hated everything that I worked on at the ABC ... I found the process so dry' (Fenech 2014). Fenech was particularly critical of the flagship ABC sitcom *Mother and Son*, whose production process he had been able to observe: 'They rehearsed the jokes so much, it was like theatre on stage ... There was no spontaneity' (Fenech 2014). Reacting against the house style of the time, as the *D-Generation* group had also done, he began to experiment in what was an emerging 'short film' scene in the mid-1990s, using comedy in that format to probe issues around race and ethnic diversity. On collecting his award at Tropfest for *Pizza Man*, a comedy featuring the brown-skinned employees of a suburban pizzeria, he declared 'this one's for all the Chockos!' (Fenech 2014).

Fenech's case also demonstrates the value of plurality within public service broadcasting, as his career has been significantly shaped by differences between the ABC and the second broadcaster SBS. The ABC will always be central to the ecology of creative production in Australia, if only because of its size and resources. As the 'national broadcaster', it also has a special role in validating fringe performers by giving high-profile exposure. For Fancy Boy, for example, success on the ABC through the Fresh Blood programme was an important moment of recognition – one, as group member Mark Conway (2015) put it, when you could hear parents saying 'Oh, my son's actually achieved something!' But the lower profile of SBS has had its own advantages, allowing freedoms to comedians that the ABC has not always been able to extend. Fenech has benefitted from this, along with other mavericks such as the creators of *Wilfred* Adam Zwar, Jason Gann and Tony Rogers, and the aforementioned John Safran.

While it was established in the 1980s as a 'multicultural broadcaster', SBS developed in the 1990s to more closely resemble the UK's Channel 4. It receives much less government funding than the ABC, particularly following a change in legislation allowing it to take advertising, and programming decisions are not subject to the same intense public scrutiny. Its 'under the radar' identity has allowed it to commission edgier programmes, often from small and emerging production companies, as well as keeping an active eye on the risky leading edge of international developments, from the Korean wave to US cable breakouts such as the *Larry Sanders Show*, *Deadwood* and *South Park*. Fenech's commission in 1999 to make the series *Pizza* arose from a desire in SBS to find an Australian *South Park*. It offered freedom to explore radical, in-your-face alternatives to the wordy absurdist humour of the satirical British-derived tradition he had observed at the ABC. Fenech (2014) favours a fast-cut kinetic physical and visual comedy, explaining 'I didn't like talky humour, I liked action comedy'. He counts as influences the American physical comedy of the Three Stooges and John Landis, the saucy English 'Carry On' movies and Benny Hill, and the vernacular 'Ocker' comedy of Paul Hogan.

SBS has also provided, in the form of SBS Independent (SBSi), what is probably the best example in Australian public service broadcasting of a quasi-permanent outreach to fringe cultural practices. SBSi was designed and funded as part of Creative Nation, the federal Labor government cultural policy of the mid-1990s that we discussed in Chapter 1. SBS was chosen for the initiative as nimbler and more open to new challenges than the ABC, where higher overheads, a

Fringe to Famous

larger bureaucracy and relative cultural homogeneity were seen as resulting in a certain conservatism. Running from 1994 to 2007, SBSi sought out projects from emerging talent and small creative companies across drama, comedy and documentary, which it then funded, developed and broadcast. It sat alongside more general state and federal government grant schemes and tax concessions directed at specific projects that included film and television comedy. It was SBSi that first commissioned Fenech for *Pizza*.

Experimenting with audiences

What happens when comedians who have developed their art in small fringe spaces find themselves projected onto a larger screen? A crucial question here is how they develop relationships with new audiences. In the Melbourne case, as we have seen, what began as performances for small audiences of peers within universities and small venues was honed in middle-tier comedy venues in front of audiences from the suburbs. It was then taken on to hybrid festivals, mass media platforms for sketch and variety in front of studio audiences and associated live tours. In cases such as Denton, John Doyle and Greig Pickhaver, a sense of the audience was developed first through Theatresports or art-house theatre, then enlarged through youth-oriented FM radio, affording opportunities to dialogue with listeners through talk back.

Those inclined to romantic ideas of the fringe as a pure space of creativity have often represented the move to larger audiences as a dilution of an original idea or 'dumbing down'. This interpretation was strongly rejected by our interviewees. Denton (2014) observes, for example, that while he never cut his cloth to audience expectations, all his experience had taught him that 'the audience is way smarter than people tend to think':

> Never, ever assume that the brickie on the building site doesn't love the really obscure thing you just did, and the barrister doesn't love the smutty thing ... I have always found, in everything I've done, that the lowest common denominator view that we have of the Australian audience is misplaced.

Similarly, The Chaser was surprised by the positive response they received from audiences following their break into television. They had thought of their comedy as a 'niche product', unlikely to resonate widely, but discovered that the mainstream audience was much more receptive than they had expected. As Morrow (2015) put it, 'audience tastes were actually better aligned to what we liked'.

Figure 20 Andrew Denton, 2008. Photograph by Mark Calleja/Newspix. Courtesy Newspix.

An important strategy in developing a relationship with television audiences has been to bring a representative sample into the studio. For Denton's first series for the ABC, *Blah, Blah, Blah,* producers Andy Nehl and Mark Fitzgerald bussed in an audience from Sydney's working-class western suburbs, a demographic not usually targeted by the national broadcaster. This significantly changed the tone of the show, an experiment in crossing social issues journalism with carnivalesque subversion and play. It built on the previous success of Nehl and Fitzgerald with *vox pop* outreach to the suburbs in the ground-breaking ABC youth series *Beatbox* (1985–87), part funded by the federal government's Community Employment Program. Denton (2014) describes *Beatbox* as

> a largely unmediated conversation with the public ... It was authentic. You know television is smoke and mirrors. It's not meant to be authentic. So, when something honest happens on it, people take notice.

When later joining the production side of The Chaser, Nehl saw that the shows would benefit from the energy and engagement of a live audience. This element was lacking in the group's first television show, *CNNNN*, for which the programmes were recorded out of sequence with multiple takes. Nehl pushed for their second show, *The Chaser's War on Everything*, to be produced 'as live' in front of a studio audience. In the year leading up to *The Chaser's War on*

Everything, the group also presented the first in a tour of live theatrical shows around Australia to develop their relationship with a growing and dispersed fan base.

An ongoing engagement with mass audiences has also been central to Fenech's practice. While his initial commission by SBS Independent might suggest a preference for a niche audience, he has revelled in opportunities to connect with large, diverse audiences from the outer suburbs. Far from seeing this relationship as diminishing the artistic vision of his early experiments in short film, he has embraced it as a source of inspiration. Like Denton, he has avoided second guessing what people might want, consistently seeking to challenge the audience. His work offers provocative representations of the communities from which the audience is drawn, in contrast to the corporate distractions that are often served up to it. But the relationship is one that is built on respect. Indeed, for Fenech (2014), the outer suburbs are where the 'real culture' is to be found: 'Culture is not created by rich people and the middle classes; it's the mass.' He engages suburban working-class audiences in a language they relate to, with energetic physical and sexually explicit themes, vernacular slang, embodied vulgarity and stories of small triumphs by 'battlers' over officialdom.

Figure 21 The *Pizza* cast at Elvis Pizza Restaurant in Sydney's Rushcutters Bay, 2005, featuring Paul Fenech (centre, seated), Rebel Wilson (centre, standing) and other cast members. Photograph by Ross Hodgson/Newspix. Courtesy News Ltd/Newspix.

Part of this strategy has also been in casting. Fenech has a sharp eye for potential actors in the communities he represents on screen, creating roles for Arab, Polynesian, Indigenous and Asian actors as well as for disabled people and all body shapes. *Pizza* was the breakthrough role for Rebel Wilson, who played the lead part of lusty Greek-Australian Toula, and Turkish-Australian comedian and actor Tahir Bilgiç who played her indifferent husband Habib. 'If I have one mission', Fenech (2014) says, 'it's just to make media that looks like our society'. In fact, he exceeds and complicates the SBS mission to reflect multicultural Australia, by engaging with the fluid ethnic hybridity of the suburbs.

Fenech's approach to audiences could be seen as building on the Australian comedic tradition sometimes referred to as 'wogsploitation' (Speed 2005). An earlier example, emerging in Melbourne in the late 1980s, was the live sketch show *Wogs Out of Work*, which resonated widely as an irreverent representation of Australian multiculturalism. *Wogs Out of Work* was adapted into the iconic Channel Seven situation comedy *Acropolis Now* and the hit film *The Wog Boy*. A number of live spinoffs through the 1990s and early 2000s became launchpads for comedians from Asian, Arab and other non-Anglo backgrounds. At the heart of the original live show was a robust dialogue with its heckling audiences, particularly young people from Mediterranean and Middle Eastern migrant communities. Fenech has found a similar connection through live touring shows, taking the characters and action off the mediated streets of his sitcoms into large theatres where he interacts with a largely working-class fan base across Australia.

But of our interviewees, it was Vizard who perhaps offered the most detailed account of how fringe content is negotiated with mainstream audiences. He has always been interested in reaching the widest possible audience, leading him from the outset to make overtures to commercial television rather than the ABC, as some of his associates from the inner Melbourne student and fringe scenes had done:

> Doing it at the ABC seemed more conventional in a way, at least to me, because there's an existing community there that's attuned to risk, an established audience of like minded people … But how do I get to everyone else? How do I speak to those who don't agree with me? Those I've never met? That's the question.
>
> (Vizard 2014)

There is an obvious *business* interest in reaching audiences for commercial media and Vizard has done very well in business terms. But it is important to recognize that there can also be a cultural or creative interest. As Vizard (2014) points out, there are questions raised by the crossover between fringe and mainstream that deserve to be considered in their own terms:

> What is the internal structure between the familiar and the challenging? Between mainstream and fringe? ... This is why I reject the idea of the polarities as being offerings that should exist at one end or the other ... I'm interested in hybrid places that woo or disrupt or challenge people – blur simplistic binaries. So what audiences and critics, performers and producers might otherwise have regarded as risky or fringe at the outset is not that at the end of the experience.

Vizard's frustration here is with a kind of purism that wants the fringe and mainstream to be kept in separate boxes. Reflecting on *Fast Forward* today, he describes it as 'a weekly one hour nationally broadcast site of liminality, creating instability':

> We seduced the audience with the appearance of familiarity: it looked like a normal TV world that inhabited most viewers' living rooms. At the same time, we destabilised the known world, by changing channels, by segueing into unrelated sketches, by juxtaposing the familiar with the unknown, by playing with space and time.
>
> (Vizard 2014)

As we observed in Chapter 1, however, Vizard's position also brings into question the tendency in creative industries arguments simply to *refuse* polarities between fringe and mainstream. It would be impossible, for Vizard, to understand crossovers between the two without recognizing significant differences between them. It is certainly possible to bring them together, but it requires imagination and effort to do so.

As we have already observed, sketch comedy is a genre particularly suited to such a project, offering a framework that enables the mixing of the familiar and challenging. In the case of *Fast Forward*, this mixing was organized by rapid cuts between sketches, mimicking the short attention span of the remote-control wielding channel surfer. Sketches were often cut into smaller segments to which the viewer was returned at different points throughout the hour. As Vizard (2014) puts it:

> The great thing about a sketch comedy show is that you're given permission to canvass a hundred things if you're minded to ... So I can canvass material that's broad-based comedy slapstick and hardly challenging at all, and then within a minute I can do something highly political, or highly charged and complex. But

I've only invested that much – I've only scared people that much. I'm not going to lose them.

Vizard describes this strategy, which he sees as necessary in commercial television, as 'sugar coating', a term that might admittedly suggest a 'dumbing down' of an original creative idea. However, he has always worked with a longer time horizon and greater ambition than a single show. Over time, he argues, 'I can … actually inoculate people, as to what might have been contentious or even offensive, by the end of a season, becoming mainstream. I can challenge, shift, broaden and educate an audience' (Vizard 2014). The challenge is different from playing to an audience of peers who will immediately 'get' an allusion or comic idea. But for Vizard it is a challenge that is, if anything, more exciting:

> If I take an audience that were already largely there, and I leave them largely where they were, that's an interesting exercise … but to me it's not nearly as valuable as taking that audience – a bigger audience – to a place they might not normally go, at least not willingly, and saying, 'have you thought about looking at things this way?'
>
> (Vizard 2014)

Like many who have moved between fringe backgrounds and mainstream audiences, Vizard has sought to shift the borders of what is permitted and what is regarded as legitimate. In doing so, he expresses in an Australian idiom a similar insight to that which Bourdieu (1993 106–10) derived from his work on the European avant-garde and the 'heretical displacement' of boundaries: '[I]t's the experimentation that gives rise to the sugar coating of tomorrow' (Vizard 2014).

If experimenting with audiences involves risk, it is important to acknowledge the downsides. Risky plays, by their nature, can backfire. We discussed a couple of examples with Craig Reucassel and Julian Morrow from The Chaser. The first was one of their best-known stunts – one indeed that attracted international attention – in which Morrow and Chas Licciardello masqueraded as the Canadian delegation to the 2007 Asia Pacific Economic Forum (APEC) at the Sydney Opera House. It involved driving a motorcade through multiple security checkpoints, showing clearly bogus identities along the way, before disgorging Licciardello dressed as Osama bin Laden and feigning outrage that he had not been invited to the summit. It breached highly sensitive security protocols, was denounced by politicians and public officials and led to the arrest of eleven cast and crew. The second example was a 2009 sketch satirizing the

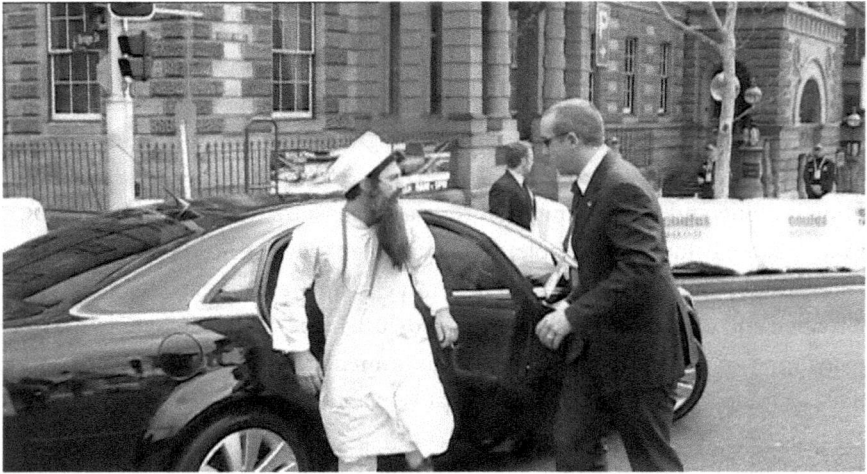

Figure 22 Chas Licciardello (left) and Julian Morrow filming a segment for *The Chaser's War on Everything* inside the security zone at the APEC conference, Sydney, 2007. Courtesy ABC.

Make-A-Wish Foundation, an organization dedicated to granting the wishes of children with critical illnesses. It was seen by many as insensitive to the children, leading to a significant backlash.

Both The Chaser and ABC management stood by the APEC stunt. As Reucassel (2015) points out, the public 'loved it' and, while it caused acute embarrassment to politicians and officials by revealing the laxness of security, the very fact of doing so could be seen as aligning with the public interest. It was, as Morrow (2015) puts it, 'an example of good luck, where the outrage happened but we were right'. By contrast, the Make-a-Wish skit is acknowledged by the group as a mistake. Morrow sees the incident in the context of their ongoing efforts to adjust to a mass audience. When they had been running a small satirical newspaper, they had been accustomed to doing 'all sorts of crazy over the top jokes', but 'as you get to bigger and bigger audiences you just take on a bigger responsibility'. He is frank in acknowledging that with Make-a-Wish 'we didn't handle it well': 'We were grownups, we had a TV show, and it was our job to get that stuff right. We got it wrong.' Having accepted, however, that there should be 'failure criteria' and that it is important to acknowledge mistakes, Morrow points out that taking risks will always result in some 'glorious failures'. The other side of the rich cultural seam to be found in taking fringe content to mass audiences will always be that you 'fuck some stuff up' (Morrow 2015).

Fenech has also been accused of making fun of those at the social margins, a charge that has been made particularly of *Housos*, a second series for SBS set among the artful dodgers, welfare recipients and anti-authoritarian inhabitants of an outer suburban housing estate, and *Bogan Hunters*, a mock nature documentary investigation of suburban and regional working-class communities for the commercial streaming service Seven Mate. The criticism is one that Fenech (2014) rejects, pointing out that 'real housos' have been some of his greatest supporters:

> If you watch *Bogan Hunters* or *Housos* and you don't get it, it means you are disconnected with the vast majority of Australians, because there's more cultural nuance in that than there is in … the fucking *The Voice*, or *Dancing with the Stars*, or the news … That's where the real flavour is – in those outer suburbs.

Fenech (2014) sees the criticisms as reflecting a longstanding middle-class prejudice against his style – 'all the critic-y, sort of uni-educated satire lovers fucking hated it' – and he has mostly been supported by the SBS and the other media organizations with whom he has worked. The example underlines the point, however, that offence is an ever-present possibility. If the tension between fringe content and mainstream audiences can produce moments when the culture 'sings', it can also produce moments of conflict and dissonance.

Experimenting with institutions

The other obvious development, as comedians move from the fringe to the mainstream, is that they become enmeshed in complex institutional arrangements. This is the point, to recall Brett Mills (2017: 155), when 'large numbers of people come into play'. It is also the point when understandings of the relation between fringe and mainstream most often fall prey to the abstract interpretative frameworks we discussed at the beginning of the chapter. In one influential tradition – the Frankfurt School and its successors – large-scale organizations are conceived as 'capitalist' (or where government is involved 'bureaucratic'), the implication being that they are the antithesis of the creativity of the fringe. In another tradition – the 'left optimism' that found its fullest expression in the 1980s – they are seen as no more than neutral hosts for the carnivalesque eruptions of popular culture. More recently, the creative industries perspective has sought a more nuanced understanding by refusing strong distinctions between the fringe and mainstream but has done so at the cost of a wilful suspension of critical distance from the commercial cultural industries. Left culturalism has in turn re-established such distance but has also revived flat Frankfurtian stereotypes of the mainstream, concepts such as 'neoliberalism' coming to serve a similar function to that of the 'culture industry'.

As we have suggested elsewhere in *Fringe to Famous*, a starting point in addressing these problems is Bourdieu's (1995) analysis of the idea of artistic autonomy, particularly as outlined in *The Rules of Art*. This analysis offers a way of recognizing the agency of fringe formations in relation to large-scale cultural production without falling back on romantic assumptions about the transcendence of the aesthetic domain. For Bourdieu, the autonomy of the artist should be attributed not to some pure aesthetic inspiration but to social strategies through which they mark out and defend their distinctness. The perspective offers a way of framing the relation between fringe and mainstream that avoids abstract oppositions between 'art' and 'industry'. A further important contribution is a generational model of positions within the field of cultural production. As Bourdieu (1993) points out, many of the structures encountered by those emerging within the 'field of restricted production' are institutional accretions of earlier fringe formations. Today's establishment is often yesterday's avant-garde. Examples from Australian comedy might include the way in which performers such as Chris Lilley and Barry Humphries, once considered risky or cutting edge, have been represented recently by a younger generation as out of touch incumbents, to be 'deplatformed' for racist or sexist views.

However, Bourdieu's perspective also has significant limitations. As David Hesmondhalgh (2006) has pointed out, Bourdieu showed surprisingly little interest in mass or large-scale production. His emphasis on autonomy is valuable, opening up questions that are generally passed over in Anglophone work on media and cultural industries. But it is 'simply astonishing', as Hesmondhalgh (2006: 217) puts it, 'how little Bourdieu has to say about large-scale, "heteronomous" commercial cultural production, given not only its enormous social and cultural importance in the contemporary world, but also its significance in determining conditions in the sub-field in which he is clearly much more interested, restricted production'. What Bourdieu does say suggests an unreconstructed view, not all that far from the Frankfurt School. The most dedicated work on the cultural industries within his circle was in fact undertaken by associates such as Patrick Champagne. In Champagne's formulation, one that Bourdieu himself drew upon, 'the mass media produce standardized products on a large scale, designed to respond to pre-existing, external demands' (Champagne 2005: 55–6; cited Hesmondhalgh 2006: 223).

It is not the place here to attempt an alternative general account of the cultural industries. What we will do instead is put scholarly perspectives into conversation with those of practitioners who have actually negotiated relations between fringe and mainstream. The picture that emerges from the latter, in the case at least of the comedians we spoke to, might be described as a kind of heterodoxy. It is possible to find examples in our interviews that align with almost all the theoretical positions we have mentioned – from Frankfurtian pessimism to pop cultural optimism, from creative industries enthusiasm for commercial production to left cultural scepticism – but they appear not as characterizations of the cultural industries *as such* but as contingent observations on particular situations or tendencies.

This may of course be simply because practitioners *are* practitioners, not theorists. We should not expect them necessarily to have fully developed accounts of institutional and economic totalities. But it may also be that the cultural industries simply are multivalent. In the terms we have been using throughout the book, they are hybrid, partaking at the same time of the qualities that Bourdieu (1993) ascribes to the fields of 'restricted' and 'large-scale' production. If this is so, the value of considering the perspectives of practitioners is that they are more likely to see this complexity. For those immersed in it, it is a complexity that is impossible to avoid. This would align with a suggestion by Hesmondhalgh (2006: 228) that the most satisfactory scholarly accounts of the mainstream cultural industries are those that use mixed approaches – for example, combining political economy, organizational studies and hegemony theory. It also accords with our sense that what appears as theoretical inconsistency in Mills' approach to comedy may be a sign not of weakness but of strength.

It is largely taken for granted by comedians moving from fringe scenes to mainstream media that the move will involve conflict. In Chapter 1, we cited the example of Vizard's differences with executives at Channel Seven. As he expanded further on this theme:

> The very essence of comedy shows, our shows and our success involved pushing the boundaries, comedically, socially, culturally, even legally. The very destabilizing contentiousness which was at the heart of the success of our shows was also the source of disruptive uncertainty that broadcaster administrators struggled to manage.
>
> (Vizard 2014)

The causes of this conflict, furthermore, are broadly consistent with critical scholarly analyses of commercial media. The orientation to profit privileges economic over artistic considerations, limiting the scope for imagination and leading to a bias towards well-worn formulae. As Vizard (2014) puts it,

> very few people are capable of seeing something off a piece of paper. They always want it to be like something else. And networks are identical – in fact, they're worse now. That's why they buy formats of overseas shows … They're in risk minimisation or arse protecting mode.

Similar frustrations were aired by those who have worked for public service broadcasters. Craig Reucassel from The Chaser describes a 'constant battle' over the extent of risk and experimentation at the ABC (Reucassel 2015). The problem in this case might be described as 'managerialism' – in line with critical perspectives on government (Klikauer 2013; Madsen 2020) – with struggles taking place over tolerance of risk:

> [T]here's always people in the ABC desperately trying to get the next edgy thing on there … going to the comedy club, or looking on YouTube, or finding the new thing and trying to get it on … And there's also always people who, when the edgy material leads to problems, are dealing with it – and they're always pushing back the other way.
>
> (Reucassel 2015)

Perhaps the most poignant statement about these struggles was an admission by Fenech (2014) of sheer exhaustion:

> Even though I've been really lucky … and I've had a great career, it's been so hard to maintain it, and to get ahead. And I've been doing it since I was 19 … It was like trench warfare. Every little inch had to be really hard … and I've lived it year after year. So you think you're going alright, you've got a run, and then some person changes in a position of power, or something happens … and then you're there again. It's very tough.

At the same time, there is nuance in these accounts. The organizations in question are represented not as monolithic or homogeneous, but as having an internal complexity. Vizard (2014) acknowledges enlightened managers at Channel Seven, such as Gary Fenton, who commissioned many risky, non-traditional shows. One of the Executive Producers, Chris Greenwood, was also 'fantastic', a notable exception to the 'arse protecting' tendencies more generally observed. Greenwood had a certain authority, having worked for ten years at the highest level of television in the UK, including on the iconic *Parkinson*, making him a valuable ally. Similarly, Denton pays tribute to the young producers Andy Nehl, Mark Fitzgerald and Martin Coombes, who he was fortunate to work with on his first show, *Blah, Blah, Blah*, for the ABC. This group, who had earned some credibility through their earlier success with *Beatbox*, 'put up a shield' around him, protecting him from the 'shit that may have been coming down' (Denton 2014). It is also clear from Fenech's (2014) reference to the importance of 'people in power' that there has been a similar complexity in the SBS and the other organizations with whom he has worked. While institutions may be organized around certain dominant principles, their actual concrete form always involves a range of personalities.

It might be possible to preserve the idea of a consistent character to mainstream institutions by representing those with sympathies for the fringe as renegades, infiltrating spaces where they do not really belong. The idea has a theatrical appeal and there is certainly material in our interviews that could be used to support it. Vizard (2014) describes his strategy at Channel Seven as 'smuggling', using subterfuge to introduce ideas that would have been rejected if presented upfront. Similarly, Fenech (2014) suggests that the novelty of *Pizza* helped him to fly under the radar at SBS:

> [T]hey didn't know how to criticize it because they didn't know how I made it or why it succeeded ... It was a bit like being a unicorn at the zoo. People just went 'Oh, just leave it alone. It's probably OK because we don't really understand it'.

Robyn Butler of Gristmill suggests that comedy might be thought of generally as a form of disguise. When making *The Librarians* and *Upper Middle Bogan* for the ABC, she found that the organization left the creative team alone as 'just carny people' (Butler 2016). Such descriptions recall Greene's (2008) account of avant-garde television comedy in the United States, in which figures such as Andy Kaufman and Soupy Sales are cast almost as undercover agents in spaces otherwise dominated by anodyne commercial formulae.

To frame such incursions of fringe comedy as exceptions, however, is to assume that the 'normal' state for mainstream institutions is a singular pattern or logic. As Hesmondhalgh suggests in response to Bourdieusian representations of large-scale commercial media, such an assumption is questionable. As noted above, Bourdieu and his collaborators saw commercial media as pursuing profits by catering to 'pre-existing' external demands. Bourdieu himself was fascinated by market research, seeing its growth in the twentieth century as evidence of a relentless expansion of profit-oriented strategies in the field of large-scale

Figure 23 *The Librarians* television series (ABC, 2007–10), featuring Robyn Butler (front centre, seated), Wayne Hope (second from right, crouched) and other cast members, n.d. Courtesy Gristmill.

production. But as Hesmondhalgh (2006: 225) points out, 'it isn't at all clear that we can talk securely in this way about the demand for goods existing before goods are made'. Despite the enormous resources invested in audience research, the cultural industries remain notorious for their rates of failure. Demand is not a secure point of reference but a tenuous construct, 'perennially failing … to impose order on a chaotic market'.

It is in this context that practices emerging from the field of restricted production can gain real influence within the field of large-scale production, fusing with the latter to produce hybrid formations. There is a paradox here that needs to be fully grasped. Fringe practices are organized around values that are different from those of mainstream institutions, giving them an appearance of detachment or even antagonism. Vizard (2014) admits to having sometimes done things to test the limits, knowing that it would probably 'shit the network'. An example was an occasion when he put to air an unedited wedding video of one of the crew: 'And it wasn't shot for that purpose. It was, like, shithouse … handheld, it was the worst hour of television.' Yet this very detachment often allows the objectives of institutions to be realized in ways that would not otherwise be possible. In the case of *Fast Forward* and *Full Frontal*, Vizard and his associates delivered a ratings bonanza to Channel Seven that the prescriptions of the executive hard heads at the network could never have achieved. In doing so, they were able to shift mainstream practices. When we suggested to Vizard that he may have stretched the network as much as the audience, he agreed: 'I think we did, actually, by virtue of doing what we did. As well as stretching ourselves.'

Denton (2014) provides a similar account of institutional hybridization at the ABC where, he suggests, outsiders have been 'essential to renewal':

> I think it requires people sitting outside the system to be so energized by what they see is there or isn't there that when they come into it the rules that may exist aren't necessarily going to stop them. Or they see those as things to be bent or broken or changed. So those people coming in with a mixture of clarity, determination – often anger.

Figure 24 *Fast Forward* cast photo, *c.* 1990. From left: Magda Szubanski, Jane Turner, Marg Downey, Michael Veitch, Peter Moon, Ernie Dingo and Steve Vizard. Courtesy National Film & Sound Archive.

It is important again to grasp the subtlety of this position. The mention of anger might lead us to assume that rules are experienced by fringe entrants as a purely negative force. For Denton, however, management pushback can actually be productive. While frustrating in the moment, it sets up a creative tension that is enabling: 'It's very good to have stuff to push against, because if you're coming in with … that urgency to say something, or say it in a particular way, then to have people throwing up brick walls is just a further invitation to focus that laser beam to burst through' (Denton 2014). To return to the idea of negotiation, gatekeepers open gates as well as close them.

The independents … and their animateurs

We could summarize the above by saying that the comedic fringe has been a source not only of new content for mainstream media, but also of innovations in the way the mainstream itself is constituted. It is not stretching the point too far to say that one of Australia's leading commercial television networks – Channel Seven – has traces somewhere in its institutional DNA of Betty Burstall's radical fringe theatre of the 1970s. This perspective is one that helps to address some of the theoretical quandaries we considered at the outset. On the one hand, it allows us to affirm the central proposition of critical scholarship on media institutions: that the structure of the mainstream media has a major influence over the culture that is produced. The problem with the optimistic 'populist' impulse in cultural studies – such as Docker's 1980s work on carnival cited earlier – has been its tendency to minimize or deny this. Terry Eagleton (1981) was, in a sense, correct in insisting that carnival is always 'licensed'. None of the television comedies we have been considering would exist if it had not found institutional sponsors. On the other hand, the perspective allows us also to mute the 'cultural pessimist' conclusions that have generally been drawn from this. It is a mistake to see the mainstream as representing a simple dominant principle to which all those who interact with it are immediately subordinated.

The perspective is also useful in interpreting more recent developments in the institutional structure of cultural production. One of the most important of these has been the rise of what Charles Leadbeater and Kate Oakley (1999), writing of the British scene at the end of the 1990s, called 'the independents' – small businesses in the cultural sector, drawing on informal networks and placing a high value on autonomy and creativity. Many examples have emerged in Australian comedy over the last thirty years, coinciding with an acceleration of co-production and outsourcing arrangements in the major media organizations. The direction was set in 1989 with the establishment by Vizard and Knight of Artist Services, and by Denton, Anita Jakoby and Peter Thompson of Zapruder's Other Films. Over the next twenty years, artist-led 'comedy companies' specializing in television and sometimes film production became the common pattern. Other notable examples include Working Dog Productions established by *The D-Generation* principals Santo Cilauro, Jane Kennedy, Rob Stitch and Tom Gleisner (1993); Gina Riley and Jane Turner's Riley Turner Productions for the making of *Kath and Kim* (2002–2007); Paul Fenech's Antichocko Productions (2005); and Robyn Butler and Wayne Hope's kitchen table production house Gristmill (2004).

The response to this general development in academic and policy writing was marked, initially, by a certain euphoria. For Leadbeater and Oakley (1999: 11), the independents had freed themselves from the need to seek institutional patronage, finding a way to rely only on their own 'creativity, skill, ingenuity and imagination'. An important subplot in this narrative was the rapid development at the time of digital media and the internet, which appeared to offer direct access to mass distribution for a new generation of 'cultural entrepreneurs' (20). The analysis, and others like it, opened up a substantial new research and policy agenda in the early 2000s, engaging media and cultural studies in novel and interesting ways with topics such as business models, copyright law, cultural geography, online distribution and the affordances of digital media. At the same time, it could be seen as reprising the tendency of popular cultural studies in the preceding period to minimize the significance of large institutions. There were, indeed, some direct continuities. The most notable example in Australia would be the work of John Hartley, who moved from popular cultural studies in the 1980s and 1990s to writing on the creative industries in the 2000s and 2010s, becoming a key figure in both fields.

As in the case of other theoretical perspectives, however, the creative industries analysis of independent production intersects only at points with those of practitioners. It is certainly the case that the promise of greater autonomy has been a significant motivation for the formation of independent businesses. In some cases, this motivation has been in relation to legal rights over content. One of the reasons Denton formed Zapruder was the realization that the intellectual property for his early work was held by the ABC or the commercial production house McDonald Eastway which had partnered on his projects for Channel Seven. In other cases, the autonomy being sought has been in relation to aesthetic control. For *The D-Generation* ensemble, the catalyst for forming Working Dog was a production dispute with the ABC over the shooting style to be used for *Frontline*, their mock documentary satire of television current affairs. The team wanted to shoot on Hi 8 video to give the show a gritty 'reality' appearance, while the ABC insisted that in-house productions use the formulaic 'quality' style developed for comedies such as *Mother and Son*.

In many ways, however, independent production has only offered new ways to address old problems. Denton (2014) is explicit about this:

> I always had this vision of Zapruder as being like a formal version of what Mark Fitzgerald and co had done for me [at the ABC], which is 'I'm going to put a buffer around you, and I'm going to take away that group of people who are going to instil fear and questions marks into you, and I'm going to give you every opportunity to do your thing'.

This vision was codified jokingly in a 'pimping agreement' signed with The Chaser, which included the undertaking from Denton (2014): 'I, as producer, endeavour to protect you from all non-essential dickheads.' The important point to note here is that such an agreement would not have been necessary if it had not been felt that the 'dickheads' remained a very real presence and one that could not be ignored. It is clear from Denton's comparison with his early years at the ABC that he is referring to institutional gatekeepers – similar to Vizard's (2014) 'arse-protectors' in the commercial sector – who respond to new entrants only with reflex demands that they conform to established norms. Yet it is from precisely such gatekeepers which, according to the creative industries arguments of the early 2000s, 'the independents' were supposed to have been freed.

It might be objected that Zapruder is not quite the kind of independent that Leadbeater and Oakley had in mind. At the time the company was founded, Denton was mainstream media royalty, so the company might be seen simply as hiving off established functions. However, relations with mainstream institutions have also been important to those we might dub 'true' independents, small start-ups established by a younger generation who would also qualify as 'digital natives'. An example is Checkpoint Media, the production company of the Fancy Boy ensemble cited earlier. Checkpoint had no prior relation to the broadcasters, trading initially on a reputation established through viral videos on YouTube. Yet it has also been shaped from the outset by relations with large institutions. For the group's Mike Nayna (Nayna & Conway 2015), YouTube might be thought of as the 'open mic of television comedy'. It offers an important new platform for fringe expression but does not fundamentally alter the question of relations between fringe and mainstream.

If seen in these terms, Fancy Boy's trajectory is very recognizable from previous generations of comedians. The group has roots not only in online media, but also in the cultural ecology of Melbourne described earlier: before breaking out with their own acts, the group ran a comedy room, Checkpoint Charlie, in the city – from which the company name is derived. Upon launching the company, they took on video production work from corporates and government agencies to pay the bills while exhibiting at festivals – particularly WebFest, an adaptation of the festival format for the internet generation – and looking for support from institutional sponsors such as Screen Australia and the ABC for more ambitious projects.

Online distribution has clearly seen the creation of a whole new ecology in which emerging comedy acts find sheltered, risk-taking spaces. Other notable examples include the Bondi Hipsters, Kate McLennan and Kate McCartney and the surrealist comedy troupe Aunty Donna, formed at the regional University of Ballarat's Arts Academy. For most of these artists, a break into television is not a culminating end game, but only one option to be pursued alongside an ongoing streaming practice and live performance. Aunty Donna submitted a pilot in the same round as Fancy Boy of the ABC's Fresh Blood but the group was not commissioned for a series. Undeterred by this, they built a large youthful following through a titular YouTube series then a dedicated YouTube channel. When they did finally make it to broadcasting, with a premiere of *Aunty Donna's Coffee Café* on the ABC in 2023, it was almost as a bespoke complement to their online profile. This points to the recent emergence of a new platform hybridity, in which the dialectic between fringe and mainstream is as much internal to online platforms as aligned with the distinction between online and broadcasting. This is the media landscape that is being explored in Australia by scholars such as Guy Healy (2022).

The last decade has seen increasing attention to the fact that the online platforms are themselves owned by large multinational corporations, ones indeed that have come to dwarf the broadcasters. This has been accompanied by a sharp pendulum swing from the creative industries optimism of the late 1990s and early 2000s. Small independent producers are now widely represented as subordinated to the profit-oriented designs of 'platform' or 'surveillance' capitalism (Srnicek 2016; Zuboff 2019). There is a risk in this context that debates over cultural production in the 2020s may find themselves in similar blind alleys to those of the 1980s and 1990s, flip-flopping between the equally implausible extremes of simple-minded voluntarism and grim institutional determinism. There can be little doubt of the need today for critical perspectives on 'big tech'. The corporations in question – Facebook, Apple, Amazon, Netflix and Google – are global behemoths with enormous influence, over not only cultural production, but many other aspects of our everyday lives. At the same time, however, we should avoid repeating the error of assuming that large institutions are easily reducible to a single or simple principle.

It would be interesting in this context to consider the commissioning and curatorial practices of the online platforms. How is it, for example, that a match was made between global streaming giant Netflix and Hannah Gadsby's stand-up show *Nanette* (2018), riffing on edgy themes of gender inequality, mental illness and the experience of growing up queer in small-town Tasmania? Might a similar story of hybridization be told in this case as the one we have told above for Channel Seven and the ABC? But to focus only on the 'macro' (the global tech company) and the 'micro' (the individual comedian) tends to favour simple oppositions between structure and agency. The story of *Nanette* involved many actors that might better be described as 'meso'. The Netflix show was an adaptation of earlier stage versions developed through extensive engagement by Gadsby with creative directors and audiences at festivals and live events, both in Australia and internationally. Her comic performance had also been honed through experience on television, through involvement in the ABC comedies *Adam Hills Tonight* and *Please Like Me* as well as her own three-part series *Hannah Gadsby's Oz*. The fact that analogue *distribution* is in precipitous decline should not distract us here from the continuing importance in *production* of the 'art worlds' associated with broadcasting.

We finish the chapter therefore with a brief account of the contribution of mid-level 'animateurs' in the development of comedy in Australia. There are many examples we might choose from, even if we limit the scope just to ABC staff commissioners, executive producers and department heads responsible for comedy since 2000. Most of the latter have had substantial connections with fringe scenes: Andy Nehl, whose formation was in punk music and radical community radio (4ZZZ, Radio Skid Row); Dennis Watkins, who cut his teeth in university revue, theatre sports and fringe theatre; Guy Rundle, who combined comedy writing for Max Gillies with radical journalism and editing of the left-alternative *Arena* magazine; Katrina Sedgwick, who had directed the Adelaide Fringe; and Richard Fidler, who had performed, written and produced as part of the avant-garde *Doug Anthony All Stars*. But we will focus here on Courtney Gibson, Head of ABC TV's Arts and Entertainment from 2003 to 2007, a period of significant outreach and popular experimentation in comedy. Gibson (2014) has consistently seen the ABC as an 'off Broadway' space where new talent, and experimental formats, genres and styles can be developed and trialled before more open-minded audiences without the immediate pressure of having to demonstrate ratings.

Gibson came into media through journalism, starting as a seventeen-year-old 'copy girl' at News Ltd. She then moved into television in the UK, working for Channel 4's *The Big Breakfast* and as London 'stringer' on Vizard's *Tonight Live*. Returning to Australia, she joined forces with Andy Nehl to produce the boozy, rambunctious chat show *Mouthing Off*, hosted by Fidler, for Vizard's Artist Services and The Comedy Channel. After co-creating and producing pop culture series *The Hub* for Pay TV channel Arena, Gibson became Deputy Commissioning Editor of documentaries at SBS Independent in 1998. She later translated aspects of the SBSi model to the ABC, first as a Commissioning Editor, then as Head of Arts and Entertainment. Gibson's (2014) role at both broadcasters has been liminal, 'moving between roles' making television within the independent production sector and 'working inside the channels'.

The highlight for Gibson (2014) at SBSi was 'working with emerging program makers ... you would spot new talent and projects all the time'. The imperative during her tenure was commissioning from marginal and emerging talent, notably first-time Indigenous filmmakers, teaming them with experienced production people. Comedy making for screen is a collective enterprise; coordination between creative and technical teams is crucial – even on lower budgets – in bringing programmes to fruition at a production standard that will attract an audience. Commissioning editors within public broadcasters have leverage over the composition of these teams, even where the comedian is working within an independent company. For Gibson, combining emerging talent with experienced cinematographers, editors and producers was the key to enabling creative risk-taking within a financial envelope that the institution could sustain. Getting the balance right between experience and new approaches is, as she puts it, about 'taking the risk out of them in order to get the best work'. This can be a win-win arrangement, as 'the first-time director is incredibly well supported', while the experienced production team 'learn new skills and ways of seeing things' (Gibson 2014). This became the best practice modus operandi at SBSi and was brought to ABC Arts and Entertainment by Gibson in the early 2000s.

Working closely with former SBSi colleagues Debbie Lee and Amanda Duthie, Gibson's responsibilities as Head of ABC Arts and Entertainment included commissioning and developing new voices and talent from comedy venues and festivals, sourcing funding for programmes from multiple sources (in part to spread the risk), locating emerging talent and ideas, and putting together production teams with a workable balance of experience and new talent, and editorial oversight on behalf of the broadcaster. Gibson's ABC projects included *The Chaser's War on Everything*, Chris Lilley's popular cycle of narrative comedies beginning with *We Can Be Heroes* and *Summer Heights High*, the late-night cult series *Double the Fist* and multiple series by Shaun Micallef, Laurence Leung, and Robyn Butler and Wayne Hope's Gristmill.

Another contribution of the comedic animateur is to negotiate deals with co-production partners, such as state and Federal screen finance agencies (VicScreen, Screen Australia, etc.) and international media organizations to invest in novel projects led by new players – a function that has become crucial in an environment of shrinking public funding in Australia since the 1990s. This is where, as Mills (2017) suggests, negotiating finance for production deserves to be seen as a creative contribution. Gibson (2014) outlines a process where young people with great ideas are supported by 'bring[ing] other interests to the table … getting people enthused about the projects'. In Gibson's (2014) experience, the big difference between comedy on public broadcasters compared to commercial television is that they are almost all co-funded: 'In public broadcasters one of the things you need to do is get people on board, and sometimes that can take years and years … That's sort of part of the [commissioning] gig.'

In conclusion then, the successes of comedy in Australia since the 1980s cannot be attributed solely to the creativity of the fringe or to the institutionalized forms of large-scale production through which comic performance has been popularized. Both ingredients are necessary, but neither is sufficient on its own. Without a robust field of restricted production, mainstream forms would be empty and anodyne, lacking a capacity for renewal. It is crucial for the development of comedy, therefore, that there be sheltered spaces in which such a field can develop. These spaces may be physical, as in the case of student revues or fringe theatre, or mediated, as in the case of niche publications, radio programmes or online forums. Too much attention can sometimes be paid to the medium: what is important is the function they serve as crucibles for alternative values. It is also essential, however, that there be opportunities for crossover and exchange between fringe comedy and mainstream institutions. These opportunities can be found in mid-level spaces, such as theatre restaurants or festivals, or through producers or animateurs, such as Courtney Gibson, with a talent for brokering relationships. The important point, again, is one of principle: the potency of comedy needs to be understood as a complex ensemble effort by players distributed across both fringe and mainstream locations.

As we suggested at the beginning of the chapter, this point may be easier to see in the case of comedy than it sometimes is for other cultural forms. Concepts such as the carnivalesque provide a fertile framework within which to develop an appreciation of hybridity. At the same time, continued work is required to prevent a hardening of categories such that fringe comedic performance and mainstream institutions come to appear as structurally opposed. In the shadow of the counterculture, the concept of carnival was often captured to a trenchant anti-institutionalism which sought to discount the cultural agency of figures in mainstream locations. This tendency has been met by a tough-minded institutional realism which suggests that however subversive carnival may appear on the surface, it is in fact always 'licensed', merely serving the interests of those in power. Our argument above has been that neither perspective is satisfactory. The most important element in this is a recognition that both fringe and mainstream are complex formations that can never be entirely reduced to a single, simple principle. While the distinction between the two remains important, actual social and historical entities will, in both cases, always be interlaced with threads that are owed to the other.

5

Alternative visions: The Indigenous wave and Australian independent cinema

One of the more celebrated 'fringe to famous' moments in Australia over the past twenty years has been Warwick Thornton's *Camera d'Or* win for *Samson & Delilah* at the 2009 Cannes Film Festival. The achievement was received in the arts and cultural pages of local media as confirming the arrival of a 'new wave' of Indigenous filmmaking (Boland 2009: 6; Kalina 2009: 12; Rosemary 2009: 6). In press coverage of the many triumphs of *Samson & Delilah* – first at Cannes, then with critics, at the local box office and later its shortlisting for the Academy Award for Best Foreign Language film (a feat made possible because more than 60 per cent of the dialogue was in Warlpiri) – the discussion also emphasized the *improbability* of the film's success. The content was considered too difficult and too unpalatable for most audiences. Thornton is a Kaytetye man, born and raised in Alice Springs in central Australia, thousands of kilometres from the country's major cities. He was a first-time feature director who had also written and shot the film, the budget was tiny, the actors untrained locals and the production unconventional. Interviews with Thornton focused on the parallels between his own tumultuous teenage years growing up around Alice Springs and the dysfunction and substance abuse portrayed on screen (Dow 2009: 8; Maddox 2009: 19; Rosemary 2009: 6). According to popular discourse, *Samson & Delilah* had succeeded entirely against the odds.

Yet this narrative belies the fact that the film was the result of a long-term programme of screen policy initiatives expressly developed to establish a commercially successful Indigenous screen sector in Australia. There can be no doubting Thornton's achievement in bridging between remote Indigenous communities and urban, cosmopolitan audiences both in Australia and internationally, but his career did not come out of nowhere. Like that of Rachel Perkins, Ivan Sen, Wayne Blair, Sally Riley and other key filmmakers, producers and policymakers associated with Australia's Indigenous film and television

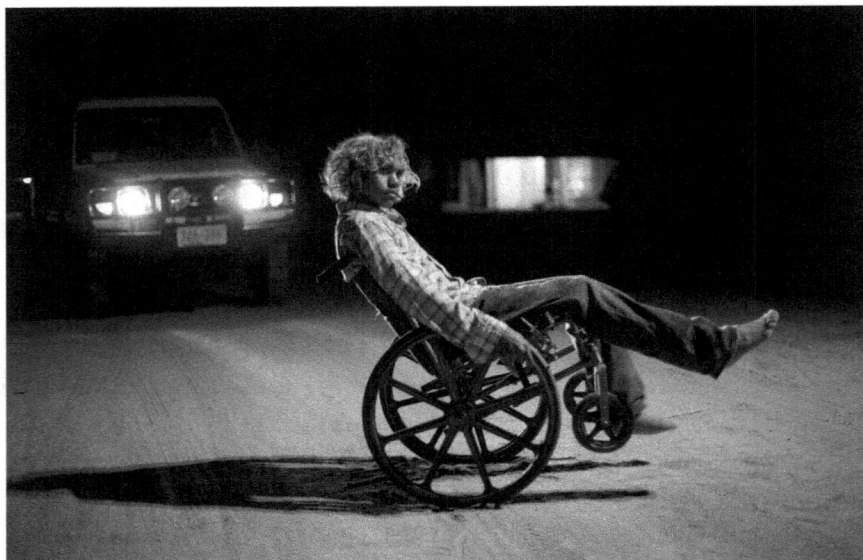

Figure 25 Rowan McNamara in *Samson & Delilah* (2009). Photograph by Mark Rogers. Courtesy Scarlett Pictures.

sector, it has built on a long process of crossover and exchange between Indigenous cultural production and mainstream institutions and audiences. The 'Blak wave' movement is a case in which oppositions between 'fringe' and 'mainstream' are heightened by colonial legacies of race, taste and geography. Yet the success of a film like *Samson & Delilah* can also be traced to histories of creative fusion and hybridization, not only at the level of filmic expression and narrative form, but also in the institutional, organizational and economic arrangements that have supported them.

In this chapter, we examine an important development in Australian screen practice, tracing its trajectory from a position of social, industry, policy and often geographic marginality, to varying degrees of commercial and critical success, locally and internationally. At the level of both scholarship and practice, Australia's cinematic 'Blak Wave' challenges many of the ways we have conceptualized margin/mainstream relations as they exist between independent and commercial production, and between First Nations, national, global and Hollywood filmmaking traditions. Traversing comfortably across populist genre pleasures, contemporary art, international art-house cinema, and with roots in local Indigenous community art and media-making scenes across the breadth of the country, Australia's Indigenous film *naissance* represents an ideal case study for reimagining margin/mainstream relations in the contemporary period. As one of the country's clearest and surest policy success stories to emerge from many decades of government subsidized screen culture, it also offers an opportunity to consider what broader lessons can be learnt from the architecture of the policy, its implementation and its evolution alongside the filmmaking culture it helps to support.

Mapping the field

If Australian movies themselves aren't mainstream, 'then we're on the fringe of the fringe of the mainstream'.

(Sally Riley, quoted in Hawker 2002: 1)

There are certain challenges in bringing the perspective of the book to Indigenous screen. We have sought in *Fringe to Famous* to question a widespread insistence in scholarly work on cultural industries that the 'fringe' or 'independent' be regarded only as discursive constructions. It is important in developing the idea of a hybridity between fringe and mainstream that we allow these terms to point to actual differences, whether they be in scale, social location, forms of expression, organizational structure or economic arrangements. Indigenous cultural production might seem, at first, a perfect example. If we consider a case such as *Samson & Delilah*, the differences in context from those of the major centres of international screen production could hardly be more obvious. Yet this obviousness also risks returning us to the kind of romanticism that we have wanted to avoid from the outset: one for which the fringe is conceived as a radical 'outside' to the mainstream, representing an 'authenticity' or 'purity' that is not to be found elsewhere. The very starkness of the opposition between the Hollywood studio and the remote Indigenous community therefore presents its own kind of dangers.

The point is important not only for the way we conceptualize relations between the fringe and mainstream, but also for the ethics of writing or speaking about Indigenous cultural production. For a group of non-Indigenous authors – as we are – to invoke an Indigenous 'reality' might easily lead to the kind of ventriloquism identified in the 1990s by American literary/film scholar Marianna Torgovnick. 'The primitive', as Torgovnick (1990: 9) called it, 'does what we ask it to do. Voiceless, it lets us speak for it'. The approach is made more problematic still by the association between a supposed authenticity in Indigenous screen and the fact that the communities being represented are often *poor*. To attribute a positive value to such authenticity comes perilously close to the 'slum voyeurism' (Gonzaga 2017) or 'favela chic' (Goldschmitt 2020) that has been rightly criticized internationally in screen and cultural studies. It is probably for good reason that Indigenous artists have often sought to resist such interpretative frames, using humour or playing with conventions of genre fiction to puncture expectations of otherness and confound easy ascriptions of marginality.

The safest course in this context would no doubt be to revert to the critical consensus that the fringe or independent be considered only as discursive categories. Doing so would align us with a major body of scholarship that has developed over many decades in relation to a range of cultural industries – indie cinema and indie music cultures in the UK and the United States in particular (Newman 2011; Perren 2012; King, Molloy and Tzioumakis 2013; Hesmondhalgh et al. 2015). 'Mainstream' and 'independent' are understood in this literature as interdependent concepts defined not in relation to actual phenomena but through and against each other. If mainstream is used to imply 'a large-scale commercial media industry' oriented towards profit (Newman 2009: 16), and a corporatized approach to culture making that is 'vertically integrated, well-financed and *big*' (Hesmondhalgh and Meier 2015: 94), then the independent is defined by the negation of all these things: production that claims a virtue in being small-scale, artist-driven, autonomous and motivated by art, personal vision, passion, politics or ethics. These oppositions are generally seen as aligning with orientations in relation to power: 'mainstream media support the dominant ideology while alternative media oppose it' (Newman 2009: 18).

There are problems internal to this approach when applied to Australia, as the discursive positions are less distinct than they are elsewhere. Most Australian screen content is heavily government subsidized and in the ultra-risky realm of feature film production, it is an enormous feat for a title to make back its original budget. It is difficult therefore to see any part of the Australian screen sector in terms of dominance, profitability or mass audiences. As Geoff King (2014: 53) has argued, the currency of the term 'independent' is weakened outside of North American contexts because '*any* nationally based production is likely to have the status of a Cinderella in comparison with the global dominance of Hollywood'. King suggests that American independent cinema therefore has the most clear-cut claim to 'indieness'. The status of independence makes sense only through sharing the same geographic space as Hollywood. The definition of cinematic independence as 'not-Hollywood' means something sharper and more distinct in the United States, but the further away from the centre you are, the looser and more ambiguous the label becomes. It is not that all Australian films are independent so much that no Australian film, globally speaking, could ever be properly mainstream.

The mainstream in Australia is widely understood to be elsewhere, principally in the form of Hollywood studio blockbusters with budgets in the hundreds of millions, or the content produced by newly powerful American players such as HBO, Netflix and Amazon, or to a lesser extent in the form of quality British screen productions from the BBC and Channel 4. This means that Australian films generally become most clearly marked as 'independent' or 'fringe' when they circulate internationally. The paradigmatic examples here are low-budget, Indigenous art-house films such as *Samson & Delilah*, which appear even smaller, more niche and more marginal in markets outside Australia, doubling down on their outsider status in a way that enables them, paradoxically, to gain audiences on international art-house circuits.

But an outsider status is often assigned internationally also to films that would not be considered marginal in Australia itself. So, for example, a popular genre film such as the crime drama *Animal Kingdom* (2010 dir. David Michôd) – which had a budget of approximately AU$5 million, a cast that was very well-known locally and direction from an experienced filmmaker with a normative career trajectory – was represented in the global context as a low-budget, indie underdog (Hynes 2010: 44; Kern 2010: 25–5). In a similar vein, the Indigenous-led musical comedy *The Sapphires* (dir. Wayne Blair, 2012) had an even larger budget of AU$8 million (Maddox 2012), a wide cinematic release and a cast including Australian celebrities (established actor Deborah Mailman and pop singer Jessica Mauboy) and international talent (comedian Chris O'Dowd). By any local measure *The Sapphires* was a big, successful mainstream film, but in the ensuing coverage of its international release, the multi-million-dollar, feel-good, based-on-true-events blockbuster morphed into an unlikely underdog, 'the little Aussie film that could' (Christie and Harris 2013: 43).

There is admittedly a standard way to preserve the discursivist perspective in the face of such paradoxes. This is to introduce a principle of relativity according to scale. Such a principle is embedded in Bourdieu's (1993) concept of the 'field of cultural production' which we have drawn on, to some extent, throughout

Figure 26 L-R: Deborah Mailman, Shari Sebbens, Jessica Mauboy and Miranda Tapsell in *The Sapphires* (2012). Courtesy Goalpost Pictures.

the book. To determine the status of any instance of cultural production, for Bourdieu, we need first to specify the field within which it is being considered; the position of a particular cultural production will automatically change when its reference points shift. The perspective can be used to explain examples, such as the ones above, where the same phenomenon can appear as 'mainstream' in one context and as 'fringe' in other contexts. Indeed, the relativity in the use of such terms might be seen as adding weight to the idea that 'mainstream' and 'fringe' are no more than discursive categories. It further suggests that such terms are not anchored in 'real' differences but refer only to rhetorical or performative positions adopted within the field of cultural production by some actors in relation to other actors.

However, the example of Indigenous film also provokes us to consider the limits of such discursivism. While the arguments for avoiding reality claims may be clear, there is a certain absurdity in following them to their logical conclusions. Are we really to deny that there are concrete differences between the production contexts of Thornton's *Samson & Delilah* and a Hollywood blockbuster? Nor do ethical considerations for non-Indigenous authors weigh only in favour of restricting ourselves to the analysis of discursive oppositions. A rigorous discursivism may address concerns about the dangers of speaking for others, but it also prevents recognition of the impact of Indigenous perspectives on mainstream Australian cultural forms. If all that can be referenced are 'constructions' or 'performances' of Indigeneity, we are condemned to a hall of mirrors in which the agency of actual Indigenous artists is ultimately denied.

Some of the strongest arguments for a recognition of this agency have come from Indigenous scholars and artists themselves. One of the most prominent has been Marcia Langton, who has sought to draw attention over more than thirty years to Indigenous contributions to Australian cultural expression and public life. An essential aspect of this project has been to establish that what might be seen as 'fringe' Indigenous cultural forms have their own internal organization independent of any relation they may have with the white mainstream. In her influential essay of the early 1990s *Well I Heard It on the Radio and Saw It on the Television ...*, Langton devotes a chapter, for example, to the Warlpiri Media Association in the remote Northern Territory community of Yuendumu. Drawing on the work in the 1980s of American anthropologist Eric Michaels, she describes 'specific Aboriginal cultural modes of sociality' (Langton 1993: 59) which are brought to bear in how Warlpiri people make video and television. The media technologies used by the Warlpiri have, of course, been adopted from the outside. What needs to be understood, however, is what Michaels called the 'process of incorporation' by which the Warlpiri socialize these technologies in their own distinctive ways.

Langton is acutely aware of the problems of romanticism. *Well I Heard It on the Radio ...* is full of caustic observations about 'the constant stereotyping, iconising and mythologising of Aboriginal people by white people who have never had any substantial first-hand contact with Aboriginal people':

> These icons of 'Aboriginality' are produced by Anglo-Australians, not in dialogue with Aboriginal people, but from other representations such as the 'stone age savage', the 'dying 'race'', the 'one penny stamp Aborigine, the Pelaco Shirt Aborigine, Venus Half Caste, the Cinesound News Service caricatures, Crocodile Dundee I and II, the 'received wisdom'.
>
> (Langton 1993: 34)

But even in the way she presents these criticisms, Langton urges us to consider alternatives to purely discursive understandings. Besides cultural and textual constructions that emerge internally within Aboriginal communities and within the non-Aboriginal communities, there is also a 'third category' that arises when Aboriginal and non-Aboriginal people engage in 'actual dialogue':

> In these exchanges, as in any social interaction, the individuals involved will test imagined models of the other, repeatedly adjusting the models as responses are processed, to find some satisfactory way of comprehending the other. It is in these dialogues ... that working models of 'Aboriginality' are constructed as ways of seeing Aboriginal people, but both the Aboriginal subject and the non-Aboriginal subject are participating.
>
> (Langton 1992: 35)

While Langton has no patience for those who seek to deny legacies of racism and colonialism, she is also critical of those who see these legacies as so determining of relations between Aboriginal and non-Aboriginal people that dialogue is impossible: 'In some films, television and video, the director/editors/writers/producers, black and white, seem to want Aboriginal people to iconise "the oppressor" ... These filmmakers want to see "Europeans" portrayed only as oppressors and all the complexities eliminated. They fail to admit the intersubjectivity of black/white relations' (Langton 1992: 37–8).

Langton's concept of intersubjectivity could be seen as corresponding to the model we have sought to develop in *Fringe to Famous* of hybridity between fringe and mainstream. It shares an understanding of marginal, small-scale cultural production as embedded in concrete historical formations which have their own distinctive qualities. To recognize this distinctiveness is not to suggest that the qualities in question are radically 'other', incomprehensible to those who come to them from the outside. It is significant that Langton seeks to normalize dialogue between Aboriginal and non-Aboriginal subjects as similar to those 'in any social interaction'. Indigenous screen cultures are woven through with figures, techniques and narrative devices that are familiar to non-Indigenous audiences. Indigenous screen cultures have a long history of absorption of outside influences: even in very remote communities, regular film screenings were an established institution from at least the 1950s (Langton 1992: 19). At the same time, remote Aboriginal people have, as Langton puts it, 'their own production values, distinct aesthetics and cultural concerns' (14).

When Indigenous screen content is exhibited to large, predominantly non-Indigenous audiences, it carries with it some of these values, aesthetics and concerns. This is not to deny that Indigenous filmmakers may often make strategic use of more abstract discursive oppositions between fringe and mainstream, particularly in international art-house contexts. The significance at Cannes of a film like *Samson & Delilah* may have been, to some extent, as a kind of 'not-Hollywood', representing a 'rawness' and 'authenticity' not generally seen in mainstream cinema. But even in cases such as these, the creative expression cannot be entirely reduced to position-taking within the field. Thornton's work draws on more than thirty years of experimentation in film and video in Central Australia. His success in the international art-house circuit has been a success also of projecting the values generated by this experimentation onto a larger screen.

An intersubjectivity between Indigenous and non-Indigenous elements is even clearer in films, such as *The Sapphires*, pitched more at the Australian domestic market. It may indeed be facilitated by the fact, as we have remarked above, that the lines between 'fringe' and 'mainstream' are fuzzier in this market than in the international domain. Rather than seeing this fuzziness as a lack, it might be more productive in the context of our argument in *Fringe to Famous* to see non-metropolitan locations such as Australia in more positive terms as crucibles of hybridity. The weakness in the definition of mainstream production reduces the charge of 'otherness' associated with fringe locations, allowing them to enter into more dialogic relations.

Indigenous artists take pleasure, just as non-Indigenous artists do, in seeing their ideas represented within the mainstream. When asked about his hopes for the future of the Australian film industry, director of *The Sapphires* Wayne Blair (quoted in Siemienowicz 2014) said, 'It would be great for non-Indigenous filmmakers to cast Aboriginal actors in key roles, and also for Indigenous filmmakers to have budgets of 20 or 30 million,' equivalent to those of other local blockbusters like *Mao's Last Dancer* (2009, dir. Bruce Beresford).

The last fifteen years have seen a huge collective effort directed towards realizing such aspirations. The result has been that Australia's Indigenous filmmaking has moved closer and closer to occupying an indisputable position within the local industry, in terms of box office receipts, ratings, budget, craft, aesthetics, and critical and industry recognition. Indeed, 'mainstream success' is one of the central motifs in how these films and practitioners are talked about, in both the media and in academic scholarship (Dolgopolov 2014; Davis 2017; Griffin, Griffin and Trudgett 2017; Keast 2018; Siemienowicz 2018). 'Crossing into the mainstream' has now become a central part of the story of the rise and rise of Australian Indigenous filmmaking.

A wave?

To appreciate the scale of the boom in Indigenous filmmaking in Australia, it is important to acknowledge just how little Indigenous authored screen material, of any genre, length or format, existed prior to the 1990s. Indigenous characters and stories were, overwhelmingly, fodder for non-Indigenous filmmakers. The late 1970s saw increasingly vocal demands for better representation of Indigenous people, more support for Indigenous self-representation, and a small number of non-Indigenous filmmakers began to seek greater input from Indigenous artists and communities. Often-cited examples include *Backroads* (1977, dir. Phillip Noyce) which stars Aboriginal actor and activist Gary Foley, *My Survival as an Aboriginal* (1978, dir. Essie Coffey working with Martha Ansara) and *Two Laws* (1981), a collaboration between Borroloola Tribal Council and white filmmakers Allesandro Cavadini and Carolyn Strachan. Autonomous Indigenous authorship, however, remained almost non-existent until the mid-1980s.

The extent of the absence of Indigenous voices from Australian film is documented at length in Brian Syron's (1996) book, *Kicking Down the Doors*. Syron is often credited as the first Aboriginal director of a feature film for his work *Jindalee Lady* (1992) (Donovan 2002: xi). The film was an ultra-low-budget feature that never received commercial distribution. Syron was unsuccessful in his efforts to get funding support for the film from the federal funding agency, The Australian Film Commission. The rejection of the funding application eventually resulted in a hearing between Syron and the AFC at the Human Rights and Equal Opportunity Commission. *Kicking Down the Doors* functions as part memoir and part counter-narrative of Australian film history. For anyone with even a passing knowledge of Australian film from this period, all the key moments are there: the establishment of the Australian Film Development Corporation, then an Australian Film Commission, a dedicated Australian Film and Television School, specialist funds for women filmmakers and experimental filmmakers, the 10BA tax incentives of the late 1970s and 1980s, and the establishment of the multicultural Special Broadcasting Service (SBS). But with the passing of each film historical milestone, Aboriginal filmmakers, writers, producers and technical talent were relegated to the fringes of Australian filmmaking by the myriad public institutions created to support local screen culture.

A constant theme in the decades that Syron describes is a perception that, no matter whether the filmmaker was Indigenous or not, films concerning

Indigenous issues, or the so-called 'Aboriginal problem', were considered 'box office poison' (Syron 1996: 19; 78; 148). The concern is one that lingers still, to be found everywhere in the background to conversation about the 'surprise' box office success of *Rabbit Proof Fence* (by non-Indigenous filmmaker Phillip Noyce, 2002), and later *Samson & Delilah* (2009), *Bran Nue Dae* (2009) and *The Sapphires* (2012). Regardless of who was behind the camera, the popular consensus until relatively recently was that dealing in any way with Indigenous themes, people or stories was antithetical to mainstream success.

In the late 1980s, institutional silence and inaction gave way to tentative policy, and eventually significant Indigenous programming and production initiatives at the public broadcasters and the federal and state screen funding agencies (complemented by support for Indigenous media, culture and heritage available via other areas of government policy, primarily via the 'communications' portfolio). The Australian Broadcasting Commission (ABC) and SBS introduced dedicated Indigenous programming and production units in the late 1980s (Peters 1994). Newly formed remote Indigenous media organizations such as the Central Australian Aboriginal Media Association (CAAMA), Imparja Television, Broome Aboriginal Media Association (BAMA) and the Warlpiri Media Association became increasingly active producers of short video and documentary. In response to growing scrutiny, the AFC commissioned a report into 'Promoting Indigenous Involvement in the Film and TV Industry' (McPherson and Pope 1992) and published Langton's (1993) essay, cited above, *Well, I Heard It on the Radio and I Saw It on the Television ...*, on the politics of representing Aboriginal people and stories. In 1993, at long last, the AFC established an Indigenous Branch and in May the same year Tracey Moffat's experimental Indigenous horror triptych *BeDevil* debuted in *Un Certain Regard* at the Cannes Film Festival (although the film's development pre-dated the establishment of the AFC's Indigenous Branch). It was both the first feature film written by an Aboriginal person to receive government funds and the first to receive commercial distribution (Donovan with Lorraine 2992: 163–4). *BeDevil* is also the first and one of the only horror anthologies directed by a woman (and likely a good many other 'firsts' besides).

What followed was a series of sustained and significant training and production initiatives involving the Indigenous Branch of the AFC (later Screen Australia), often in partnership with the public broadcasters and state film and television funding bodies. The initiatives included the long running National Indigenous Documentary Fund along with *From Sand to Celluloid* (1996),

Shifting Sands (1998), *Crossing Tracks* (1999), *Dramatically Black* (2005), the *Long Black Feature Program* (2004) and *The New Black* (2009) among numerous others. These initiatives supported film projects that were required to have Indigenous people in a minimum of key creative roles, and they were designed to support aspiring filmmakers and producers (who may have little or no professional screen credits) move from community-based media production to longer documentary formats, short dramas and eventually feature-length films. The intention was to provide stepping-stone initiatives that allowed for 'carefully mentored and monitored development' (Australian Film Commission 2007: 2), with successful alumni of the first programme later returning to mentor a new round of aspiring filmmakers.

According to ABC's Head of Indigenous Sally Riley, who was both a participant in early incarnations of the programmes and later ran them as Manager of the Indigenous Branch at the AFC, the plan was 'to create a pathway for people. So we would start with 10-minute films and we'd go to half-hour films, [then] hour films. We did an initiative of one-hour films and then eventually we went to features'. The programme sought to operate like a 'mini film school', compensating in part for the historical absence of Indigenous students from NIDA and AFTRS, the nation's primary training institutes for the screen and performing arts industries (Riley 2017). The activities of the Indigenous Branch represent cultural policy at its most interventionist and hands on and are closer in design and implementation to the earliest state interventions into Australian screen policy in the late 1960s and 1970s, which had been central to the emergence of an Australian 'New Wave'. Much like the first 'new wave', the beneficiaries of the AFC's Indigenous Branch's activities over the last twenty-five years include all the key names of the 'Black Wave' and among them many of the most celebrated filmmakers and producers working in Australia today.

In the years after the establishment of the AFC's Indigenous Branch, there was an initial ripple of feature films which received limited commercial releases – *Radiance* (dir. Rachel Perkins, 1997), *One Night the Moon* (dir. Rachel Perkins, 2001) and *Beneath Clouds* (dir. Ivan Sen, 2001). Although they were all critically well received, the films were not commercial successes, leading the new Manager of the Indigenous Branch Sally Riley to express concern that the slate of Indigenous films were not reaching broad audiences. As Riley (quoted in Hawker 2002: 1) put it, '[t]hey do well in festivals but you really want people to see them'. That wider level of success came with a second more substantial wave of productions in the form of feature film debuts from the programme's alumni including *Samson & Delilah* (dir. Warwick Thornton, 2009) and *The Sapphires* (dir. Wayne Blair, 2012); and follow-up films from Ivan Sen including *Toomelah* (2010), *Mystery Road* (2013) and *Goldstone* (2016), and Rachel Perkins' *Bran Nue Dae* (2009).

These features have been accompanied by a growing presence on television, involving a range of high-profile and often highly rated television shows (Knox 2012; 2016a; 2016b; 2018) including telemovie bio-pic *Mabo* (2012, ABC), hard-hitting drama *Redfern Now* (2012–15, ABC), sketch show *Black Comedy* (2014 & 2016, ABC), reality television show *First Contact* (2014 & 2016, SBS), dark superhero fantasy *Cleverman* (2016–17, ABC) and the television spin-off series based on *Mystery Road* (2018–22, ABC). When the Indigenous Branch at the AFC was first established in 1993, there had been, over the course of the previous twenty-five years of public funding for Australian film culture, just two feature films written or directed by an Aboriginal Australian and only a handful of shorts. In the subsequent thirty years, there have been many dozens of feature films, shorts films, documentaries and prime-time television.

'Authentic' Indigenous auteurs on the international art-house circuit

In late 2008 at an industry conference on Queensland's Gold Coast, Australia's premiere Greenfield destination for off-shore Hollywood productions, the then president of the Screen Producers Association of Australia Antony Ginnane lamented the nation's 'appalling' box office record of late. The reason local films were taking such a slim share of box office receipts was, he argued, because '[w]e've been making, in the main, dark, depressing, bleak pieces that are the cultural equivalent of ethnic cleansing. Nobody goes to see them' (Ginnane 2008). Ginnane was far from the only one to make such claims about Australian cinema at the time. Columnists, critics and industry insiders complained that contemporary Australian films were too 'dark', 'disturbing', 'dreary', 'unpleasant' and they didn't connect with audiences or the box office (Schembri 2008; Buckmaster 2009; Hoskin 2009). Dark themes, it seemed, were the enemy of a robust national cinema. Yet barely six months later, Warwick Thornton's dark, difficult and confronting love story between two marginalized Indigenous youth, won critical acclaim, the *Palm D'Or*, scooped the major prizes at all the

Australian screen awards, and became one of the top 100 grossing Australian feature films of all time.

In the surrounding Australian media coverage, *Samson & Delilah* and filmmaker Warwick Thornton were discussed in terms which were very much in keeping with the well-established virtues of authentic indie cinema: scale, autonomy and oppositionality. Much was made of the film's outsider setting in the desert north-west of Alice Springs – which was described as 'a different world', remote, isolated and somewhere 'few people know or understand' (Parkes 2009: 23) – and of its low budget, minimal script and pared back production which saw local kids cast as the film's leads, family members in key roles and crew doubling as extras. Again and again, these choices were framed as deliberate artistic preferences rather than the by-product of financial constraints:

> Thornton says they could have had a lot more money, but they didn't want it because it would have caused trouble. Without a lot of hands in the pot, Thornton was able to shoot the film himself and control every other aspect of its creation. He was able to keep it simple and this is the key to its success. Every gesture, every landscape and every word are made to count.
>
> (Parkes 2009: 23)

The decision to shoot on a small scale, with a small budget and in remote Australia was taken as evidence of Thornton's artistic integrity. It demonstrated his opposition to the bigger, slicker commercial productions of Hollywood or even Sydney: 'We didn't want that big clown show ... the marquee for 150 people for lunch,' said Thornton (quoted in Kent 2009: 17) when promoting the film's release. And it gave Thornton greater artistic autonomy – fewer prying eyes, fewer commercial concerns and less interference from White Australia. As Thornton (quoted in Parkes 2009: 23) said at the time, 'we wanted to work with people who weren't going to come up to Alice Springs and go all culture shock on us'.

The film's dark and confronting subject matter was a constant theme, with film reviews and interviews often resorting to itemizing all the ways the film's content was 'antithetical to Hollywood storytelling': 'petrol sniffing, the cycle of poverty, the lack of services, prejudices against Aboriginal people and the treatment of women' (Parkes 2009: 23; Rosemary 2009: 6). The film and its writer/director were celebrated for their 'bruisingly honest' approach, for being 'unashamed', 'fearless' and 'courageous' in tackling these 'hard' issues realistically, 'without trickery or artifice' (Parkes 2009: 23; Rosemary 2009: 6). There were references to Australian cinema's underdog status too, with commentators noting that

Figure 27 L-R: Rowan McNamara, Warwick Thornton and Marissa Gibson on set of *Samson & Delilah* (2009). Photograph by Mark Rogers. Courtesy Scarlett Pictures.

the film faced an 'uphill battle' against blockbuster Hollywood fare (*Samson & Delilah* opened alongside a reboot of the *Star Trek* franchise and new *X-Men* instalment, which had 'marketing budgets exceeding the total cost of his film' (Kent 2009: 17)).

Released the following year, Ivan Sen's *Toomelah* (2010) was described in very similar terms to Thornton's feature debut. A 'spiritual cousin' to *Samson & Delilah* (Maddox 2011a: 11), *Toomelah* is set in a tiny Aboriginal community in western New South Wales. It centres on the life of a young Gamilaroi boy Daniel (Daniel Connors), a precocious ten-year-old who postures as a gangster and seems destined to end up, like so many of the young men in his community, in a life of violence, petty crime and incarceration. The film melds verite-style observation of daily life in Toomelah with the more familiar genre trappings of a crime movie, the story of a young recruit caught between two competing gangs. Though it did not achieve the box office success at home of *Samson & Delilah*, *Toomelah* debuted in *Un Certain Regard* at Cannes and received a theatrical release in art-house cinemas in Australia where it was widely praised.

Scale, autonomy and oppositionality were key again to the film's positive reception. Much was made of the film's authentic setting in Toomelah, a former

Figure 28 Daniel Connors in *Toomelah* (2011). Photograph by Ivan Sen. Courtesy Bunya Productions.

Aboriginal mission which was described as 'a speck on the map between Moree and Goondiwindi' (Downes 2011: 35), a 'sad and dysfunctional' community 'where the only thing that breaks the monotony is tragedy' (Dent 2011: 123). The press kit provided details of Toomelah's difficult history, including its notoriety as having 'some of the worst living conditions in Australia', which reviewers dutifully repeated. Once again, the media coverage for the film emphasized its unconventional and extremely DIY production, which included a tiny budget of AU$500,000, a cast consisting almost entirely of young, first-time actors drawn from the community, dialogue cribbed verbatim from conversations Sen had observed during the months he spent researching the film, and an extraordinarily lean shoot in which Sen doubled as writer, director, cinematographer, editor, composer, as well as researcher, interviewer and community liaison.

As was the case for Thornton's work on *Samson & Delilah*, these production methods were framed as deliberate artistic preferences and markers of the film's authenticity and independent spirit. Shooting the film as 'a virtual one-man crew' (Maddox 2011a: 11) was necessary for Sen to win the trust of his young cast of non-professional actors, and to get the level of intense realism and authenticity he was after. 'It was a gamble', Sen said in interviews, 'but I felt it was the only way I could get close to the performance level I wanted'

(Maddox 2011a: 11). More broadly, these choices are indicative of Sen's virtuoso talent, his solitary and obsessive approach to filmmaking, and his status as Australia's 'foremost auteur' (Bodey 2011: 15), themes which have been central to how Sen is talked about dating back to *before* his first feature film, when he was widely heralded as the next great hope for Australian cinema ('Ivan Sen' 1999: 94; Taylor 1998: 2; *7.30 Report* 2001). Almost without fail, press coverage emphasized Sen's personal connection to 'the mish'; Toomelah was where his mother was born, where her family comes from and where Sen spent a lot of time as a young child. Like *Samson & Delilah*, *Toomelah* was praised for its 'confronting', 'uncompromising' and 'unflinching' portrayal of difficult themes – racism, intergenerational poverty, dysfunction, violence and substance abuse – which Sen, with his long connection to the community, was able to capture with 'raw authenticity' (Dent 2011: 123; Downes 2011; Maddox 2011a: 11; Maddox 2011b: 3).

Overseas, the same qualities widely described as non-commercial and likely to turn audiences off helped the two films secure a clear market position within international festival and art-house circuits. International critics discussed the films in broadly similar terms, emphasizing the films' shoestring budgets, the visual beauty of their outback locations, authentic if 'wrenching' depictions of poverty and community dysfunction (Simon 2011: 23), their impressive use of non-professional young actors and the auteur credentials of the two directors. As a result, the films were squarely positioned in the realm of art-house or festival cinema by trade magazines. *Toomelah* was an admirable (if familiar) example of outsider cinema about the treatment of cultural minorities which would likely do well in Australia, on the international festival circuit and with alternative venues, but otherwise had 'very limited commercial prospects' (McCarthy 2011; Simon 2011: 23). *Samson & Delilah* had somewhat better prospects, described as being 'destined to become a pillar of the fest circuit' while the addition of Thornton's talented direction combined with 'cultural curiosity' for the subject matter meant it would likely do very well on art-house circuits (Edwards 2009: 90).

Despite the extreme cultural specificity of the two films, their non-commercial qualities – unpleasant and confronting content, uncompromising auteur vision, lack of a conventional narrative, atypical film style and extremely DIY production methodologies – proved readily transferable to an international market for marginal culture. Thornton's penchant for long, wordless takes was likened to festival auteur darlings Tsai Ming-liang and Apichatpong Weerasethakul (Edwards 2009: 90). However, *Toomelah*'s apparent deviations from an art-house formula attracted some criticism. Reviews emphasized the documentary aspects of the film, describing *Toomelah* as more 'ethnographic portrait than polished narrative' (Simon 2011: 23) and an 'observational study as much as a dramatic story' (McCarthy 2011). The film's few concessions to more commercial possibilities – its one professional actor, a hip-hop inflected soundtrack and a loose crime-genre plot – are dismissed as too 'predictable' or 'unnatural', conspicuous Hollywoodisms in what should have been straight up marginal cinema.

In both domestic and international reception, the films were applauded for their geographic, production and cultural distance from mainstream filmmaking. However, both Sen and Thornton are the beneficiaries of what are now long-standing programmes and policies that have specifically sought to enable Indigenous films and filmmakers to cross over into the mainstream, having participated in some of the earliest short drama initiatives from the AFC's Indigenous Branch. Moreover, both filmmakers have also discussed their interest in commercial viability, genre storytelling, and a desire to engage and reach wider audiences. While Warwick Thornton makes clear that *Samson & Delilah* was a deeply personal and political film, in interviews he readily acknowledges that the film, his first feature, also needed to be a stylistic calling card that would establish his auteur credentials and, if at all possible, be a commercial success (Thornton 2012). This pragmatism is evident, for example, in the creative and strategic decision to use Warlpiri language and minimal dialogue, which enabled the film to be an official entry to Academy Awards best foreign language (according to producer Kath Shelper, Kalina 2009: 12). It is also evident in the film's ambiguously happy ending, which was a constant selling point in reviews attempting to convince a broader public that the film was worth seeing, despite being a 'dark, petrol-sniffing documentary soaked in guilt and depression' (Harvey 2009: 30).

In a conversation with Marcia Langton (Thornton 2012), Thornton is asked about the reception of *Samson & Delilah* and in particular the tendency for (white Australian) critics to celebrate, in Langton's view incorrectly, the film's 'happy ending.' 'I thought, *have we been watching a different film?*' says Langton; 'I don't think the urban Australian audience got it, that the story is about two petrol sniffers ... and it's actually an incredibly depressing ending'. Thornton replies, 'The irony of that film is just being alive is a happy ending ... They were there and sort of safe and alive. And how tragic that that could be a good outlook for an Indigenous person in central Australia. That's my take on it.' The otherwise lyrical and meandering *Samson & Delilah* adopted the format of a love story in order to reach a wider audience. If the successful heterosexual coupling at the end of the film is the most conventional of all Hollywood tropes, ambiguity is the most familiar convention of art cinema. As such, the end for the young lovers in *Samson & Delilah* is not explicitly happy but ambiguously optimistic. This creative pragmatism – balancing auteur brand, personal storytelling and strategic concessions to commercial interests – is all clearly at play again in Thornton's most recent feature film, *Sweet Country* (2018). This time the unconventional aesthetics and bleak horrors are tempered not by a love story or the possibility of a happy ending, but through genre storytelling (a period Western), star power (Sam Neill, Bryan Brown) and, courtesy of *Samson & Delilah*'s success, Thornton's status as an auteur of 'uncompromising vision'.

Ivan Sen has also discussed at length his efforts to negotiate the commercial logic of independent culture. At the time of his much-vaunted debut feature film *Beneath Clouds* (2002) – a slow, restrained road movie about two young Indigenous teens hitchhiking across country NSW – the young filmmaker discussed his desire for future productions to be more mainstream. His next film promised to be a genre film, a noir-ish *X-files*-style film set in Roswell, New Mexico, in which he hoped to cast the likes of (at the time, indie cinema darlings) Johnny Depp and Cate Blanchett. In multiple interviews, Sen explains that while he was very happy with *Beneath Clouds*, he in no way wanted to be

Figure 29 Sam Neill and Shanika Cole in *Sweet Country*. Photograph by Daniel Foeldes. Courtesy Bunya Productions.

restricted to films or stories about Indigenous themes. As with earlier breakout artists like Tracey Moffatt, Sen talks of wanting to establish himself first and foremost an Australian filmmaker and hoped 'the Indigenous filmmaker tag will get left behind' (Maddox 2013: 6; Sen quoted in Naglazas 2002: 8).

After *Beneath* Clouds, Sen spent the better part of a decade making documentaries to self-fund his pet project, *Dreamland*, which had since morphed from the sort of high-end American indie that might star Blanchett or Depp, into an experimental work shot with just Sen and one actor, camping out in the Nevada desert. Whatever its artistic accomplishments, the film largely disappeared after a handful of screenings. In the words of one reviewer, 'mainstream acceptance is out of the question' (Kuipers 2009: 19). If *Beneath Clouds* had been a meandering, personal drama of the kind that regularly appears in festival and art-house circuits, then *Dreamland* pushed further out into the margins of an artist's film or moving image art, more likely to be found in a gallery than an independent cinema.

According to Sen, *Toomelah* was the first part of a deliberate strategy undertaken with his long-time producer to move back into mainstream and commercially viable filmmaking after an unsuccessful foray into more personal filmmaking. This new approach involved making 'genre films for bigger audiences but still with some sort of cultural perspective somewhere in them' (Sen quoted in Bodey 2011: 15). In one interview, Sen describes *Toomelah* (and his plans for what would become *Mystery Road*), as 'giving people what they want', which appears to mean both more conventional storytelling and greater acceptance of the Indigenous filmmaker label that he once fought to cast off.

This desire to move into the mainstream via a blend of genre and Indigenous stories was made clearer again in his subsequent films, *Mystery Road*, its sequel *Goldstone* and most recently the television spin-off series *Mystery Road* (ABC, 2018–2022). Taking inspiration from the likes of the Cohen Brothers film *No Country for Old Men*, Sen's recent works meld auteur style and Indigenous-themed stories, with substantially increased budgets, sizeable crew, bankable international stars, accessible genre storytelling and even a multi-platform franchise. Whereas *Toomelah*'s rough use of certain crime film genre tropes was criticized by some international critics for jarring with the film's otherwise observational and documentary tones, the reception for *Mystery Road* and *Goldstone* suggests he has got the mix better, with both films picked up for art-house distribution in the United States and Europe. The Hollywoodisms

Figure 30 Aaron Pedersen in *Mystery Road* (2013). Photograph by Ivan Sen. Courtesy Bunya Productions.

dismissed as inauthentic in *Toomelah* are sufficiently couched in the language of knowing genre revisionism (of masculinist cinephilic favourites the Western and Noir genres) to position *Mystery Road* and *Goldstone* closer to the realm of crossover independent film.

Indigenous entertainment as social enterprise

Films are made to be seen, that's why they're made, they're made to be consumed by the public, and so you want your film to get the biggest audience it can …
And particularly because a lot of our work is Indigenous-based or social issue-based, we do it for a reason. It's not just entertainment. You want it to have the biggest impact it can.

(Rachel Perkins 2017)

Released only a few months later than *Samson & Delilah*, Rachel Perkins' 2010 film *Bran Nue Dae* was parallel and opposite. A comedy musical road-trip movie adapted from a much-beloved stage musical by Indigenous playwright Jimmy Chi, the film features lashings of bawdy humour, young love and a cast of Australian pop stars and comedians jostling for attention alongside well-known thespians gleefully hamming it up. In Australia, *Bran Nue Dae* was celebrated for its 'feel good' qualities, its easy pleasures, joyfulness and sense of fun (Bodey 2010: 11; Fenton 2010: 27). The reception of the film centred overwhelmingly on Perkins' unapologetic desire for a mainstream audience for Indigenous filmmaking, with reviews and interviews positioning the film as the 'opposite' of *Samson & Delilah*, even an 'antidote' to the latter's art-house miserabilism (Fenton 2010: 27).

In a now widely cited interview with film critic Jim Schembri (2010: 12), Perkins says, 'I've always thought that indigenous films could cross over into the mainstream and that it was the content that was making them not do that.' She goes on to say that 'all the black subjects were about oppression, violence, death, depression and hardship. Cinema is about entertainment'. According to Perkins, packing the film with populist entertainment conventions – musical numbers, heterosexual romance, happy endings, broad humour, bankable stars and familiar faces – was done with the express intention of obtaining as wide an audience as possible for the film, something she was all-too-aware was difficult for any Australian film, and long considered next to impossible for Indigenous stories.

> Feature films are highly risky commercial undertakings. *Bran Nue Dae*, for example, was intended to reach a really wide audience … We cast the film with as many stars as we could and we loaded it up that way with well-known identities because at that stage everybody thought that Indigenous stories never succeed commercially.
>
> (Perkins 2017)

In Australia, the approach worked. *Bran Nue Dae* had a wide commercial release, particularly for an Australian film, opening on more than 230 screens. It took almost AU$8 million at the domestic box office (Dolgopolov 2014: 79), rapidly overtaking *Samson & Delilah* as the most successful film by an Indigenous filmmaker and making it one of the top fifty grossing Australian films of all time.

In 2012, *The Sapphires* repeated and extended the success of *Bran Nue Dae*. The film was directed by Wayne Blair, another alumnus of the AFC's Indigenous Branch, and a colleague and collaborator of both Warwick Thornton (who was cinematographer on *The Sapphires*) and Rachel Perkins (as a director on the Blackfella Films television series *Redfern Now*). *The Sapphires* trafficked in many of the same populist approaches as *Bran Nue Dae* but with an even

Figure 31 Director Rachel Perkins (centre) on the *Bran Nue Dae* set with Jessica Mauboy (left) and Rocky McKenzie, 2008. Photograph by Matt Nettheim. Courtesy Robyn Kershaw Productions.

larger budget of AU$8 million and a more conventionally Hollywood approach ('Sapphires playing screens of the globe' 2012: 22). Like *Bran Nue Dae*, *The Sapphires* had been adapted for the screen from a popular stage musical. Loosely based on the experiences of writer Tony Brigg's mum and aunties, it tells the story of a troupe of four Indigenous singers and their Irish manager who tour Vietnam in the late 1960s, entertaining the troops with their renditions of soul favourites.

The film is structured as a typical backstage musical, and it features a conventional narrative, warm comedy, romance, make-overs, shimmering period costumes, dance routines and covers of well-known 60s Motown hits. While describing some of the performances as a little stilted and the plot predictable, Australian reviews roundly celebrated the 'feel-good' film for being 'warm hearted', 'wish-fulfilment fantasy' that was 'bold, bright and cheesy' and even 'a good mainstream film' that 'accommodates as many cultural tastes as possible' (Martin 2012; Wilson 2012: 15; Christie and Harris 2013: 43). The film received extensive mainstream media coverage in Australia, supported by hype around the film's Cannes debut and its swift acquisition by 'Hollywood hit-makers' The Weinstein Company. The film went on to take more than $14 million at the Australian box office, making it the highest-grossing Australian film released that year and beating *Bran Nue Dae* to become the most commercially successful Indigenous film to date (Maddox 2014: 30).

Both films, especially *The Sapphires*, were widely celebrated for their ability to balance politics and entertainment. The films acknowledge painful truths about the treatment and experiences of Indigenous Australians. *The Sapphires* opens with a reference to the 1967 referendum on the recognition of Aboriginal people as citizens and the fact that, at the time of the film's setting, they were not counted in the government census. At an amateur talent show the unimpressed, evidently racist white audience award the prize to a clearly inferior white team. As sisters Cynthia (Miranda Tapsell) and Gail (Deborah Mailman) hitchhike home from a gig, a car sails past; Cynthia asks, 'What's their problem?' and Gail responds, 'We're Black, stupid.' Incredulously, Cynthia, designated 'the sexy one' of the troupe, replies, 'Nah it's because you're ugly.' 'There's nothing I would rather be than to be an Aborigine, and watch you take my precious land from me' go the lyrics to the *Bran Nue Dae*'s standout musical number. Later, while locked up for uncharacteristically drunk and disorderly behaviour, young innocent Willie starts to panic, presuming custody to be an automatic death sentence for young Black men. *Bran Nue Dae* and *The Sapphires* reference Australia's racial divide, racist government policies, Black deaths in custody and the Stolen Generation, but they do so while operating within the parameters of light entertainment, played for dark laughs or else presented in a way deemed 'not preachy' and not allowed to drag on for 'more than a scene or two' (Horton 2012: 30; Wilson 2012: 15).

> My work is still strongly political, but I want it to be appealing and compelling, because people don't respond to being bashed over the head by something.
>
> (Perkins quoted in Sexton 2001: 3)

Beyond *Bran Nue Dae*, this balancing act has long been a part of Perkins' broader career, in policy and film production. The independent company she started in 1991, Blackfella Films, has been responsible for populist entertainment like *Bran Nue Dae* and the controversy courting and highly rated reality television show *First Contact* (Knox 2016b), together with the sombre and extremely ambitious documentary series *First Australians*, the quality drama mini-series *Redfern Now*, and a range of much smaller community-led projects and documentaries relating to Indigenous culture, politics and history. This otherwise diverse range of productions belongs to a common project of giving voice to a diversity of Indigenous experience. In interviews, Perkins describes Blackfella Films as a blend of independent film and television production company with something closer to a social justice or activist organization. The company is deliberately small (at writing, seven permanent staff), which keeps overhead costs low and means they can be picky about what they choose to do.

> A lot of the other companies will produce returning series, for example, just to bring in the money ... but for us that's not what we're in it to do. I mean obviously we'd love to make more money, that would be great and if we can make films that have impact and also make money that's fabulous. ... We're not just a production company with aims of making money, we're more of an Indigenous social enterprise.
>
> (Perkins 2017)

While Perkins is evidently very proud of strong ratings, commercial success and big audience figures, these achievements are principally couched in the language of social impact. Commercial success, bigger budgets and high production values are means to some degree of commercial sustainability for Blackfella Films, but according to Perkins, they are also part of a strategy to ensure Indigenous content can 'play in the mainstream in Australia' and that successful, quality Indigenous content is the norm not the exception (Perkins 2017). Both Perkins and Blair describe themselves as not being into 'high-brow, art-house' films for 'the half a per cent of people who watch film for a living' but as having more in common with their audience, people who just want 'films that make you shed a little tear, or make you want to fall in love ...' (Perkins quoted in Simpson 1999: 33; Blair quoted in Siemienowicz 2012).

> There are films like Ivan Sen's *Toomelah* and Warwick Thornton's *Samson & Delilah*, but why not this kind of film too? ... Aboriginal people in Australia need some joy and some love and the chance to feel human again. With my

people, comedy is the best form of healing. We wanted some positive role models, positive change, rather than negative stereotypes we see all the time. There are lots of different representations – like Warwick's, and Ivan's, and Rachel Perkins' *Bran Nue Dae*. With a film like this we can't change the world in the way governments and laws can, but we can make a difference.

(Wayne Blair, quoted in Siemienowicz 2012)

As accessible and even unabashedly populist as the films are, they are motivated in no small measure by social justice and political principles: to facilitate Indigenous self-representation, to combat negative stereotypes in mainstream media, to reach a wider public – 'The people who watch the Olympics, or one-day cricket matches' (Wayne Blair, quoted in Siemienowicz 2012) – and to deliver a message in a manner that might be better received. Moreover, the desire to demonstrate profitability is part of that same logic. Success, for both Blair and Perkins, is a form of political and social persuasion. As Perkins (2017) says, 'We either guilt-trip them or we try and say look, this is so successful we should do more of it.'

It has proven difficult, however, to translate this nuance to international contexts. *Bran Nue Dae* had a very limited release overseas, with critics by and large dismissing it as a cheesy, clumsy affair that 'glossed over' the serious issues and in the words of a reviewer for Variety it had 'no ethnic authenticity'. That is to say, a film by one of the foremost influences on Indigenous film and television policy and a celebrated lobbyist for the cause of Indigenous self-representation was dismissed as 'inauthentically' Indigenous. As was breathlessly reported at the time of its glamorous Cannes premiere, *The Sapphires* was picked up by The Weinstein Company. Given Harvey Weinstein's role as one of the chief architects behind the 1990s indie highwater mark when, at the helm of Miramax, he cultivated 'the art house film for the multiplex', expectations for the film's crossover potential overseas were very high (Perren 2012: 82). But again, as with *Bran Nue Dae*, many of the qualities that were thought to be an asset in Australia – cathartic 'feel good' fun that wasn't weighed down by too much political or historical baggage – became a liability when the film was released internationally. Again, perceived inauthenticity was a major issue.

As Therese Davis (2017: 239) writes of the film's failure to resonate with international audiences as it had at home, 'it seems that *The Sapphires* was perceived outside of Australia as "too American" as evidenced by the many comparisons it drew with *Dreamgirls*'. As Davis explains, the film was based on a stage musical by an Indigenous playwright and drew on his mother and aunties' real experiences; it was bound by Indigenous protocols that exist to guide the production of films about Indigenous people and culture and which employed members of the Yorta Yorta community as cultural consultants. Yet it was, it seems, 'too Hollywood' for international tastes (Davis 2017: 240). In recent years, genre filmmaking via the Western and the Noir, with lashings of rugged landscapes and violence all delivered in a suitably ambiguous and revisionist style, has proved a successful indie format for both Ivan Sen and Warwick Thornton, but not for *The Sapphires* and *Bran Nue Dae*'s crowd-pleasing revisionist postcolonial musicals.

After mainstream

From the very beginning, the central brief of the AFC's Indigenous Branch was to develop a 'wider audience for films written, directed or produced by Indigenous Australians' (Barron, quoted in Australian Film Commission 2007: v). Alongside developing guidelines and strategies to support Indigenous self-representation, the earliest activities of the Indigenous Branch focused on assisting filmmakers to move into drama production, ensuring distribution of screen content to the 'general public', and securing allocation of training and resources necessary to produce 'excellence' in Indigenous filmmaking (Australian Film Commission Annual Report 1994–95). Later reporting on the activities of the branch continued to emphasize the importance of wider recognition, mainstream distribution, high quality and 'competitive' production standards, and, in particular, support for longer-form drama development. In somewhat stronger and more contentious language, in its initial efforts to solicit feedback on how best to support Indigenous participation in filmmaking, the AFC is quoted as saying it would 'never' compromise on quality because to do otherwise would likely mean Aboriginal films would be 'ghettoised', which could 'seriously undermine the AFC's objectives of promoting Aboriginal films and increasing audience size'.[1]

In a 2007 publication produced by the AFC to celebrate Australia's Indigenous filmmakers and the achievements of the AFC's Indigenous Branch, Sally Riley regularly returns to the theme of mainstream success. Mainstream for her means a broader public beyond an insider niche of local filmmakers, festival-circuit

---

[1] AFC Consultant on Aboriginal and Torres Strait Islander Film Policy, Michael Pope in a letter dated 31 May 1992 to Lesley Bangama Fogarty, Director of the Aboriginal Arts Unit, quoted in Donovan with Lorraine 2002: 265.

critics or art-house audiences. Describing the success of Warwick Thornton's short drama film *Green Bush* (2005), which took home the Best Short Film award at the Berlin International Film Festival, Riley notes that it also won the Australian IF Award for Best Short Film by popular vote. 'Following on from many awards received on critical merit,' she writes, 'this was perhaps the sweetest victory' (Riley, quoted in Australian Film Commission 2007: 4).

In the Indigenous production units at the ABC, there was a similar, if belated, strategy of focusing on the development of high-quality, prime-time content. Reflecting on her involvement in early incarnations of dedicated Indigenous production units at SBS and later the ABC, Rachel Perkins said the primary obstacle facing the success of those units at that time was a matter of both resources and aspiration for Indigenous-led programming at upper-management levels:

> I think [what] really let those units down in that early period was that the people who were holding the purse strings didn't have big aspirations for Indigenous content. [...] They were satisfied to have a weekly magazine program that would be a bit of a hodgepodge of feel-good human-interest stories about Aboriginal employment schemes and whatever. [...] That was what they thought was the extent of what should be done in terms of their charter of responsibility.
>
> (Perkins 2017)

Although support for some Indigenous content was enshrined in the charters of the two public service broadcasters, Perkins describes being frustrated with the complacency around expectations for what that content could or should be. Nearly two decades later, as part of a publicity blitz for the launch of Indigenous drama *Redfern Now*, the ABC's then Director Kim Dalton talked of his desire to 'get Indigenous material out of the ghetto' (paraphrased in Quinn 2012: 22). Referring to the weekly thirty-minute magazine programme *Message Stick*, which had until that point been the primary output of the ABC's Indigenous Programs Unit, Dalton said the Indigenous content produced by the broadcaster to date had been 'good work, but it was peripheral,' and 'It sat on the edges, outside the mainstream' (quoted in Quinn 2012: 22). In other words, it was no longer good enough for Indigenous programmes merely to have a presence on the national broadcaster. With the 2010 appointment of Sally Riley from the AFC's Indigenous Branch to the ABC's newly scaled-up Indigenous department, which now had a $5 million budget to work with, the focus shifted to high-profile, ambitious and *costly* prestige drama in prime-time slots. In further recognition of her success as Head of Indigenous at

ABC TV – producing *Black Comedy, 8MMM Aboriginal Radio, Redfern Now, Cleverman*, among others – Sally Riley was promoted in 2016 to Head of Scripted Production.

Mainstreaming was embedded from the outset into the policy architecture of the AFC's Indigenous Branch, and eventually by the public broadcasters. For nearly thirty years, the desire for Indigenous filmmakers and Indigenous-led content to become 'mainstream' has remained an essential part of the vision of the likes of Sally Riley, Rachel Perkins and other key lobbyists and policy influencers. There was a clear desire for Indigenous films to circulate beyond the confines of existing, niche audiences for art-house or independent cinema, social justice documentaries, and Indigenous content narrowcast on community broadcasters (often limited to regional and remote areas). Mainstream success has been considered essential in overturning the long-held assumption that Indigenous content was 'box office poison' and to demonstrate that, with equivalent levels of funding, training and resources as had graced an earlier generation of Australian 'new wave' filmmakers in the 1970s and 1980s, Indigenous filmmakers could and would rank among Australia's best.

In 2018 the sector celebrated twenty-five years of the Indigenous Branch of the AFC, now Screen Australia, which was capped off spectacularly at the Australian Academy of Cinema Television Arts industry awards that year, at which Warwick Thornton's *Sweet Country* won Best Film and the first season of *Mystery Road*, directed by Rachel Perkins, won Best Television Series. During that time, but most dramatically in the last ten years, Indigenous screen content encompassing all styles and formats – productions ranging from art cinema to pulp genre to documentary to sketch comedy – has moved indisputably into a mainstream position *within* Australia. Internationally however, the older and more intractable indie cinema tropes of authenticity, scale, autonomy and oppositionality have, paradoxically, proved more successful in crossing over to broader overseas audiences.

6

The fringe in Freeplay: The independence of independent games

Resources help you do interesting things. Lack of resources also help you do interesting things.

— Helen Stuckey (2015)

When I took over as Director [of the Freeplay Independent Games Festival], it was sort of like 'Congratulations! Now find money, because we don't have any'.

— Dan Golding (2014a)

In September 2004, an independent games conference, titled 'Free Play', was staged as part of the Next Wave Festival in Melbourne. Developed out of a conversation between Next Wave Director Marcus Westbury and games developer Katharine Neil, the event defined itself in opposition to the large commercial studios that dominated public discussion of games in Australia at the time. By Neil's account, the culture of the studios was aggressively commercial, male chauvinist and complacent:

> We had an industry conference at the time – the Australian Game Developers' Conference – which was incredibly alienating. Like, you'd just watch your boss get up there – some fucking bean counter – and give another boss some industry award. It was super sponsored; there were booth babes everywhere. I and other people just felt that it was super alienating: big, commercial, crass.
>
> (Neil 2014)

The starting point for Free Play was a determination to create an alternative scene. The conference was held in a converted karate dojo on Flinders Street and was to be a 'kind of boss-free zone'. Word got around that 'there was some kind of rebellion going on' and one boss, from the development company Blue Tongue, managed to get in uninvited. Neil confronted him:

> 'You know, the only people getting in for free are people who are actually working on the conference. So, we have some boxes over there. Can you shift those boxes?' And he thought it was a joke. You know, they have their stupid conference which costs a million bucks to go to and is sponsored and has lots of booth babes and where they give each other awards, so I don't see why. They know as much about culture as my arse.
>
> (Neil 2014)

By marking out a different kind of space, the conference hoped to open up conversations that were excluded from the studio industry scene – about the aesthetic and political dimensions of games, about working conditions in games development and about possibilities for new or experimental forms.

Freeplay has since become an annual event, surviving in various forms for almost twenty years.[1] Its initial oppositional moment has softened and it has become part of the weave of Melbourne's cultural institutions. Yet it has continued to provide a forum for an idea of 'independence' in games. The idea is not an absolute. Freeplay has had close relations with public institutions such as the Australian Centre for the Moving Image (ACMI) and the State Library of Victoria; it has worked with universities, small games development businesses, state government and unions. Nor has the idea of independence been static: the contexts that give it meaning have shifted considerably over time. Yet it is an idea that is not without weight. It has continued to provide a focus for conversations and exchanges around games that do not often occur elsewhere.

In this chapter, we consider Freeplay as a point of entry into questions around the relation between fringe and mainstream in digital games. There are many similarities between the case of games and those considered in previous chapters. Freeplay offers a further example of the importance of hybrid forms – of crossover, translation and exchange between small independent scenes and the wider audiences, institutions and economies to which they are articulated. But there are also specificities. Scenes around games have emerged more recently and have been engaged from the outset with digital media. Games cultures have no clear anchor in the countercultural moment of the 1960s and

---

[1] From 2009, the title was conjoined as 'Freeplay'. At the same time, the event became defined not as a 'Conference' but a 'Festival'.

1970s and their generational structure is out of phase with more established cultural forms. As a 'digital first' case, games also require us to consider transformations in the relation between fringe and mainstream that are now affecting all creative fields.

The 'independent' in games

It is generally agreed that there is no single or simple way to define what is meant by 'independent games'. As Chase Bowen Martin and Mark Deuze (2009: 277) have pointed out, 'the term "independent" is used in a number of ways to describe a type of development next to, or juxtaposed with, the mainstream process of creating, marketing, distributing, and playing digital games'. It has gained currency through a literature, dedicated festivals, online communities and in the presentation of games themselves. Yet even as it was emerging in the early 2000s, it was already becoming confused by crossovers with the mainstream. Martin and Deuze cite the example, among others, of the small development studio Bungie, which in 2007 acquired majority ownership of its own stock in order to ensure their creative freedom and 'return to their independent roots' (Martin & Deuze 2009: 277). Yet the studio remained closely engaged with Microsoft, which had been for a while its corporate owner. Bungie was the creator of Halo, a 'quintessential blockbuster of the video game medium' that was carried on Microsoft's Xbox line of consoles.

Most of the confusion between 'mainstream' and 'independent' has been the result of these kinds of exchange. As Brendan Keogh (2015: 152) points out, international corporate publishers 'now compete with – and draw influence from – smaller teams or individuals that are finding their own critical and commercial success in vibrant independent scenes'. The interface between the two has broadened as these scenes have multiplied. In the 1990s and early 2000s, digital games were generally associated with a fairly narrow social base – male, geeky and organized around competitive formats and technological expertise. But digital distribution and the migration of games onto smartphones and tablets have greatly expanded the diversity of game players. At the same time, the removal of barriers to entry in production has allowed new groups to become involved in games development, leading to what experimental games developer and writer Anna Anthropy (2012) has called the 'rise of the videogame zinester'. The creative side of games has been opened, as Anthropy puts it, to 'freaks, normals, amateurs, artists, dreamers, drop-outs, queers, housewives, and people like you'.

Exchanges between mainstream and independent games are most often noted at the level of style or aesthetics. As Jesper Juul (2014) has argued, independent developers have always faced the problem of how to produce games that do not look simply like cheap versions of big-budget titles. Their response has generally been to make a virtue of necessity, deliberately eschewing production quality in favour of other values: 'By emphasizing the small, personal and simplistic, Independent Style makes the claim that limited budgets are not a limitation but rather a better, and more authentic, way of making games' (Juul 2014: 46). But as this approach has gained a following, the style has been appropriated by mainstream players. As Nadav Lipkin (2013: 3) puts it, '[o]nce a style emerges and displays profit potential, mainstream forces use their resources to emulate the style of indie media production artificially'. Many games released by large publishers therefore bear the stylistic hallmarks of independent games.

But the impact of independent games on the industry can be seen at other levels too. As Keogh points out, mainstream or 'Triple-A' businesses have looked to independents not just for creative ideas or aesthetics but also for innovation in forms of organization and modes of distribution. For example, 'as indie developers explore new ways to fund themselves, these monetisation practices feed back into the industry' (Keogh 2015: 156). A notable case is the popularization of 'alpha' access by the runaway indie success story *Minecraft*. The Triple-A industry has recognized the value of this approach in creating a player base 'that both provides free testing labour and funds further development of the game' (156). Other borrowings from the independents include the use of the 'pay-what-you-want' model for bundles of games and the adoption of crowdsourcing for projects that the mainstream publishers will not invest in.

It goes without saying that there have been major influences in the other direction too – *from* the mainstream *to* the fringe. Many of the pioneers of independent games drew, initially, on knowledge and skills acquired from working in the Triple-A industry. At the time of launching Freeplay, Katharine Neil was a commercial games developer with Infogrames, the predecessor of Atari, working on titles such as *Grand Prix Challenge*, *Looney Tunes Space Race* and *Superman: Shadow of Apokalips* for PlayStation 2, Dreamcast and GameCube. The technology required for games development in the early 2000s was expensive, making involvement in the Triple-A industry the only viable route to expertise. Much of the interest in independent games revolved around 'modding' or modifications of games released by the major commercial publishers. Even when full independent authoring of games became possible in the later 2000s, the technology was not always used to assert an independent aesthetic or ethos. Many small developers conceived of their work as portfolio pieces, hoping to gain entry to the Triple-A industry.

A common response to this exchange between independent and mainstream has been to question the very meaningfulness of the distinction. For Martin and Deuze (2009: 290), 'a logic of opposition between mainstream and alternative gamework is somewhat deceptive'. Some have gone further, suggesting that the idea of independence is merely a kind of symbolic posturing within what is really a single, continuous terrain. For Juul (2014), for example, independent games are a product of 'authenticity work'. The idea of independence is 'a careful construction to appear as a counter to large-budget game productions, and to give the appearance of a direct connection between players and game developers'. 'Independence', for Juul, does not denote any real phenomenon; it needs always to be understood as belonging in scare quotes.

The arguments here are similar to those we have seen in earlier chapters in relation to other fields, but the games case also presents some differences. Many of these relate to the historical moment in which games have emerged. As Aphra Kerr (2006: 1) put it in one of the earlier attempts at a comprehensive overview of the business and culture of games, 'digital games appear to epitomize an ideal type of global post-industrial neo-liberal cultural product'. They belong to a world in which a range of previously taken-for-granted boundaries appear to have dissolved. While making use of technologies developed out of Cold War public investments in science, they emerged after the ideological divisions of the Cold War had collapsed. While associated with first world consumption, they depend on global supply chains and electronic goods manufactured in cheap labour/low tax economies in the developing world. While framed as play, games often resemble forms of work, blurring lines between different social domains (Kerr 2006: 7).

This collapse of boundaries and distinctions has put the very idea of the 'independent' or 'alternative' under substantial pressure. The effects can be seen particularly in some of the more theoretical work on games, such as Nick Dyer-Witheford and Greig de Peuter's (2009) *Games of Empire*. The 'Empire' of the title borrows from Michael Hardt and Antonio Negri's (2000) book of that name, referring to 'a new planetary regime in which economic, administrative, military, and communicative components combine to create a system of power "with no outside'" (Dyer-Witheford & de Peuter 2009: xix). There is no space within this regime, for Dyer-Witheford and de Peuter, in which to sustain alternative practices or cultural forms. The only possibility for resistance is an existential challenge to the system as a whole. While this predicament affects other fields of cultural production – indeed all of social life – it is one that comes into focus with particular clarity around games. Games reinforce the 'twin vital subjectivities of worker-consumer and soldier-citizen'; they are the 'paradigmatic medium of Empire' (xiv–xv).

A further sign of pressure on the idea of independence in the games case is the way in which independence often seems to be imaginable only at the level of the individual. An example is the 2012 documentary *Indie Game: The Movie*, by Canadian filmmakers James Swisky and Lisanne Pajot. *Indie Game* follows two independent developers, Edmund McMillen and Tommy Refenes, as they work on their respective cult titles *Super Meat Boy* and *Fez*. While supported by long-suffering domestic partners, McMillen and Refenes appear otherwise isolated. They live as high-tech hermits, driven by personal passions in an unstable and sleep-deprived world of electronic screens, black coffee and fast food. The decision against taking a position within the mainstream industry manifests as a decision also to pursue a kind of radical autonomy. The contrast with earlier countercultural visions of independent creative practice is striking. The world of *Indie Game* is one in which to be an independent is no longer to belong to a collective or movement, but to exist as a social atom.

The 'independent' in Freeplay

The meanings given to the 'independent' in Freeplay have certainly been affected by these contexts. The word has been used in a variety of ways and has been continually questioned and challenged. When asked how he defined the term, 2014–17 Director Dan Golding told us 'it's a question that the festival is always asked'. The answers, he admits, have shifted over time: 'independence doesn't mean anything like what it meant when Freeplay started. It doesn't mean anything like what it meant four years ago' (Golding 2014a). But we should not infer from this that the word is meaningless, merely a facade behind which supposedly 'real' interests are at play. Despite everything that militates against the idea of independence – the loss of boundaries of a networked world, overdetermined theories that proclaim that there is now 'no outside' – the case of Freeplay suggests that the idea can still have concrete uses that point to something more than simply 'appearances'.

To recognize such uses, we need to refuse the tendency to burden the concept of independence with impossible expectations of purity. As we argued in Chapter 1, such expectations are not inherent in the concept, but are the fallout of particular histories. It became an orthodoxy, in the shadow of the counterculture, that ideas of independence are 'romantic', invoking some kind of transcendence. But an example such as Freeplay helps us to see the contingency of such a view. Neil's marking out of a space for the conference did not hark back nostalgically to some countercultural moment – a mythical time in the 1960s or 1970s when pure independence could still be claimed. It responded in an immediate and practical way to the cynicism and sexism of the studio-based games industry in Australia during the early 2000s. It did not assume an outside from which such problems might be held to account. It *created* one from within through calculated forms of rhetoric and action.

It might be objected that the bid for independence might still be understood as an interested one. Could we not see Freeplay as an example of 'authenticity work' in Juul's sense? As producing 'the appearance of a direct connection between players and developers' in order that those involved might claim certain advantages? Similar suggestions about the stakes involved in claiming independence can be found even in Bourdieu's work on the field of cultural production, on which we have drawn extensively in *Fringe to Famous*. In an essay on the field of art production, for example, Bourdieu (1980: 261) suggests that even the most 'anti-economic' or 'disinterested' behaviours 'contain a form of economic rationality ... and in no way exclude their authors from even the "economic" profits awaiting those who conform to the law of this universe'. The argument points, at a more theoretical level than Juul, to the way in which a renunciation of the mainstream can work, paradoxically, to promote agents *within* the mainstream.

Again, however, such arguments should not be used too cheaply to dismiss the idea of independence. Juul is undoubtedly right to argue that claims to the independence of games have *sometimes* been made in a calculated way to increase their market value. It is clearly the case, too, as Bourdieu points out of art, that many of the works that command the highest price in the long run are those that were earlier associated with a renunciation of the market. Such effects are real and need to be recognized. It is another thing, however, to insist that claims to independence are *always and necessarily* self-interested, masking 'true' motivations that are identical to those of the mainstream. The latter position becomes, in effect, a kind of fundamentalism – simply a determination to see individual self-interest as the ground for all social action.

If we proceed from evidence rather than from this kind of presumption, it is not difficult to specify differences between Freeplay and the Triple-A industry against which it was initially defined. Economically, the festival refused an orientation to the commercial logics of sales, promotion and profit that governed the industry. For co-founder Marcus Westbury, this was a key motivation. Westbury remembers reflecting in the early 2000s that in the cases of music, film and writing, it was possible to hold conversations about creative products as cultural forms:

> You've got these places where you can talk about music, you can talk about film, you can talk about writing ... But there was no space to have that kind of conversation about games ... All the games events were about the *industry*. They were all based on the premise that it was about shipping units and selling products and investment. It was all about the money side of it.
>
> (Neil & Westbury 2015)

The decision to adopt a different focus was not just symbolic, but had an obvious material dimension. Freeplay has always had to operate with very limited budgets and has relied on substantial contributions of voluntary labour. This has structured the entire way in which it has taken form.

Freeplay can also be differentiated from the mainstream industry by the kind of *politics* with which it was associated. Neil was best-known at the time of the first Freeplay for *Escape from Woomera*, a games contribution to refugee and asylum-seeker activism. The game – developed as a mod of Valve Software's *Half Life* – put the player in the person of Mustafa, an Iranian asylum seeker, attempting to break out of an Australian government detention centre. The project became an object of national controversy after it was discovered that it had received a development grant of $25,000 from the arts funding body, the Australia Council (Nicholls 2003; Apperley 2008: 225–6). It came in for heavy criticism from the Federal Immigration Minister at the time, Philip Ruddock, who accused it of being an irresponsible use of public funds. However, the incident was only part of a wider pattern of political involvement. Neil had been, among other things, a union organizer and co-host of *Solidarity Breakfast*, a programme on the community radio station 3CR, covering industrial disputes and interviewing people on picket lines (Neil 2014).

Westbury's politics were less obviously aligned, but nevertheless clearly articulated. He has been a long-standing advocate and activist for structures and processes that support creative freedom and risk-taking. As he puts it, in reflecting on his initial motivations in relation to Free Play:

> I'm really interested in the capacity for people who are creative to try things, test ideas, push boundaries, experiment in sort of 360 degrees: not just try and experiment, you know, in better marketing or trying to appeal to a narrow group of people that everyone else is trying to appeal to.
>
> (Neil & Westbury 2015)

This orientation had a particular edge in relation to the games industry of the early 2000s, which was characterized by tight corporate control over creative processes. An example was the use of employment contracts to bar developers from games-related work – even unpaid – that was not directed by the studios themselves. Westbury confesses to having been shocked by how draconian these contracts were, and how different from what he knew of other creative fields:

> If you worked for a record company or if you worked for a film company, you were *expected* to have a side project. Like, that was the whole point. You have a corporate day job *to* work on a side project … In the other commercial-creative fields I knew, the expectation was that they were a somewhat casualised labour force who were always going to switch onto other projects and were developing their own projects in parallel.
>
> (Neil & Westbury 2015)

The games development studios did not accept this kind of open-weave ecology, insisting instead on an exclusive right to control the creative energies of what was generally a young and inexperienced workforce. Discontent with such policies was probably always present at some level, but became sharpened in the early 2000s following revelations internationally of exploitative employment practices, such as those that were brought to light by the so-called 'EA Spouse' scandal – in which an anonymous blogger, later found to be writer Erin Hoffman, detailed underpayment and other abuses suffered by her fiancé while working as a developer in the United States for Electronic Arts (Dyer-Witheford & de Peuter 2006).

Against this background, Freeplay sought to provide a forum for perspectives other than those of the corporate games development paradigm. As Neil puts it:

> We wanted to give a platform to the little guy – and girl. You know, the people who are not very articulate maybe. And they are not very confident and maybe they're a bit young ... And they can get up and talk about the cool maps they make and stuff. Or working conditions. We had a session on working conditions. That was very important, because it was a session with no bosses there, right?
>
> (Neil & Westbury 2015)

Neil saw her role here in a similar way to *animateurs* of independent creative practice we have encountered in earlier chapters. It was, first of all, to defend the space against encroachments from the mainstream industry – encroachments that might have stifled the emergence of alternatives. Neil's fierceness in this put her at odds not only with the games industry itself, but later even with others in Freeplay who did not take such a hard line. But it is clear that she also saw her role as nurturing the tender shoots of alternatives to the dominant corporate model. It involved finding ways to support and affirm.

An important aspect of this was the development of an alternative aesthetic sensibility. Neil drew in part here on international developments. A particular inspiration was the New York games developer and writer Greg Costikyan, who argued that independent games needed to be redefined as 'cool' (Costikyan 2005). As Neil points out, the idea was far from intuitive when it was first proposed in the early 2000s:

> Lots of people were like 'Oh that's *never* going to happen. That's impossible!' Independent games are *ugly*, they don't have great graphics, they're just ... Nerds make them, super super nerds. Everyone wants to play shiny console games ... No-one wants to play these shitty tiny little games.
>
> (Neil & Westbury 2015)

It was only later that the 'indie look' came to be widely seen as desirable and the shift depended on a number of developments that could not entirely have been anticipated at the time. One factor was the exhaustion of lines of creative development in the Triple-A industry. As Westbury suggests, the early 2000s appears in retrospect as a time when 'the whole industry was dominated by the search for ever more photo-realistic explosions and engine sounds ... The entire creativity of this giant industry was focused down to these very narrow paths' (Neil & Westbury 2015). There was always going to be a point where consumers became jaded. This coincided with the 'mobile revolution' in games, already mentioned, which was to expand and diversify the player base and create a demand for different kinds of content.

A second major aspect to the nurturing of alternatives was the creation of community. Freeplay was only one agent in this – connections were forming in a number of places – but it made an important contribution, not only in Melbourne but nationally and even internationally.[2] Neil acknowledges Westbury as bringing a particular focus to audience development: 'Marcus is really good at running festivals. And he was, like, "We've got to get serious about this. Who is the audience?"' (Neil & Westbury 2015). Four constituencies were identified: 'modders' and 'mappers'; people who were interested in games as 'art'; industrial games developers who wanted to reflect critically on the studios or to develop their work in other ways; and developers who were trying to establish businesses independently from the studios. There were differences between these constituencies – a 'game art' contributor unsettled some at the first conference by showing images of pornographic modelling she had been involved in – but there were also sufficient commonalities of interest for vibrant conversations to take form. The conference was pitched to those who were *looking for* the unexpected, who *wanted to* be provoked by different ways of relating to games. And those who participated responded accordingly.

In summary then, Freeplay was established on the basis of different stated values and interests from those of the Triple-A games industry, it was associated with different political commitments, it was organized around different kinds of social relations, it sought to cultivate a different aesthetic sensibility and to develop different kinds of community. It would be perverse to insist that these differences, brought together in the idea of independence, should be recognized only at the level of 'appearances'. It would be equally implausible to suggest that the principals involved were using the idea of independence only as part of a long-term play to make profits within the industry. There is no evidence to support such a view. This is not, of course, to say that Freeplay was, in some absolute sense, autonomous. It was supported in part by a small grant from the government funding agency Film Victoria (now VicScreen). An important base of knowledge and expertise came from the experience of those, like Neil, who

---

[2] It is worth noting, for example, that Greg Costikyan first developed his manifesto for independent games, 'Death to the Games Industry', for a presentation at Freeplay. It was later written up in other forms, becoming a significant document in the development of the idea of indie games in the United States and elsewhere.

had worked in the Triple-A industry. To use the term 'independent' as a positive description – that is, *without* scare quotes – is only to suggest that there is a place for straightforward distinctions made on the basis of concrete observations.

The mutability of the mainstream

To suggest that these distinctions are real, however, is not to deny that they shift over time. The most obvious example, in the case of Freeplay, was a restructuring of the field brought about by the demise in Australia of the major studios. While the latter may have dominated the scene in the early 2000s, it is clear in retrospect that they were living on borrowed time. Their position was based on a 'work for hire' model that was only viable given favourable international exchange rates, enabling them to bid competitively for projects under licence for American and European publishers (McCrea 2013). These conditions had held for a decade to the mid-2000s, but came to an abrupt end following the Global Financial Crisis, when the Australian dollar became a currency haven, trading as high as US$1.10. By 2012, many of the studios had collapsed and the remainder were on life support. Income from games development in Australia had been slashed by more than half (Banks & Cunningham 2016a: 186–7).

Following this shakeout, the small independent businesses that had begun to emerge in the early 2000s became, by default, 'the industry'. It was an industry, however, with a very different identity from the one that had gone before. The change can be seen in a sharp repositioning of the representative organization, the Game Developers' Association of Australia (GDAA), particularly through the leadership of its CEO in the aftermath of the crash, Antony Reed. Reed took the position in 2010 because he thought it would be 'challenging'. This is perhaps an understatement. As he described the situation:

> The industry was in a pretty miserable position. We had lost about 60 to 70 percent of our talent overseas. At the time, the GDAA had three members and I think we had a little over 300 participants in the sector.
>
> (Reed 2015)

Reed decided that the only way forward was to break decisively with the 'work for hire' model and all that had been associated with it. While his own background had been in distribution and marketing for international publishers such as Sega and Virgin, he had become interested, before the crash, in the potential for greater creative input into commercial games development in Australia. He became an internal critic of the narrow focus of the studio industry and ran a conference in 2007 seeking to generate interest in the development of original IP. When he came, himself, to direct the GDAA, his aims for the organization were similar, in many ways, to those of Freeplay:

> I could see an indie community starting, I could see what they were doing and that was a lot of the inspiration of what I wanted to do going forward. And I think, for the talent that remained, it was working out how we bring that together as a community ... I reframed the GCAP [Games Connect Asia Pacific] conference. I took it away from trying to be an intense skills development conference, because it was failing at that anyway, and made it more conversational.
>
> (Reed 2015)

One of the most significant achievements of the GDAA under Reed was the creation of 'the Arcade', a shared workspace for small games development businesses in South Melbourne. Opening in 2013 with twelve resident organizations, it had grown by 2017 to accommodate thirty-four (Foley 2017). Reed has always been keen to point out that the Arcade is not an 'incubator'. It has refused the top-down directive model that had characterized the studio industry, seeking instead to facilitate bottom-up creativity and horizontal exchange.

Games developers we spoke to in the Arcade testified to the value of the space in supporting and stimulating their work. As Simon Joslin, co-founder and creative director at the Voxel Agents, put it:

> When you're in The Arcade, you know, you're constantly spending time with [other developers] and becoming close friends ... Throughout the year you're constantly learning from each other by being in each other's spaces and hearing about their games and seeing the ... struggles they're up against. And you're sharing your own and you're constantly having a little bit of banter back and forth about how to improve.
>
> (Joslin 2016)

Joslin has also been a regular participant in Freeplay – at the time we spoke, the Voxel Agents had participated every year since starting out in 2009 – and has also found it an important stimulus to his work: 'Definitely in the earlier years it was eye-opening to see how many other people were out there and making interesting experiences in Melbourne and Australia and to be encouraged to explore, to be encouraged to venture into new land and take chances.' The Arcade, in Joslin's view, just took this further, allowing exchanges to move beyond the intermittent mode of the 'forty-minute presentation' to 'normal everyday practice'.

Given this mutation in the meaning of 'the industry' in Australia, the 'independent' identity of Freeplay was also bound to change. In the immediate aftermath of the crash, while a number of the studios remained, there was little to distinguish the positions of the GDAA and Freeplay. Katharine Neil – no longer directing Freeplay – saw the convergence and was concerned about a weakening in the defence of an independent identity. She had a difference with one of her successors, Paul Callaghan, over relations with the GDAA. By Neil's account, Callaghan had reservations about airing certain topics at Freeplay on the grounds that Reed had thought it might be 'bad for the industry':

> And I was, like, 'this is bad?'. For me, that's not independence. You can't have someone on speed dial from the Triple-A industry telling you what to put in your so-called independent conference.
>
> (Neil 2014)

Callaghan's own recollections are a little different from Neil's, but irrespective of the details of the case, the oppositional identity that she had earlier established for Freeplay would have been difficult to sustain. The dominant presence against which she had developed that identity had largely evaporated. While Reed may have come out of the Triple-A industry, the programme he had developed for the GDAA had much in common with Freeplay.

Independence from 'indie'

An obvious conclusion that might be drawn from this is that the distinction between 'mainstream' and 'independent' had lost its meaning. It is here that the perspective of Juul, and others who question the distinction, could be seen to gain some traction. As noted above, the perspective has emerged in response to just such a confusion of positions and identities. It is one we have also encountered in previous chapters in relation to other fields. The mid-2000s was, in fact, a high-water mark in general ideas of what might be called 'non-contradiction' in cultural economies. They gained widespread influence, for example, in the creative industries paradigm in cultural policy and cultural studies at the time – one that proclaimed an end to historical tensions between culture and commerce, urging the two to come together in a new 'win win' (Hartley 2005a: 19). Reed's reforms to the GDAA were very much of this moment. As he put it when we met at the Arcade, '[t]here is no reason that commercialization and creativity cannot coexist. I believe it' (Reed 2015).

But in the case, at least, of the games scene in Australia, this moment was no more permanent than the one that preceded it. There was always a potential for new lines between 'mainstream' and 'independent' to form. Despite the similarities between the GDAA and Freeplay, there was also an important difference: the horizon of the GDAA remained unabashedly commercial. In the 'coexistence' between commercialization and creativity, in other words, commercialization was always assumed as primary. This is not to deny the significance of Reed's reforms to the GDAA: they shifted its identity from a narrow business focus to embrace questions of creativity. It is only to say that creativity was always seen as being *in the service of* commercial outcomes. This was partly because of the remit of the GDAA – its very *raison d'etre* was industry development – but it also reflected Reed's formation in the Triple-A industry. His interest in the creative aspect of games had been framed, from the outset, by a perception of commercial opportunity.

The difference did not present itself immediately as significant. For a period during the collapse of the studios, commercial and non-commercial agents in the Melbourne games scene were generally seen as belonging to the same community. All were involved in experimenting with alternatives to the work-for-hire model. Over time, however, commercial interests around mobile games began to define new kinds of canons or orthodoxies. The tendency is described by Paul Callaghan, co-director (in his fourth year solo director) of Freeplay from 2009 to 2012:

> Over those four years, the industry started to reassert itself, and started to tell specific stories about things. While the larger studios disappeared, a lot of the mobile studios were very successful – so Firemonkeys and Halfbrick. And I think, certainly in our last two years, we responded to that ... So, yeah, I guess ... in those last two years it was 'how do we react to this new industrial narrative that's emerging?'
>
> (Callaghan 2014)

The success of the mobile studios gave rise, as Callaghan puts it, to 'a new mainstream story about what it meant to be an Australian developer'. It was a story that continued to focus on small games for mobile media as an alternative to the high-capital console business of the international publishers but was nevertheless a story that was 'heavily industrialized'. It was 'all about "oh, you've got to make an iPhone game and that iPhone game has to be a hit'" (Callaghan 2014).

The development also had an international aspect. From the late 2000s, 'indie games' were becoming increasingly incorporated into the mainstream in Europe and North America. An example is the increasing prominence of indie booths at major games expos such as PAX, Eurogamer Expo (EGX) and Electronic Entertainment Expo (E3). PAX has probably been the leader in this, having been associated from the beginning with forms of cultural crossover. The franchise was launched in Seattle in 2004 by Jerry Holkins and Mike Krahulik, previously known as the authors of the popular games-oriented web-comic, *Penny Arcade*. While offering a showcase for Triple-A blockbusters, PAX has also been porous to more spontaneous popular cultural forms – encouraging cosplay, for example, and providing spaces for board games and other low-tech or vernacular forms of play. 'Indie' games have always had a place within the format, but have increasingly been redefined from fringe attractions to a part of the main game. A turning point was reached in 2012 – shortly before PAX was extended to Australia – with the launch of an 'Indie Megabooth' at PAX East in Boston, allowing small games developers to gain a collective presence similar to that of the major publishers (Parker, Whitson & Simon 2017).

Callaghan describes the broad development as 'almost a corporatization of independence' (Callaghan 2014), nominating it as one of the main challenges that he and Co-director Eve Penford began to face after taking over the organization of Freeplay in 2009. Like Katharine Neil, both Callaghan and Penford had worked for the studio developer Infogrames (Melbourne House) in the early 2000s. Both were energized by the revolt against the studio paradigm and the opening up of a project of creative experimentation around games. Penford (2016) describes the early Freeplays as having 'blown our little minds'. For the collective of people in Melbourne generally, 'it was so out of the norm for people that it really stopped them in their tracks'. In developing and expanding the project, however, it became increasingly important to articulate a distance not from the major studios but from the 'indie' formation that had come to replace them.

Callaghan (2014) is explicit in drawing the line:

There's a difference between 'indie' and independent, I think. In Australia that's definitely true. So, for us it was always about how we could get as many people talking about their independent practice as we could, so that people looking at it

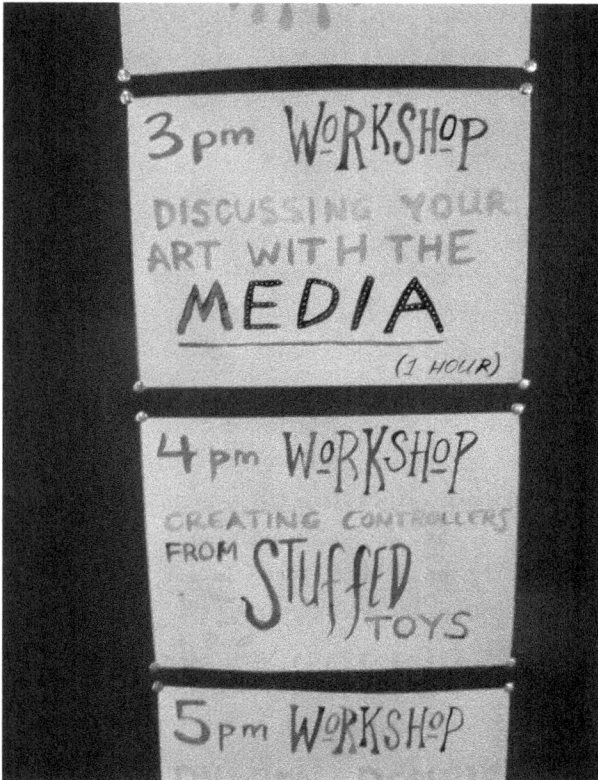

Figure 32 Independence from 'Indie'. Freeplay session posters, 2015. Photograph by Hugh Davies. Courtesy Hugh Davies.

can go 'oh, I'm more like this person, or this person, and I can see these multiple paths', rather than just, 'I need to go to work at EA', or 'I need to have a big IGF-winning game'.[3]

The project of defining an independence from 'indie' led to a number of departures from the original model developed by Neil and Westbury, but most of these could be seen as an adaptation to changing circumstances of the same underlying commitments. They continued to place a value on Westbury's '360

[3] EA refers here to Electronic Arts Inc., based in California – the second largest games publisher in Europe/North America. IGF refers to the Independent Games Festival, the largest event of its kind in the world. The IGF, held annually in San Francisco, is centred around competitions and awards, aspiring to be the 'Sundance Film Festival for games' (https://igf.com/about-igf).

degrees' of experimentation. As Penford (2016) put it, 'I think it's important to do things that aren't "games as we know them", because otherwise we go down a track, a rail'. There were also clear continuities in Callaghan and Penford's attempts to create platforms for less established voices – Neil's 'little guy or girl'.

Two strategies are worth mentioning here. The first was the development of new audiences. It might seem surprising, at first, that this could have any relation to independence. Under Callaghan and Penford's direction, Freeplay was staged at the Victorian State Library and reached out to a larger and more general audience than the earlier events. Between 2009 and 2012, the attendance increased from 600 to more than 2000 (Callaghan 2014). This might appear more a strategy of *mainstreaming* than an effort to regain independence. Neil, again, was somewhat critical of the move, seeing it as re-defining Freeplay from a focused conference for games developers to a 'kind of cultural festival' (Neil 2014). It was associated with the establishment of a board, some of whose members seemed to be, for Neil, 'well-meaning, do-goody people' from the arts. While recognizing the right of those who put in the work on the event to define it as they pleased, she was concerned that Freeplay might have lost a certain edge.

However, the development of new audiences was associated with a strategy of keeping the identity of Freeplay open, preventing it from going down the 'track' or 'rail' of a singular, prescriptive idea of indie. The industry prism was dislocated, for example, by the simple act of putting games in a public display space in the library. As Penford (2016) describes it:

> I doggedly ran around every single game company in Melbourne and said 'give me copies of your games because of a festival'. And some of them didn't understand why we were doing this. You know: 'this isn't GCAP, this isn't Las Vegas, what are you doing?' And I'm sort of there trying to explain that we're showcasing these things to the public and they might actually want to put something out there. And it's to show, you know, the Victorian games that we were making ...

Public exhibition worked, as Penford puts it, to 'crack' or 'fracture' the industry narrative, drawing those involved in the creation of games to see themselves in different terms. Yet it did so in a way that sought to avoid alienating or antagonizing. Penford saw open opposition as potentially destructive: '[W]e (mainstream and indie) needed to be more collaborative, and a little bit more secure in each other's company so that there could still be discourse and agitation and criticism without it destroying or imploding the environment for making games in general, and importantly (and also more likely), without the mainstream destroying the indie space' (Penford 2016).

The paradox of Freeplay under Callaghan and Penford is that it was much less hostile to the industry than it had been under Neil, but also more distant from it. The independence cultivated by Callaghan and Penford was not an independence of antagonism, but of detachment or aloofness. The identity was later captured in an initiative of Dan Golding, one of defining some of Freeplay's programmes around 'parallels'. The idea was inspired by a suggestion by games scholar Paolo Ruffino that, in considering the meanings and values associated with independent games, we shift the perspective from the games themselves to the 'social understanding' surrounding them. As Ruffino puts it, narratives of independent production which take this perspective avoid 'naïve oppositions or forms of engagement with an alleged mainstream/dependent industry', seeking instead to 'offer themselves as parallel practices' (Ruffino 2013: 119). It is a perspective, for Golding, that helped to clarify the kind of independence that Freeplay was seeking to represent: 'It's not like a subsection, and it's not necessarily pushing away or isolating itself. It's just parallel. It's different' (Golding 2014a).

A second strategy in developing the idea of independence was the establishment of awards to recognize achievements in games development in terms other than commercial success. It could be described, in Bourdieusian terms, as a strategy of 'consecration', similar to that which contributed to the autonomization of art in Europe in the eighteenth and nineteenth centuries. The emergence of academies, salons and other agencies bestowing critical recognition was crucial, Bourdieu (1993: 112) argues, in giving art a 'truly cultural legitimacy'. The legitimacy conferred by the Freeplay awards may not have reached quite these heights. For Penford, they were often merely a small corrective to abusive relationships within the games industry – relationships that sought to exploit dependence:

> I hope that … you know, standing up and being able to say 'I did this thing and other people thought it was alright' was useful. Because I think it's an industry that doesn't want you to believe you're any good. There was very much that sense working in the established companies, where if you were in any way good they couldn't tell you that … 'You're nothing without me.' Lots of us – lots of people were really quite broken by that.

(Penford 2016)

Despite their moderate ambitions, however, the Freeplay awards have performed something of the function of consecration described by Bourdieu. They have provided a focus for articulating alternative ideas of value.

Figure 33 Presentation of awards by Director Paul Callaghan, Freeplay 2010. Photograph by Liam McGuire. Courtesy Liam McGuire.

Cultural policy and post-countercultural independence

The relative modesty of the idea of independence represented by Freeplay might lead us to overlook its significance. It is an idea that lacks the clarity of the European modernist ideas of artistic autonomy analysed so sharply by Bourdieu. More proximately, it lacks the hard-edged definition inherited from the counterculture around cultural forms such as music and film. The difference is one that is probably general to games as a 'post-countercultural' phenomenon. Even those with more radical ideas of independence in games, such as Neil, have not imagined that they might overthrow or supplant the Triple-A industry. Establishing a place for the independent has been not so much a revolutionary as interstitial practice. It has involved creating small spaces for doing or thinking differently within a larger culture shaped by the commercial mainstream.

Yet the 'weakness' of the idea of independence in games also has definite strengths. It has meant, in particular, that crossover between independent and mainstream is less prone to purist inhibitions around 'selling out' that have so often affected other cultural forms. Freeplay is interesting in this context in that it has managed to normalize exchange between independent and mainstream over an extended period. While the 'independent festival' is a familiar format, common across many cultural fields, it is one that has tended to oscillate between the divergent poles of 'collapse' and 'capture'. As Canadian management scholar Donald Getz (2002) has observed, festivals often have short lives, foundering due to various combinations of a lack of organization and strategy, financial problems, volunteer burnout and other factors. Those that achieve longevity have generally done so by joining with or supplanting the mainstream against which they were originally defined. The paradigm example internationally is probably the Edinburgh Fringe – a case, as British arts critic Michael Billington (2002) puts it, in which 'the child has outgrown the parent', becoming a cultural behemoth of its own (see also Frew & Ali-Knight 2010). Against this background, Freeplay is noteworthy in having survived well into a second decade while continuing to offer alternatives to whatever the mainstream has become.

The achievement can be attributed in part to practical arrangements around governance. A key factor has been the relation between the board and directors. As described by 2013 Co-director, Harry Lee:

> Freeplay is a non-profit organization with a board and directors and they are two separate entities with separate roles and the way that they work together is really fascinating. So, the board is saying 'let's make sure that Freeplay doesn't burn and crash' and the directors are saying 'let's burn and crash everything'. Which is really fun!

> (Lee 2015)

Lee identifies two kinds of imbalance that can occur within this structure: one in which the 'director has no leash and the board becomes their lapdog', the other 'when the board becomes so stifling that creative vision is lost'. Freeplay is perhaps particularly remarkable as a long-running festival in avoiding the latter problem. Lee and co-conspirator Katie Williams were in their early twenties when they were given the directorship and both were untested in festival programming and event management. Lee freely admits that he was one of those who wanted to 'burn and crash everything'. Freeplay's controlled exposure to risk-taking of this kind has had significant payoffs for renewal. The changes brought by the 'young ones' – Lee and Williams – to the 2013 festival brought a new range of voices and a new sea of faces (Golding 2014b).

To draw the larger lessons of the games case, however, we need also to acknowledge a more conceptual innovation – an innovation in the way independence is understood. It is significant that Lee could represent the tension between organizational stability and creative experimentation as 'fun'. 'Burning and crashing' clearly has quite different resonances for a young cultural activist

Figure 34 The 'young ones'. Harry (Shang Lun) Lee giving instructions for a location-based game, Federation Square, Melbourne, at Freeplay 2012. Photograph by Katie Harmsworth. Courtesy Katie Harmsworth.

in the games space in the 2010s from those that might have been associated with a countercultural figure of the 1960s or 1970s. It does not suggest an existential struggle between opposing principles but something that might be better described as a dance of difference. The kind of independence that emerges here is one that is aware of its limits, knows that it will be countered at some point and respects pushback even as it seeks to expand its influence.

Where might this understanding of independence take us in policy terms? A useful way of answering this might be first to consider some work in the mid-2010s by John Banks and Stuart Cunningham (2016a; 2016b) proceeding from a project on sources of innovation in the interactive entertainment industry in Australia. Developed in partnership with the Australia Council for the Arts, the work exemplifies both the strengths and weaknesses of the creative industries position discussed in relation to Cunningham in Chapter 1. It is in addressing the weaknesses that the perspective gained from Freeplay may help us to move forward.

Banks and Cunningham's analysis starts from a determination to avoid crude oppositions between mainstream commercial production and smaller players at the fringes or margins. Games development in Australia is considered as a 'diverse ecology' (Banks & Cunningham 2016b: 128), in which the two are entangled in complex ways. In some cases, the relationship may be weighted towards mainstream economic interests. In Sydney, for example, employment for games developers has continued to be mostly in work-for-hire projects commissioned by corporate clients. In other cases, however, small players have been able to gain greater creative control. In Melbourne, notably, there are a number who have established successful businesses around original IP. Even at the ends of this spectrum, actual organizations and projects are, for Banks and Cunningham, fusions, formed by processes of crossover and exchange.

This recognition of complexity and hybridity has been important in bringing greater visibility to and support for 'bottom up' processes in games production in Australia. By emphasizing continuities over contradictions or oppositions, Banks and Cunningham are able to represent the value contributed by small players in terms clearly recognizable within the mainstream. In a paper covering much the same history discussed earlier in the chapter, they suggest that the collapse of the major games studios in Australia might be seen in Schumpeterian terms as part of a process of 'creative destruction' (Banks & Cunningham 2016b). While jobs and income were decimated, the collapse set the scene for renewal. The perspective is used to advocate for the small businesses or 'indies' we encountered above. The latter are inscribed within an industry development narrative, their contribution being measured according to similar criteria – jobs and income – that had been used to represent the value of the large commercial players. The analysis aligns closely with the position of the GDAA – Antony Reed is indeed a key witness – and has succeeded in engaging the interest of policy and funding agencies, from the Australia Council to state government departments such as Creative Victoria.

Notwithstanding these achievements, the policy programme also has significant limitations. As discussed in Chapter 1, the sensitivity of the creative industries paradigm to crossover and hybridity has been bought at the cost of economic reductionism. While Banks and Cunningham appear, at one level, simply to be offering an analysis of the games industry, their position is also animated by a wider agenda. In the introduction to the paper mentioned above, they cite Toby Miller's (2016) characterization of commercial cultural production as dominated by a 'global regime of huge media conglomerates' (Banks & Cunningham 2016b: 127), a characterization that calls up the possibility of others or outsiders. Miller's perspective becomes a negative point of reference – taken to exemplify much of 'critical media, communication and cultural studies' generally – structuring the analysis in significant ways. Always just below the surface runs a suspicion of attempts to open up distinctions between economic and non-economic values. The result is a systematic blindness to aspects of the field that cannot be represented in economic terms.

A similar point might be made in relation to actual government programmes. The Victorian state government is widely regarded as the most supportive in Australia of small games developers – the envy, indeed, of developer communities in other states. It has long supported the development of original content through grants awarded through Film Victoria. Yet as Paul Callaghan points out, this support has been directed almost entirely to existing businesses. While Director of Freeplay, Callaghan reviewed Film Victoria's funding decisions in games, finding that the 'vast majority of the funding was going to established studios'. Grant guidelines have heavily favoured business experience over evidence of actual innovation. Support for the creation of original IP has indeed often been extended to those who have only ever developed content under licence:

> So you're sort of throwing this money expecting magic to happen, and a lot of those projects are just never emerging. And basically, there was no way for anyone to get access to that funding without having been in the studio system ... So there's no meaningful access to funding for people to migrate from the fringe to the mainstream. There's no awareness of what it means to build fringe practice in games, even when that's pointed out.
>
> (Callaghan 2014)

Like Banks and Cunningham's analysis, the policy in question here has been developed within an avowedly progressive framework. It has been designed to support bottom-up processes in the cultural industries and to recognize the contributions of small players. Yet it also exhibits the same characteristic hardening against anything that cannot be recognized as already internal to the economic field.

What explains this hardening? The obvious answer is that attempts to identify alternative values to those of business are widely seen as a reproach to economic aspirations. This perception can be seen, for example, in responses by the GDAA to such attempts on the part of Freeplay. For Antony Reed, the turn taken by Freeplay in the 2010s took it down a path that was 'anti industry':

> It was designed to be a cultural conversation and unfortunately it lost its way a little bit. So there hasn't been much interaction between GCAP and Freeplay. I

have disagreed with a number of things that the conference has said ... I think trying to impose guilt on people who make money out of their games is the wrong way to go.

(Reed 2015)

An apprehension in relation to 'anti industry' perspectives also appears to inform the determination of Banks and Cunningham to restrict their focus to business development. It is an apprehension, to be fair, that is not entirely without foundation. While the problem may not extend to the whole of 'critical media, communication and cultural studies' – a hazy category, in any case – it would be fair to say that there is a small academic industry in charging the creative industries with complicity in social inequality, imperialism, environmental destruction and various other ills (see e.g. Miller 2009).

It is here that the perspective gained through Freeplay may have a contribution to make. It is a perspective that recognizes an outside to the economy without taking a position *against* the economy. This is not to suggest that the relation between Freeplay and the games industry has always been harmonious: it is possible that things have sometimes been said, to use Reed's phrase, that 'impose guilt on people'. But there is little evidence that Freeplay has been, in a systematic sense, 'anti industry'. As described by Callaghan, the festival has been opposed only to the idea that any single path should be assumed as normative:

The conversations that we would always have internally were that [independence] was about people being able to choose what they wanted to do, and pursue that actively, and us supporting them in that. So, if people wanted to get a job in a studio, that was totally valid. That's them asserting their independence. And if people wanted to make weird glitch-art games, that's fine as well. And if people wanted to find a middle ground between those two possible career paths, that was fine.

(Callaghan 2014)

The ideal represented here is of an acceptance of multiple values. 'Art' and 'industry' are seen as different rather than opposed, leaving open the possibility of productive forms of crossover and hybridization.

Such crossover can be found in the Melbourne-independent games scene, even in the absence of policies to support it. A good example is the work of experimental games designer Alexander Bruce, best known for the non-Euclidean first-person puzzle game *Antichamber*. While the game has been a commercial success, selling more than 100,000 copies since its release on Steam in 2013 (McElroy 2013), it began as a philosophical art piece, *Hazard: The Journey of Life*, developed while Bruce was a student at Swinburne University. The movement from the fringe was facilitated initially not by business development programmes but by the independent festival circuit. An important early breakthrough was the inclusion of a prototype in a showcase at Senses of Wonder Night in Japan, the focus of which Bruce (2015) describes as 'weird experimental things'. This was followed by a string of other awards, including a number at Freeplay. It was only following this recognition – in what Bourdieu would call the cultural field – that Bruce began to consider how the game might be developed commercially.

The business development for Antichamber was undertaken in autodidactic mode by Bruce himself, drawing only on informal mentorship from others in the games community. His experience confirms Callaghan's analysis of the limitations of existing government programmes:

> When Screen Australia had their $20 million for the games sector, I went to a couple of the discussions there just to see what kinds of things they were talking about – because they had this strong focus, saying 'we want to help foster independent development in Australia' … But what they really meant was still the old Australian studio model. You know: 'We want people who are making jobs in Australia. We want to give money to studios so they can employ people'. Which was very different to the kind of thing I was doing.
>
> (Bruce 2015)

As Bruce points out, the investment required for Antichamber was in fact very small: 'I only needed, like, $10,000, or something like that, which is probably too small for the scope of what Screen Australia was thinking'. It was more practical, given this, to approach the Indie Fund, a programme set up internationally by a group of independent developers more in touch with the realities of bottom-up commercialization.

But if policies around games development in Australia have limited relevance to figures such as Bruce, there is no reason why they must continue to be. If the tired opposition between economy and culture can be put aside, then Banks and Cunningham's 'ecological' approach might be extended to include sites where innovation in games is actually occurring. The important move required here is a recognition of the specificity of the cultural field. A key factor in a career such as Bruce's is what might be called the 'economy of regard'. This is not a money economy, but an economy of recognition and respect – the crucial vector that first allows an obscure work by a student developer to gain some currency. It is an economy that is nurtured in small independent spaces such as Freeplay, but also in public institutions such as the Australian Centre for the Moving Image and the Victorian State Library. An essential part of this infrastructure is also, of course, education. It was while studying at Swinburne that Bruce was first able to put his work into circulation: 'As a student, I was showing it just to other students, I was showing it to lecturers – because we'd have subjects that were about feedback and how to process that' (Bruce 2015).

It is possible that the games case has something distinctive to contribute here to our understanding of contemporary cultural production more generally. The dominance of the industrial definition of games has meant that those interested in the cultural dimension have had to work harder than their counterparts in other fields to affirm its specificity. If this can be seen in examples such as Freeplay, it can also be seen in scholarship on games. An excellent recent example is Brendan Keogh's (2023) book *The Videogame Industry Does Not Exist*, which brings a nuance to our understanding of relations between industrial and cultural production that could have value beyond the games case itself. An essential starting point for this is a recognition of the two spheres as distinct. Drawing on Bourdieu, Keogh argues that we need to recognize a 'videogame field' with a degree of autonomy from the 'industry'. The point in doing so, however, is not to magnify the differences between them but to understand how one informs the other. Alternative sites of games production do not simply exist alongside and separate from the industry: 'They instead form the foundation of skills, cultures, genres, communities, technologies, and aesthetics that are a necessary precursor for any industrialized videogame production to occur' (Keogh 2023, 6).

To take this perspective is in some ways to call for a return to some of the traditional priorities of cultural policy and education in the creative arts. But doing so should not be thought of as therefore opposed to economic priorities. The argument we have sought to advance in *Fringe to Famous* is lost if it appears to be an argument merely for 'art for art's sake'. To state the obvious, it is important for games developers – and for the economy more generally – that people are able to find employment. The sharp end of cultural innovation does not always produce immediate economic benefits. In relation to the example above, Alex Bruce is the first to admit that *Antichamber* has not directly generated many jobs in the industry. There is, however, a clear relation between a general *sphere* of innovation and the capacity of economies to develop and respond to change. Indeed, there would not now *be* a games industry in Australia if there had not been an independent sector at the time of the collapse of the major studios and the work-for-hire paradigm. Against this background, a strong cultural policy should also be recognized as sound economic policy.

Conclusion: Designing osmotic ecologies

Fringe to Famous has examined the circulation of art and artists between small fringe scenes and mass popular markets in Australia over a forty-year period from the last two decades of the twentieth century to the present day. Our aim in doing so has been to draw attention to the value of this circulation and of the hybrid forms it has produced. The argument is one that has required a balancing act. On the one hand, we have sought to recognize *differences* between the fringe and mainstream – differences not only of scale, but also of institutional forms, characteristic relationships, ideas of value, aesthetic sensibilities and political commitments. On the other hand, we have sought to highlight the importance of *exchange* between fringe and mainstream formations. Such exchange often involves tensions or frictions. We have attempted to show, however, that the relation between fringe and mainstream is as much symbiotic as it is conflictual. Hybridization between them produces outcomes – both cultural and economic – that neither could achieve on their own.

This positive account of hybridity offers an alternative both to a romantic tendency to see fringe and mainstream as irreconcilable opposites and to an anti-romantic reaction that questions the validity even of attempting to distinguish between them. The often-heated arguments between these two tendencies should not distract us from what they share: a purified idea of the fringe that forces a choice between seeing differences from the mainstream either as absolute or as nothing at all. The idea is one that can be traced most immediately to the counterculture of the 1960s and 1970s, or more precisely to intellectual positions that have been abstracted from it in the half century since. In seeking alternatives to this tradition, we have looked to more empirically grounded conceptualizations that can be found in historical writing and in the perspectives of creative practitioners themselves. As our interview evidence has shown, there is little doubt for most artists that there are significant differences between small scenes of cultural production and the mainstream, but there is little doubt either of the potential for mixing between them.

In terms of recent debates around the relation between culture and economy, the position we have taken might be described as 'post-creative industries'. It is important, we have argued, to resist the tendency of creative industries to represent cultural and economic value as always or necessarily aligned. There is overwhelming evidence of differences between them in contemporary cultural production – not only in fringe arts practice, but also in the mainstream cultural industries. To fail to recognize this fact is to distort our understanding of the field. We emphasize, however, that a post-creative industries perspective is not an *anti*-creative industries perspective. There are many cases where a 'win win' between cultural and economic aspirations can indeed be found. The creative industries idea has inspired an enormous amount of work over the last twenty years in identifying such cases by governments, academic researchers, international agencies and peak bodies in the arts and cultural sector. The positive contributions of this work should not be denied.

We have therefore kept a certain distance also from the perspective we have called 'left culturalism', a perspective that has tended to *over*state differences between fringe and mainstream. There is, again, much that we share with this perspective. It has been important in drawing attention to conflicts or antagonisms over differences between cultural and economic values, and to the fact that the interests of artists and the institutions that employ them do not always coincide. The problem, however, is that it has often gone beyond this, exaggerating the differences and representing them in structural terms such that a win on one side is, by definition, a loss on the other. Given the social dominance of institutional and economic logics, the result for anyone who cares about cultural values can only be depressing. This pessimistic tendency has been met periodically with criticisms, both for its inability to offer constructive programmes for action and for overdrawn factual claims. Yet it has also proven remarkably resilient. While the grim twentieth-century prognostications of the Frankfurt School may now be seen as a historical curiosity, many of its animating ideas have found a new home in twenty-first-century critiques of neoliberalism, surveillance capitalism and managerialism.

It might have seemed at times that our position is merely fence-sitting, lacking the conviction to choose one or other side. Our argument, however, is that the choice between creative industries and left culturalism is ultimately a false one. In finding positive ways forward for art and culture in Australia, we need to embrace *both* the critical insight that the values generated within small fringe scenes often differ sharply from those of the mainstream *and* the creative industries suggestion that 'contracts between art and commerce' (Caves 2002) can be very much to the benefit of both. We have argued throughout the book that the two sides of this position are, in fact, complementary. As we put it in Chapter 1, the idea of a generative hybridity between fringe and mainstream requires that we recognize a difference to be hybridized. This means that we must sometimes defend the idea of difference even as we are also affirming the value of mixing and exchange.

The risk in this position is always of leaning too much to one or other side, bringing the balancing act unstuck. There are two general strategies we have used to guard against this. The first has been to focus on concrete examples of hybrid formations. These have included self-managed creatives in the music industry, such as singer-songwriter Courtney Barnett; streetwear fashion label Mambo, which combined an open studio structure with a keen sense of the commercial possibilities of subcultural expression; artist-led television comedy production houses, from Working Dog and Zapruder's Other Films to The Chaser, Gristmill and Paul Fenech's Antichocko Productions; Indigenous filmmakers such as Warwick Thornton, Wayne Blair, Ivan Sen and Rachel Perkins, who have brought First Nations perspectives to international festival circuits and suburban multiplexes; and the Freeplay-independent games festival, which has provided a platform for small Australian games cultures to connect with public institutions and gain broader recognition. What is shared among all of these is that they are hard to place in abstract terms. They have been independent in ethos but have also reached out to mainstream audiences.

The second strategy in maintaining balance has been to use the example of others as a guide. A key inspiration from the outset has been Frith and Horne's *Art into Pop* (1987). Another, with certain qualifications, has been Bourdieu's (1993) attempt to develop a nuanced understanding of relations between the 'field of restricted production' and the 'field of large-scale production'. But as we argued in Chapter 1, the exhaustion of the creative industries paradigm offers opportunities for connecting also with a wider range of sources. At the centre of the paradigm was always a certain accelerationist logic. In eliminating any space for the fringe in the sense abstracted from the counterculture, it exploded the terms that have governed debates around politics and culture from the 1970s to the early 2000s. At the very points where it tended to grandiosity, it also created the conditions for more modest, empirically sensitive ideas of the fringe to re-emerge. It becomes possible, in this context, to recapture some of the inspiration of earlier moments – the 'cultural industries' moment in scholarly work during the 1980s, for example, or, in Australian cultural policy, of the Keating government's Creative Nation or of institutional outreach to fringe arts practice under Whitlam in the 1970s.

The perspective is one that allows a cautious optimism. It is important to acknowledge a pervasive malaise in the early 2020s, a mood that has been exacerbated by the fatigue associated with the COVID-19 pandemic. It would also be foolish, in view of the dark political clouds of the last decade, to dismiss Justin O'Connor's (2016: 51) warning that 'interregnums breed monsters'. We have argued, however, that much of the sense of 'stuckedness' (Hage 2009) of recent years can be attributed to the exhaustion of a cycle of cultural-political development initiated in the 1960s and 1970s. The creative industries idea might be seen, in this context, as an 'end of history' moment for ideas around cultural politics. As the case of geopolitics has shown, however, history has a way of starting again (Hochuli, Hoare & Cuncliffe 2021). This is not to say that the way it does so will always be positive, only that we might see the future as again genuinely open, 'unstuck'. Against the tendency of creative industries to forced optimism and of left culturalism to reflex pessimism, we have attempted to recapture a sense of historical contingency.

What possibilities might there be then for Australian arts and culture in the 2020s and 2030s? Where might we look for fresh hybridizations between fringe and mainstream formations? This is the point in the book where we hope that readers will have their own ideas. Any answers to these questions will reflect the backgrounds, identities, contexts and values of those who consider them. As a way of concluding, however, we suggest a general framework that might offer productive ways forward.

Affirming the fringe

A starting point would be to recognize that fringe cultural formations in Australia are now significantly undervalued. The major context for this, we have suggested, has been a protracted response to a late-twentieth-century moment in which they were *over*valued. We have not wished to deny the necessity of a correction. Many of those who were active in the counterculture and left political movements of the 1970s came, themselves, to reject the mythologization of the fringe and its burdening over time with impossible expectations. The problem has emerged only as the critique of these tendencies has evolved from a corrective to its own kind of orthodoxy. Fringe formations today show few signs of attachment to the ideas of purity that came to be associated with the counterculture, yet they continue to be besieged by the cultural-political antibodies that emerged against those ideas. The immune defences that once protected against pathogenic forms have become instead the disease.

It is easy to blame distrust of the fringe on conservative reaction. The recent Coalition government in Australia (2013–22) showed a lack of sympathy for the arts in general. Examples include funding cuts to the public broadcasters and the Australia Council for the Arts, the suspension of Australian content quotas supporting local film and television production and, most symbolically, the burying of the Commonwealth arts portfolio within the resolutely utilitarian-sounding Department of Infrastructure, Transport, Regional Development and Communication. As Ben Eltham (2015) pointed out at the height of this maelstrom, a particular antipathy was reserved for small-scale independent practitioners. The premise of the cuts to the Australia Council was in part to shift funding, in the name of 'excellence', to large arts organizations such as Opera Australia. A hardened indifference to fringe arts practice was further confirmed in the design of the pandemic employment support package JobKeeper which, despite pleas that the most vulnerable arts workers were those in unstable or insecure jobs, shut out precisely those workers.

In a wider perspective, however, many of the most active agents in the delegitimization of the fringe have been at least nominally progressive. While recent Coalition policies at the national level may have been particularly callous, they built on shifts overseen by centre-left forces – Labor governments, arts managers, progressive thought leaders and academic cultural theorists. The stripping of the arts of an independent status in the naming of ministries might indeed be seen as merely formalizing a widely held view in these circles that any claim for the independence of culture is naïve, that the only way it can still be recognized is as fully incorporated, functional to governmental or economic needs. A major variant of this view has been the idea that the arts should be framed as an 'industry' (O'Connor 2020), but this is only one of a family of positions that developed in the shadow of the counterculture around the idea that there is 'no outside'. A key example in cultural theory has been the Foucauldian argument that there is no outside to relations of power – in centre-left politics, the argument that there is no outside to the market economy.

These arguments were amplified in the early 2000s by the fact that they seemed to be confirmed by developments in the world at large, particularly those captured under the concepts of 'globalization' and 'digitization'. It was always widely acknowledged that these phenomena have been complex, uneven and variable, but a powerful consensus nevertheless emerged around a central theme. As the American journalist and business commentator Thomas Friedman (2007) put it in one influential formulation, it was that 'the world is flat'. The idea is one that came to Friedman during a trip to India. As the CEO of a technology company in Bangalore explained to him, '[w]e could be sitting here, somebody from New York, London, Boston, San Francisco, all live. And the implementation is in Singapore, so the Singapore person could also be live here ... That's globalization' (Friedman 2007: 5). The lesson from such stories for Friedman was that new media technologies, combined with the evaporation of Cold War divisions, had created a seamless flux of information and capital – a world without topography.

If this imagined trajectory is now being reassessed, it has often been regretfully, with reference to developments such as the souring of social media, nativist revolts against international agencies, the Russian invasion of Ukraine and the emergence of geopolitical tensions between the United States and China (Dupont 2022; Hartley 2022). There is much in these developments that is of course deeply troubling. But a return of topography – or rather of a topographic conception of cultural and political realities – may also have more positive potentials. Fringe cultural formations did not do well from flat world thinking. At the high tide of that thinking, they might be seen indeed as having suffered a double torment: first from the overhang of a reaction to the counterculture (a charge of romanticism); second from the idea that cultural or political divisions had become irrelevant, dissolved in a global, digital continuum (a charge of atavism). A reversal of the tide might suggest an easing at least of these charges, opening the possibility of a more positive valuation of the fringe.

There are some signs in Australia of a retreat from the narrow utilitarianism of recent years. Following its election in 2022, the incoming Albanese Labor government embarked on a consultation process towards the development of a new national cultural policy. Among five pillars in setting a framework for this policy has been the 'centrality of the artist' (Burke 2022). The pillar is significant in recognizing a dual identity of the artist – as 'worker' and as 'creator of culture' – opening the way to the kind of pluralist understanding we have advocated for in *Fringe to Famous*. There are ways, however, that this move could

Figure 35 Prime Minister Anthony Albanese with Missy Higgins at The Esplanade Hotel at the launch of the *Revive* cultural policy, following a performance by Higgins of the Triffid's classic *Wide Open Road*, 2022. Courtesy Prime Minister's Office.

also be strengthened. So long as the focus remains on 'the' artist in the singular, the specifically cultural dimension of the policy direction remains weak, being left to rest on dubious ideas of creative genius. As our case studies have found, artists depend crucially on interactions with peers and audiences. Examples include the theatres and clubs that have provided the seedbed for much of Australian comedy, the small venues that have launched so many rock bands, media-making circles in Indigenous communities and the fringe festivals that have catalysed exchange around digital games.

A first suggestion in conclusion therefore is that we more positively affirm these fringe formations. This is a programme that could be undertaken not only in politics and policymaking but also in many other fields – journalism, education, business, arts management and public administration. We are not suggesting that perspectives on the fringe should be uncritical, only that they be freed of systematic prejudices. There is nothing *inherently* naïve or romantic in recognizing the importance of value formation in small scenes in the 'field of restricted production'. These scenes can certainly become pretentious or self-indulgent; they will always be embedded, too, in specific social contexts that can never be fully representative of the society at large. But to make these shortcomings the basis for a generalized judgement against them is to lose sight of their wider contribution. Whatever their faults, they are an essential source of cultural and economic renewal.

Osmotic ecologies

Neutralizing prejudices is not sufficient, however, to establish a framework with which to move forward. The perspective we have developed in *Fringe to Famous* presents a challenge that cannot be solved by simple acts of affirmation. At the heart of this challenge is a central contradiction. Our perspective suggests, on the one hand, that fringe cultural formations need a certain insulation from the economic and managerial logics that govern mainstream institutions, an insulation sufficient at least to ensure that their difference can be recognized. Yet it requires, on the other hand, that they be *exposed* to precisely those logics, brought into contact in ways that allow them to mix or combine. The contradiction is not as stark as it seems, as neither insulation nor exposure needs to be understood in absolute terms. The compromise solution might be thought of as a semi-permeable or osmotic membrane allowing exchange between the fringe and mainstream to be both enabled and constrained. But how might such a model work in practice?

In our interviews for *Fringe to Famous*, some of the most explicit reflections on this question emerged in relation to business structures by figures, such as Steve Vizard, who have had experience at the hard, commercial end of mainstream media. Pressures on the relation between fringe and mainstream are, in this context, intense. As Vizard (2014) put it in relation to television, 'the purpose of commercial TV is to deliver a profit … So if you're going onto their turf … then you have to work out a mechanism of how you can maintain their audience'. But the bluntness of this ultimatum has the advantage at least of forcing a certain clarity. As we saw in Chapter 4, Vizard's relation to the executives at Channel Seven was sometimes one of open conflict. The function of his company, Artist Services, was in part to regulate the relationship, providing baffles or protections that would make it more manageable. The formal premise of Artist Services was, like the network, business, but it was a business bent to the needs of the field of restricted production. The strategy is one that has also been important for the other artist-led comedy production houses we have discussed.

An obvious question arises here about the public broadcasters, whose very purpose has been to offer shelter from commercial pressures of the kind that Vizard encountered at Seven. What role do they play in facilitating exchange in Australia between fringe and mainstream? The ABC and SBS have appeared at many points in the book and mostly in positive ways. Breakthroughs for fringe cultural expression in major commercial media are probably only possible for those with certain backgrounds, personal qualities or resources. Vizard had the advantage of working from a very robust field of restricted production, Melbourne's small theatre scene of the 1970s; it is also significant that he had been primed for mainstream institutional encounters through professional experience in the law. The public broadcasters have presented a less forbidding face than the commercial networks, allowing entry to a wider range of fringe formations. An example would be the role that Triple J has played in outreach to fringe music cultures, many of them nascent or fragile. We would concur, in this context, with the proposition of ABC chairman of the 2010s, James Spigelman (2012), that Australia's major public broadcaster could reasonably claim to be also its 'most important, single cultural institution'.

But commercial imperatives are not the only barrier to exchange between fringe and mainstream. The counterpart in public broadcasting is a deadening managerialism and aversion to risk, which can be just as effective in cruelling creativity and blocking entry to the fringe. We encountered examples in our case studies, indeed, where it was *business* structures that offered shelter, not against commercial pressures elsewhere but against chloroforming managerial tendencies in public broadcasting. An example was Andrew Denton's (2014) formation of Zapruder as a way of insulating fringe entrants such as The Chaser from 'non-essential dickheads' at the ABC. It is also important to acknowledge the role of the SBS, which has offered another kind of refuge from the frequent conservatism of its larger, more established sibling. It has allowed entry, for example, to 'unicorn' talents like Paul Fenech and hosted significant innovations such as SBS Independent – still one of the best examples in Australia of public sector outreach to fringe cultural practices.

A general lesson might be drawn here about the value of varied institutional arrangements in the cultural industries. This theme often emerged at the height of the broadcasting era in relation to the mix in Australia of American commercial models and European-style public service institutions (O'Regan 1993). But the commercial/public service distinction should only ever be seen as part of the picture. The distinction is important but can easily become fetishized, as seen for example in arguments by groups such as the Friends of the ABC against outsourcing of production (e.g. Dempster 2011). These arguments fail to register the importance of the contractual leverage of independent production houses in maintaining spaces for exactly the kinds of creative freedom and experimentation that it is imagined commercialization will put at risk. It is for this reason that we have remained agnostic in *Fringe to Famous* about the private versus public dichotomy. Our findings suggest that it is often as important to consider differences *within* sectors – for example between the ABC and SBS or between Channel Seven and Artist Services – in efforts to ensure an open, plural system.

The example of broadcasting is a useful one, then, in considering general principles for what might be called 'osmotic ecologies'. From the point of view of our argument in *Fringe to Famous*, the critical factor in the relation between fringe and mainstream is the degree of permeability of the membrane between them. If this membrane is too permeable – or if indeed there is no membrane at all – then the distinction between fringe and mainstream is lost. If it is not permeable enough, then fringe and mainstream are unable to communicate, coming to be defined as existential opposites. What is lost in both cases is the potential for hybridization between them. Given the significance we have assigned to hybridization, we have some sympathy for the nightmare visions often conjured up in writing on the cultural industries of, alternatively, an abject submission of culture to the logics governing mainstream institutions or of an 'art for art's sake' preciousness that threatens to disconnect and isolate sites of cultural renewal. We see limited value, however, in addressing these problems through abstract arguments about the nature of capitalism or doctrinaire injunctions against the idea of an 'outside' to the mainstream. We suggest that they be considered instead at the more practical level of institutional design.

This approach could be brought to the other sites of exchange between fringe and mainstream we have discussed in the book – small record labels, independent bookstores, pubs and clubs and regional entrepots between remote Indigenous communities and metropolitan cultural institutions. There are two more general forms that should also be mentioned here: festivals and educational institutions, which are significant across many different fields. We gave most direct attention to the festival format in Chapter 6, on the Freeplay Independent Games Festival. As we saw there, relations between fringe and mainstream in festivals often resolve into questions of governance, such as the definition of roles for creative directors and boards. Harry Lee's (2015) identification of two kinds of imbalance in these roles – one where the 'director has no leash and the board becomes their lapdog', the other 'when the board becomes so stifling that creative vision is lost' – is a good example of the considerations involved in the design of osmotic ecologies. A similar care in institutional design can be seen in other cases – the Melbourne International Comedy Festival, music festivals and the international film festivals that have provided an osmotic membrane for Indigenous film.

Educational institutions have figured prominently throughout the book, a sign of their general importance. They were a particular focus in the cases of music and comedy, where art schools and university revues have provided a crucible for fringe formations and where campus venues, publications and radio stations have offered bridges to larger audiences. But they have been an element in our other cases too. Even Dare Jennings of Mambo – famously a university dropout – leant to some extent on educational infrastructure such as the Tin Sheds studios at the University of Sydney. Like public broadcasters and festivals, educational institutions are a site of constant tension between openness and closure in relations between fringe and mainstream. The momentum of the last twenty years has often appeared to be strongly on the side of openness, as in bids for institutional reform aligned with creative industries arguments (see e.g. Montgomery et al. 2021). However, the osmotic ecology of educational institutions depends equally on efforts to preserve degrees of closure, particularly by those resisting crude forms of vocationalism or the erasure of distinctions between culture and economy.

The paradox that needs to be grasped in recognizing the importance of these efforts is that it is in the interests even of business that there be an outside to business. We have seen many examples of this in the book, from the hot commercial properties that emerged from art school bands and student revues of the 1980s to breakout successes in games emerging from experimental student projects in the 2010s. A further striking games example is *Untitled Goose Game*, released in 2019 by independent Melbourne-based developer House House. Selling over a million copies in its first year (Moyse 2019), the game had creative roots not in a games development programme but in the School of Art at RMIT

University. As explained by one of the company's founders, Michael McMaster (2019), the value of this educational formation was not in transferring directly relevant vocational skills but in 'the slow development of taste'. The critical factor, as we have seen throughout *Fringe to Famous*, is close engagement with peers and intimate audiences. It is the 'ability to look at your own work with perspective and clarity, and to support the work of others, to engage in a wider community practice'. For creative work, McMaster suggests, the value of tertiary education is not so much, as the old adage has it, in teaching you 'how to think' as in teaching you 'how to care'.

Domesticating the digital

What role might online media play in the future evolution of relations between fringe and mainstream cultural production in Australia? What possibilities might they offer in the development of 'osmotic ecologies'? To pose these questions late in a conclusion risks drawing attention to what some readers may have seen as a significant absence in *Fringe to Famous*. As we conceded in the Introduction, the book has relatively little to say about the shifts in the cultural and media landscape that have occurred since the 1990s in response to digitization. We defended this decision there on the basis, first, of the value of a historical approach and, second, of increasing evidence that digital media have not transformed the cultural industries as radically as was earlier predicted, the implication being that lessons from the past may be more relevant in the present than might have been expected even a decade ago. In suggesting frameworks for the future, however, the digital is clearly a topic that is important to address.

A complication here is that an interest in digital media has often been entangled with anti-romantic ideas of the kind we have wanted to avoid. The most influential recent variant of these ideas – the creative industries arguments we have visited at various points throughout the book – has been strongly associated with work on digital media, to the point that the two have sometimes become effectively identified (e.g. Turner 2012: 83–121). Indeed, the major legacy of these arguments in Australia, at least in the academic arena, appears no longer to be in approaches to the cultural industries so much as in digital media studies. Examples include projects by erstwhile creative industries principals (Cunningham and Craig 2019; Hartley, Ibrus and Ojamaa 2021), the emergence of the Digital Media Research Centre as the major successor to creative industries research at Queensland University of Technology and the establishment of the ARC Centre of Excellence for Automated Decision-Making and Society – an initiative that has involved many of the same people and institutional DNA as the Centre of Excellence for Creative Industries and Innovation of the late 2000s.

As suggested by our comments above on the themes of 'globalization' and 'digitization', there are obvious reasons for an affinity between the anti-romanticism of creative industries and an interest in digital media. One of the most striking features of digital media during the first wave of reception in the 1990s and 2000s was their capacity to dissolve boundaries – not only between analogue media (the phenomenon that came to be known as 'convergence') and geographic territories ('globalization'), but also more generally between cultural, political and institutional forms that had developed within the analogue media system. It is a feature that resonated strongly with efforts during the same period to dent the authority of ideas of an outside to the economic and governmental logics of mainstream institutions. It becomes difficult, in this context, to distinguish between supposed objective properties of digital media and willed imaginings emerging from critical responses to the legacy of the counterculture.

Whether objectively determined or willed, the erasure of boundaries associated with digital media clearly answers the 'exposure' requirement for osmotic relations between fringe and mainstream. The energy and optimism of creative industries arguments at the turn of the millennium can be attributed in part to a recognition of their potential, still new at the time, to enable fresh hybrid formations, connecting sites of cultural and economic activity that would otherwise have been relatively separated. The growth of the internet was an important context, for example, for Leadbeater and Oakley's (1999) vision in *The Independents*, discussed in Chapter 4, of new kinds of integration between small creative enterprises and the mainstream economy. Where such digitally attuned arguments have been weaker, however, is in attending to the 'insulation' requirement. While it was often hoped in the early vertiginous period that general models for online interaction might be adapted from the intimate, participatory modes typical of small scenes (e.g. Jenkins 2008), the longer-term effect of boundary erasure has more often been to flatten distinctions between these modes and the economic and governmental logics of mainstream institutions.

If our findings in *Fringe to Famous* bear on these questions, it is in questioning the actual extent of boundary erasure associated with digital media, particularly as it concerns relations between fringe and mainstream. Our attempt to historicize anti-romantic arguments has brought into question the *desire* to refuse distinctions between fringe and mainstream, locating the context for that desire in a moment that has now passed. But we have also questioned the idea of erasure in more straightforward empirical terms. The most relevant case study here has been, again, the Freeplay Independent Games Festival. As we saw in Chapter 6, games have been particularly subject, as a 'digital first' case, to pressure on the distinction between fringe and mainstream. Presumption against the distinction has come not only from breezy, pro-business creative industries arguments, but also in a darker mode from critically formed arguments such as those of Hardt and Negri's *Empire* (2000). As Freeplay demonstrates, however, it is quite possible, even in a field organized around digital media, to construct spaces for values and practices that are distinct from those of mainstream institutions. The widespread insistence that such distinctions cannot be observed begins to appear in this context as little more than dogma.

A conclusion that could be drawn here is that digital media are better thought of as reshaping than fundamentally altering the cultural industries. It may be relevant here to recall the description by Fancy Boy principal Mike Nayna (Nayna & Conway 2015) in Chapter 4 of YouTube videos as the 'open mic' of television comedy. Such comparisons between new and old technologies are routine among creative practitioners, underlining the fact that it is not the technologies that are important so much as the functions they serve in organizing human relations – in this case between comedians and audiences. While the boundary dissolving functions of digital media are certainly striking, they are not unique: broadcasting and the printing press were hailed in their day as revolutionary and for not dissimilar reasons. At the same time, more attention should probably be paid to 'insulating' practices in digital media, from the careful nurturing of online co-creator groups to the role of moderators in screening out disruptive or unsympathetic 'blow-ins'.

To the extent that such practices have been recognized, it has often been in negative terms, as in debates from the early 2010s around 'filter bubbles' and 'echo chambers' (Pariser 2011). As Axel Bruns (2019: 50) has argued, moral panics about insularity in small online communities have largely been misplaced: there is 'simply no empirical evidence for these information cocoons in their absolute definition, particularly in a complex, multi-platform environment'. There is a further question, however, whether some degree of insulation between online communities is even necessarily a bad thing. As Bruns (2019: 50) puts it, 'selective exposure and homophily do exist; there would be no political parties, activist movements, interest communities, fan groups, sports clubs, or other social institutions without them'. This line of thinking could be brought together productively, we would suggest, with thinking about the cultural industries. We need to understand better how 'selective exposure' in online media enables similar functions to those, highly valued in more established cultural ecologies, of small venues, cafes, niche publications or specialist bookshops.

Such an approach could be seen aligning with wider moves to normalize or 'domesticate' digital media – to neutralize exceptionalist claims that have been made on their behalf and open them to understanding in more cultural or political terms. An example would be the suggestion by Australian lawyer, political activist and technology writer Lizzie O'Shea (2020: xix) that many of the questions they pose are not as new as often assumed, that 'technological questions we are confronting today often have a much longer history – one that predates the Internet, the web, and the computer itself'. Another, in a more scholarly mode, would be the work of Amanda Lotz on digital evolutions of television. As Lotz (2021: 888) suggests, the kinds of television that have emerged through online streaming services are a 'mix of sameness and difference'. The perspective is one, like O'Shea's, that opens a space for renewed attention to the cultural and political dimension of the creative industries, a dimension that has often been displaced by a systematic anti-romanticism in earlier approaches to digital media.

Pluralizing the political

Another kind of reader may have wished that we make more of the *political* dimension of relations between fringe and mainstream. This dimension has been central to much critical work on the questions we have considered in the book, from subculture theory of the 1970s to more recent writing on exploitative labour relations in the cultural industries. It is true that we have kept some distance from aspects of this tradition, particularly its tendency to dramatize differences between fringe and mainstream in ways that foreclose the possibility of hybridity. This does not mean, however, that we have ignored a cultural politics of subversion and critique in many of the fringe scenes examined. A key theme of our music, Mambo and comedy case studies was a carnivalesque destabilization of accepted norms. Our chapter on Indigenous film examined ways in which Indigenous artists have raised issues of dispossession, racism and economic disadvantage even as they have also reached out to mainstream audiences. And our account of Freeplay drew attention to the origins of the festival in a rejection of the cynicism and sexism of the studio-based games industry in the 1990s and early 2000s.

What we have sought to avoid therefore is not the political as such, but rather the capture of the political to ideas associated with revolution, particularly flat undifferentiated conceptions of mainstream institutions – conceptions that allow the options only of unquestioning acceptance or radical opposition. As we have argued throughout the book, these ideas have been widely internalized since the countercultural moment of the 1960s and 1970s, even by those who have since sought to reject them. The result has been a narrowing of political thinking in relation to the fringe. On the one hand, there have been those who have continued to look to the fringe as a source of revolutionary potential. As the real possibility of revolution has receded since the 1960s, this tendency has become more crypto-revolutionary than revolutionary, disavowing revolutionary aspirations even as it advances themes of exploitation and oppression in ways that can only incite them. On the other hand, there have been those who have more robustly rejected ideas of revolution, but in doing so also the political as such – seeking, like creative industries advocates and 'third way' centre-left parties, to substitute it with economic, managerial and technological discourses.

It may therefore be useful to summarize alternative senses of the political that can be found in our case studies. Six at least might be identified. The first is activism to expand the possibilities for culture-making for fringe artists outside the mainstream. This has involved imaginative campaigns, organization-building, and lobbying to find resources, training and spaces – both physical and mediated – for emerging artists and cultural practitioners. Examples of this kind of cultural politics from the 1980s include campaigns for access by those on the fringe to mainstream media such as Double J and Triple J, ABC Television, SBS and state and federal screen funding programmes. The expansion of the Triple J to the regions owed everything to grassroots community demand and alliances by reformers within ABC such as Andy Nehl with youth wings of the major political parties. More recent examples would be initiatives by Freeplay to gain support of public institutions for small experimental games or the campaign by Save Live Australian Music to resist threats to Melbourne's small music venues from changes to liquor licensing regulations (Homan 2016). Advancing access for emerging artists has been complemented by campaigns for law reform and funding initiatives promoting more diverse representation within fringe and popular arts, encouraging participation and creative control for female, Indigenous, regional, non-Anglo-Celtic, LGBTIQ and others who have lacked access to the resources of the mainstream.

A second form of cultural politics centres around generational games of the kind analysed by Bourdieu. Such strategies have often been directed as much at the erstwhile avant-garde as the mainstream – for example, in punk's mockery of hippies as well as commercial music grandees. The activism around resources and access described above is often closely related to this game of recognition and competition within the cultural field. The response of avant-gardes to 'old guards' subverts the inevitable entrenchments of elites, experimental or otherwise, in ways that have long been important to cultural renewal (Moore 2012). A recent Australian example is the way Bloods lead singer Marihuzka Cornelius, a Panamanian child refugee turned punk, has challenged the traditional cultural hierarchies of the Anglo old boy ascendancy in rock 'n' roll, becoming in 2020 the face of the Sydney Festival. Bourdieu's analysis of these generational games points out the way they can help emerging players attract new audiences and grow cultural and economic capital, while renovating art within a field of market relations.

A third form of cultural politics – also related to emerging aesthetics and subject matter – has been activism to resist limitations on the making, distribution and consumption of culture, particularly government censorship of text, screen, music or digital games content. Notwithstanding the liberalization of Australia's cultural classification laws from the early 1970s, remaining state penalties for obscenity have been joined by anti-terrorist, racial vilification and other laws regulating media content, especially online. This politics has been most ambitious and intense when about upscaling experimental or risky, sometimes confronting ideas and aesthetics from the field of restricted production to mass audiences. It has involved taking on authority and established production cultures and leaders within public and private corporations and has required deft organizational politics by animateurs working within mainstream institutions (Nehl 2015). An example is the defence of The Chaser following their APEC summit stunt by ABC Arts and Entertainment commissioning editor Courtney Gibson and series producer Andy Nehl.

A fourth form of cultural politics has been organized around labour conditions in the cultural industries. Campaigns in this area have addressed issues such as wage rates, Australian content quotas, copyright recognition for Indigenous artists and a creative commons licence. The key agents have generally been artists' unions such as the Media, Entertainment and Arts Alliance and artists' collectives, who have organized, lobbied, agitated and collectively bargained to improve training, working conditions, pay and career paths of artists (Eltham and Pennington 2021).

A fifth and very visible type of cultural politics is the use of art to advance other non-art-making causes such as trade unionism, women's rights, environmental and anti-nuclear movements, anti-racism, and activism for Aboriginal land rights and sovereignty. Examples of this agit-prop approach from music include the band Midnight Oil, whose songs criticized US imperialism, environmental destruction and nuclear proliferation, lead singer Peter Garrett going on to run as a Senator for the Nuclear Disarmament Party and becoming president of the Australian Conservation Foundation and serving on the board of Greenpeace. Midnight Oil and others such as singer-songwriter Paul Kelly have also used their music to advocate on Indigenous issues, an advocacy that has gained credibility from enduring collaborations with Indigenous musicians such as Yothu Yindi and Kev Carmody. Even one of our more playful and commercially oriented case studies, Mambo, had a strong line in political artwork in their clothing designs, including a number of Hawaiian shirts protesting against French nuclear testing in the Pacific.

Finally, there is a form of cultural politics around audiences, one that has sought to involve them more fully as participants in the making of art. This has overlapped with activism around access to the means for culture-making, but the focus here has been more on the distribution of creative tools, skills and channels of distribution to ordinary people and marginalized communities, whether working class suburbanites, the long-term unemployed, people with disabilities or regional and remote Indigenous communities. It has been organized around a social democratic vision that deliberately blurs the line between artists and audiences, recognizing the contributions of the latter as peers and fans. This form of politics has antecedents in Australia in the radical nationalist literary projects of the late nineteenth century and, in the twentieth century, in the Arts and Crafts movement, the Communist Party's popular front in art, theatre and documentary, and in the Whitlam Labor Government's establishment of community radio (Moore 2012; 2020). A commitment to audience creativity has inspired many of the arts practitioners, activists and animateurs we interviewed for *Fringe to Famous*.

Ten possibilities for policy

As indicated above in relation to the affirmation of the fringe, we do not wish to limit our conclusions in *Fringe to Famous* to questions of government policy. Some of the most creative thinking around osmotic ecologies, for example, is to be found in business and community organizations such as independent production houses and festivals. We hope that lessons drawn from our case studies about the value of this thinking might feed back into these contexts. However, government clearly plays a major role in setting directions that enable – or in some cases disable – the formation of cultures and the development of cultural industries. There is also a certain timeliness in turning at the end to the role that government might play. At the time of writing, as mentioned above, a newly elected Labor government has launched a new national cultural policy. Titled *Revive* (Australian Government 2023), the policy is a five-year reset to be evaluated in three years, a roadmap anticipating further reform (Westwood 2023).

There is much in this new policy direction that could be seen as aligning with the 'post creative industries' perspective we have been outlining above. *Revive* is not indifferent to the economic value of the arts, but also pointedly affirms the importance of other values. This rebalancing was explicit in an introductory speech by Prime Minister Anthony Albanese at the launch of the policy:

> The arts are an important part of our economy. But it's also important, I think, to lift yourself above the usual economic debate. This is about our soul. This is about our identity. It is so important because it's about … being able to express ourselves. It is literally through the arts that we build our identity as a nation and a people.
>
> (Albanese 2023)

This shift in emphasis is reflected in the policy itself in a renewed focus on infrastructure and institutions, a reorientation to small- and medium-sized organizations and an attention to art forms, such as contemporary music, in which there is broad-based participation beyond elite institutions. At the same time, the shift in direction also remains exploratory. It may be useful, in this context, to sketch out some ideas proceeding from our analysis in *Fringe to Famous*. What might a cultural policy 'after the creative industries' look like?

The first and most obvious point is that it would *be* a cultural policy, not simply an industry development policy – one that recognizes the independence of culture from economic imperatives such as job creation or the generation of wealth. This aligns with increasing moves within social democratic parties, including in Australia, to rebalance policy from the narrowly market-based focus of recent decades to affirm the importance of value formation in other spheres (e.g. Chalmers 2023). It might also be well-suited to times of straitened public finances. As can be seen in a number of our case studies, the financial support needed by fringe arts practitioners is often quite small. An example is the figure quoted by Alex Bruce in Chapter 6 – just $10,000 – for the development of his experimental game *Antichamber*. As cases such as Bruce's make clear, the emphasis on dollar values within the creative industries paradigm has often led to poorly designed initiatives, leading governments to behave towards the arts somewhat in the manner of disengaged career-obsessed parents seeking to demonstrate their love for their children with expensive but inappropriate gifts.

A rebalancing towards specifically cultural values aligns with recent contributions to policy development from a left culturalist perspective. An example is a report for the Tasmanian government by Justin O'Connor on the cultural and creative sector in Australia's smallest state. While the report is a commissioned piece of work within a loose creative industries framework, O'Connor takes the opportunity to advocate openly for a recognition of non-economic values:

> Many people and communities, both national and global, are finding that economic growth, as expressed by myriad aggregated economic indicators, has simply not made their lives any easier or more secure or more meaningful. The things they value, the qualities of their lives do not seem to appear in cost-benefit models.
>
> (2018: 15)

However, the approach we are suggesting differs from left culturalism in seeing relations between the cultural and economic in more positive terms. O'Connor (2018: 10) admits that 'growing the cultural sector can be a win-win, expanding cultural activity and increasing the availability and sustainability of cultural employment', but this has more the character of a grudging concession than a positive conceptualization of the field. Our argument in *Fringe to Famous* has been that the engagement by artists with the field of large-scale production should be seen as more than a pragmatic acceptance of utilitarian logics. In contemporary market-based societies such as Australia, it can also be integral to the making of art itself.

Based on these general principles, we offer ten suggestions here for cultural policy in Australia, some of which might also be relevant to other liberal democracies. The first is the provision of institutional support for 'sheltered spaces', not immediately subject to the pressures of the market or strict managerial accounting. Such spaces, in which artists can experiment and begin to engage with peers and intimate audiences, are crucial at the formative stage where musicians, designers, comedy makers, performers and games developers are developing a distinctive voice or style. An example of such spaces in our case studies was the inner Melbourne student and fringe performance scene that nurtured emerging comedians in the 1980s. Relevant initiatives for the present might include a renewal of infrastructure in educational institutions; support for performance venues in pubs and small theatres, including reforms to liquor licensing and gambling regulation that enable such venues to flourish; community media policies building on the successes of community FM radio and Indigenous television, updating them for the internet age; and small grants to support emerging risky festivals, as distinct from the funding streams to large established institutions.

A second suggestion – balancing out the other side of osmotic ecologies – is support for exchange between fringe creative communities and institutions with the resources to work at scale. Successful models from broadcasting include SBS Independent, the ABC TV Indigenous Programs Unit, Triple J's *Unearthed* and, more recently, *Black Comedy* and Fresh Blood in television comedy. There would be value in a thorough Commonwealth review of structures and initiatives of the last few decades that have enabled exchange between the fringe and mainstream, with a view to updating them for the present. Such a review would go beyond institutional arrangements to the level of actual practices. For example, SBS Independent did more than simply expose fringe performers to wider audiences; it more actively promoted hybridization by judiciously pairing emerging artists with established professionals.

A third suggestion is a revitalization of small grants for experimental projects. The long-term benefits of such grants are often forgotten. An important seedbed for the renaissance of Australian film in the 1970s, for example, was the Experimental Film Fund set up at the beginning of the decade by the

Gorton Liberal-Country Party government (French and Poole 2011; Moore 2012). Support for small experimental projects has been a particular casualty of creative industries approaches to cultural policy. An example, discussed in Chapter 6, is VicScreen's practice of extending funds for games development only to established businesses – a practice, as Paul Callaghan (2014) pointed out, that has closed off a key source of new creative ideas. A concrete proposal at state level, therefore, would be to rebalance criteria used in the distribution of such funds from their immediate business case to their cultural contribution.

A fourth suggestion is policies to ensure that publicly funded creative work is showcased through media distribution. Our case studies in *Fringe to Famous* demonstrate a need for closer alignment between media and cultural policy. Australia's public service broadcasters have provided an important interface between fringe art and mass media audiences, often in partnership with non-government organizations such as festivals. Yet media and cultural policy remain separated – often siloed, as at present, in different government departments. A concrete policy proposal would be to mandate that any film receiving Screen Australia funding and the producer tax offset be made available, with appropriate compensation, on the free-to-air or streaming services of the ABC or SBS. A further extension would be to institute a right for Commonwealth-funded projects in other art forms – from comedy to Indigenous performance and digital games – to pitch an idea to one or other of the public service broadcasters.

A fifth suggestion is the broadening of Australian content quotas to all media, including streaming services. While twentieth-century activism saw the introduction of quotas for broadcast media, the multinational streaming platforms are not currently required to invest in local content, whether in music, comedy, drama, documentary or games. At the same time, the commercial broadcasters have used the COVID-19 pandemic as cover to weaken quotas. While the *Revive* policy has made clear it will introduce still to be determined quotas for streaming services, the principle could be extended much further. The ABC is exempt from quotas as a public broadcaster and remains heavily dependent, following a decade of funding parsimony, on a diminishing range of programming from the BBC. The possibility of introducing Australian content quotas for other cultural institutions, such as live theatre and festivals, might also be explored. Higher Australian content quotas would help to stimulate hybridization between fringe and mainstream production, particularly if calibrated to ensure diversity, with incentives to source content from emerging production teams.

A sixth suggestion is to leverage outsourcing of production to encourage dialogue between publicly funded institutions and fringe scenes. As we saw in our comedy and Indigenous film cases, small production houses play a vital role in such dialogue, buffering against risk-averse public sector management and preserving spaces for creativity. These businesses have been supported in the screen industry by policies managed by Screen Australia such as the Producer Equity Program (PEP) for low-budget documentaries and the Producer Offset tax concession for screen projects exceeding half a million dollars. However, these policies could be better designed to enable risk-taking and facilitate entry by small experimental creative teams. The Producer Offset, particularly, has often been vitiated by excessive layers of bureaucratic control and a competitive 'hunger games' application process that assumes an established business identity. A model sometimes cited among small-screen producers is Ireland's Section 481 tax concessions. The principle of the PEP and Producer Offset could also be extended to other art forms, such as games development and independent record labels. We would also advocate for a review of the criteria for pre-sale co-production commissioning by the public broadcasters to correct a tendency to favour large internationally affiliated production companies (Lowenstein 2016) and direct more of the benefit to emerging creative communities.

A seventh suggestion is to support Indigenous production for limited audiences, particularly audiences who are themselves Indigenous, as well as for the mainstream. This dual focus may sound contradictory, but First Nations contributions to Australian arts and culture over the last forty years provide an almost textbook example of the importance of maintaining such a tension. The international breakout by directors such as Warwick Thornton in the early 2000s drew *both* on twenty years of experimentation in screen production in remote Indigenous communities *and* on policy initiatives designed to take Indigenous perspectives to mainstream audiences. It is also worth referencing the Indigenous Programs unit in the ABC in the 1980s and 1990s and the Indigenous Branch at the Australian Film Institute which functioned, as Sally Riley (2017) has suggested, as a 'mini film school'.

An eighth suggestion is to develop a publicly funded cultural commons for creative practitioners. A concrete proposal here would be for the two public broadcasters to provide a clearing house through their streaming services ABC iView and SBS on Demand, enabling circulation from diverse creative communities into mainstream Australian popular culture. A 'public streaming commons' could play a similar role to Triple J's *Unearthed* and ABC TV's *Rage* in relation to independent music, providing a space where cultural producers can upload pilots, receive feedback and build a relation with audiences. This would also encourage the ABC and SBS to embrace the post-broadcast media environment, shedding outdated ideas of scarce spectrum and matching the plenty of YouTube with a richer and more varied palette of contemporary culture.

A ninth suggestion is to give greater attention to audience contributions to the making of art. As we have remarked above, cultural policy has tended to focus on 'the' artist, in the singular, overlooking the extent to which artists depend on interactions with peers and audiences. We would advocate, by contrast, that the audience be thought of not only as an endpoint or consumer of cultural 'products' but as an active participant in meaning making. The public broadcasters could again play a major role here. Rather than thinking of the ABC and SBS as distributing culture to consumers, they might be thought of rather as 'gathering' audience inputs and encouraging dialogue and exchange. Precedents can be found for this in audience-centred programmes such as the *Argonauts*, *Beatbox*, *Race around the World* and Triple J's *Unearthed*. The digital media transition offers opportunities to deepen and extend this general approach, completing a shift from the paternalist Reithian tradition inherited from the BBC to a more democratic conception of culture as created by people.

A tenth and final suggestion is to reinvigorate art schools in vocational training. Post-school education has played a generative role not only in imparting skills in graphic design, drama, film and screen, but also in nurturing aesthetic ambition. Much of the stimulus here has been extra-curricular, in opportunities to write and perform comedy, start a band, put together a student newspaper, shoot a video clip, edit zines or design posters. Commencing in the late 1970s, art schools traditionally aligned with Technical and Further Education (TAFE) transitioned to university status, conferring bachelor's, master's and PhD degrees where once diplomas had sufficed. While art schools have engaged with new practices, tools and processes (especially the digital), a creeping credentialism, coupled with an industry-compliant approach to professional practice training, has damped down the hot house social conditions for collaboration identified by Frith and Horne. This makes the system ill-suited to training in the hybridized practices of experimentation and engagement with cultural industries that we have identified in equivalent tertiary education in games and music. A narrow vocationalism leaves little space for the extracurricular activities and bohemian exchange that enabled students to develop an embodied identity as artists. A reinstatement of art school-type institutions in suburbs and regional centres across Australia would improve democratic cultural participation across exclusionary barriers of class, geography, ethnicity and Indigeneity, broadening not only the skills but also the 'techniques of the self' required for careers in culture making.

*****

In making these latter suggestions, we have been inspired in part by the social democratic vision of the late veteran Australian art historian Bernard Smith, particularly as outlined in criticisms during the 1970s of what he saw as the elitist approach of the Whitlam government to cultural education and training. Smith (1988) argued that too high a proportion of spending on the arts goes to the apex of the pyramid – to finishing schools such as the National Institute for Dramatic Art (NIDA) and the Australian Film, Television and Radio School (AFTRS) – leaving too little for the grassroots. Adopting a sporting analogy, he observed that the great Australian cricketers and swimmers have emerged from a robust participation of all children in school and local sport. An enthusiast for William Morris with a Marxist take on the Arts and Crafts movement, Smith believed that we are all innately artists. Pointing out that most young children love to draw, sing, dance and tell jokes, he argued that arts policy should build a base of democratic creative culture, starting with the public education system.

This democratic ambition shares much with the post-war British art school, which in the late twentieth century fostered the hybrid bohemian-egalitarian, public-commercial, participatory culture described by Frith and Horne. Aspects of this tradition have been kept alive over the past twenty years in democratic visions for digital media such as Axel Bruns' (2008) concept of the 'produser' or Henry Jenkins' (2008) work on 'convergence culture' and fan-made transmedia. At the same time, these recent adaptations of ideas of participation have often been allowed to rest on a narrow technological premise. As we have seen in *Fringe to Famous*, a blurring of the lines between artists and audiences is not specific to digital media but has been as much a feature of small scenes associated with broadcasting, print, recorded music and cinema. The critical factors are not technological, but institutional, political and historical. For governments, the most effective contribution that can be made in realizing the value of participation is to support structures, venues and media that enable audience involvement in the making of art. As Smith (1988: 7) observed, '[i]f your object is excellence, you begin with a broad base: elitism fails because it insists upon a narrow base, its apex fails to reach the limits of the possible'.

References

7:30 Report (2001), [TV programme], ABC-TV, 31 May.

Acropolis Now (1989–92), [TV series], Crawford Productions.

Adam Hills Tonight (2011–13), [TV series], ABC.

After Dark (1982–5), [TV series], Seven Network.

Albanese, A. (2023), Speech at the launch of the National Cultural Policy – Revive, Esplanade Hotel, St Kilda, 30 January. Full transcript available at https://www.pm.gov.au/media/launch-national-cultural-policy.

Album of the Year (2023), Pitchfork Highest Rated Garage Punk bands of All Time. Available online: https://www.albumoftheyear.org/genre/92-garage-punk/all/pitchfork/ (accessed 1 February 2023).

Albury, K. (1999), 'Spaceship Triple J: Making the National Youth Network', *Media International Australia*, 91: 55–66.

Althusser, L. (1971), 'Ideology and Ideological State Apparatuses' in L. Althusser, *Lenin and Philosophy and Other Essays*, trans. B. Brewster, 85–126, New York: Monthly Review Press.

Alvin Purple (1973), [Film] Dir. Tim Burstall, Australia: Hexagon Productions.

American Bandstand (1952–89), [TV series], WFIL-TV/Dick Clark Productions.

Animal Kingdom (2010), [Film] Dir. David Michôd, Australia: Porchlight Films.

Anthropy, A. (2012), *Rise of the Videogame Zinesters*, New York: Seven Stories Press.

Apperley, T.T. (2008), 'Video Games in Australia', in M.J.P. Wolf (ed.), *The Video Game Explosion*, 223–8, Westport, CT: Greenwood Press.

Arnold, G. (1997), *Kiss This: Punk in the Present Tense*, New York: St Martin's Griffin.

Askew, K. (2003), 'Hill Street Blues', *Sydney Morning Herald*, 29 March: 73.

Australian Film Commission (1995), *Annual Report 1994–1995*, Canberra: Commonwealth of Australia.

Australian Film Commission (2007), *Dreaming in Motion: Celebrating Australia's Indigenous Filmmakers*, Sydney: Australian Film Commission.

Australian Government (2023), *Revive: A Place for Every Story, a Story for Every Place – Australia's Cultural Policy for the Next Five Years*, Canberra: Commonwealth of Australia.

Autoluminescent: Roland S. Howard (2011), [Documentary film] Dir. Richard Lowenstein, Australia: Ghost Pictures.

Backroads (1977), [Film] Dir. Phillip Noyce, Australia: Backroads Productions.

Baker, G.A. and S. Coupe (1980), *The New Music*, Sydney: Bay Books.

Baker, N. (2019), '"Massive backwards step": Australia to no longer have a federal arts department', *SBS News*, 5 December. Available online: https://www.sbs.com.au/news/article/massive-backwards-step-australia-to-no-longer-have-a-federal-arts-department/1d19c85na (accessed 11 December 2022).

Banks, J., and S. Cunningham (2016a), 'Games Production in Australia: Adapting to Precariousness', in M. Curtin and K. Sanson (eds), *Precarious Creativity: Global Media, Local Labor*, 186–99, Berkeley: University of California Press.

Banks, J., and S. Cunningham (2016b), 'Creative Destruction in the Australian Videogames Industry', *Media International Australia*, 160: 127–39.

Banks, M., and D. Hesmondhalgh (2009), 'Looking for Work in Creative Industries Policy', *International Journal of Cultural Policy*, 15(4): 415–30.

Barry McKenzie Holds His Own (1974), [Film] Dir. Bruce Beresford, Australia: Reg Grundy Productions.

Beatbox (1985–7), [TV series], ABC.

Becker, H. (1982), *Art Worlds*, Berkeley: University of California Press.

BeDevil (1993), [Film] Dir. Tracey Moffatt, Australia: Ronin Films.

Beneath Clouds (2002), [Film] Dir. Ivan Sen, Australia: Autumn Films.

Benjamin, W. (1981), *Walter Benjamin, or, Towards a Revolutionary Criticism*, London: New Left Books.

Bennett, A. and I. Rogers (2016), *Popular Music Scenes and Cultural Memory*, London: Palgrave Macmillan.

Bennett, J. (2015), 'The Utopia of Independent Media', in J. Bennett and N. Strange (eds), *Media Independence: Working with Freedom or Working for Free?*, 1–28, New York: Routledge.

Bennett, J., and N. Strange, eds (2015), *Media Independence: Working with Freedom or Working for Free?*, New York: Routledge.

Bennett, T. (1981), *Popular Culture: Themes and Issues*, Milton Keynes: Open University Press.

Bennett, T. (1992), 'Putting Policy into Cultural Studies', in L. Grossberg, C. Nelson, and P. Treichler (eds), *Cultural Studies*, 23–33, New York: Routledge.

Bennett, T. (1998), *Culture: A Reformer's Science*, St Leonards, NSW: Allen & Unwin.

Berry, J. (2013), 'A Uniform Approach? Designing Australian National Identity at the Sydney 2000 Olympic Games', *Journal of Design History*, 26(1): 86–103.

Bianchini, F. (1987), 'GLC-RIP: Cultural Policies in London 1981–1986', *New Formations,* 1(1): 103–17.

Billington, M. (2002), 'Why I Hate the Fringe', *The Guardian*, 25 July. Available online: https://www.theguardian.com/culture/2002/jul/25/artsfeatures.edinburghfestival20021 (Accessed 30 August 2022).

Black Comedy (2014–20), [TV series], Scarlett Pictures/ABC.

Blah, Blah, Blah (1988), [TV series], ABC.

Blunt, B. (2001), *Blunt: A Biased History of Australian Rock*, Northcote: Prowling Tiger Press.

Bodey, M. (2010), 'Our Mob', *Weekend Australian*, 2 January: 11.

Bodey, M. (2011), 'Toomelah, a Step on Director's Road Back', *The Australian*, 23 November: 15.

Bogan Hunters (2014), [TV series], Antichocko Productions.

Bohemian Rhapsody: Rebels of Australian Culture (1996), [TV documentary] Dir. Tony Moore, Australia: ABC.

Boland, M. (2009), 'Rabbit-Proof Fence Praised as Trailblazer', *Weekend Australian*, 14 December: 6.

Bourdieu, P. (1980), 'The Production of Belief: Contribution to an Economy of Symbolic Goods', trans. R. Nice, *Media, Culture and Society*, 2(3): 261–93.

Bourdieu, P. (1984), *Distinction: A Social Critique of the Judgement of Taste*, trans. R. Nice, London: Routledge.

Bourdieu, P. (1993), *The Field of Cultural Production: Essays on Art and Literature*, ed. R. Johnson, trans. C. Du Verlie, Cambridge: Polity.

Bourdieu, P. (1995), *The Rules of Art: Genesis and Structure of the Literary Field*, trans. S. Emanuel, Stanford: Stanford University Press.

Bowen, C. (2015), *The Money Men: Australia's Twelve Most Notable Treasurers*, Carlton, Vic.: Melbourne University Press.

Bracewell, M. (1997), *England Is Mine: Pop Life in Albion from Wilde to Goldie*, London: Faber & Faber.

Bran Nue Dae (2009), [Film] Dir. Rachel Perkins, Australia: Robyn Kershaw Productions/Mayfan.

Breen, M. (1986), 'Popular Music: The Bands and the Media', *Arena* 74(1): 12–16.

Breen, M. (1999), *Rock Dogs: Politics and the Australian Music Industry*, Annandale, NSW: Pluto Press.

Brown, W. (2015), *Undoing the Demos: Neoliberalism's Stealth Revolution*, New York: Zone Books.

Bruce, A. (2015), Interview with Mark Gibson, Melbourne, 16 February.

Bruns, A. (2008), *Blogs, Wikipedia, Second Life and Beyond: From Production to Produsage*, New York: Peter Lang.

Bruns, A. (2019), *Are Filter Bubbles Real?*, Cambridge: Polity.

Buchanan, R. (1994), 'Where It's Happenin'', *The Age*, Saturday Extra supplement, 2 April: 14.

Buckmaster, L. (2009), 'Aussie Cinema: Doom and Gloom or Bold and Blooming?', *Crikey*, 31 August. Available online: http://blogs.crikey.com.au/cinetology/2009/08/31/aussie-cinema-doom-and-gloom-or-bold-and-blooming (accessed 2 November 2018).

Burchill, J. and T. Parsons (1978), *The Boy Looked at Johnny: The Obituary of Rock and Roll*, London: Pluto Press.

Burgess, J., K. Albury, A. McCosker and R. Wilken (2022), *Everyday Data Cultures*, Cambridge: Polity.

Burke, P. (2021), *Tear Down the Walls: White Radicalism and Black Power in 1960s Rock*, Chicago: University of Chicago Press.

Burke, T. (2022), 'Let's Get This Show on the Road: Developing National Cultural Policy', media release, 2 August. Available online: https://minister.infrastructure.gov.au/burke/media-release/lets-get-show-road-developing-national-cultural-policy (accessed 18 December 2022).

Burke, T. (2023), 'National Cultural Policy Launch – The Esplanade Hotel, Melbourne', speech transcript, 30 January. Available online: https://minister.infrastructure.gov.au/burke/speech/national-cultural-policy-launch-esplanade-hotel-melbourne (accessed 7 February 2023).

Butler, R. (2016), Interview with Tony Moore and Mark Gibson, 20 January.

Callaghan, P. (2014), Interview with Mark Gibson, 10 October.

Cameron, D. (1992), 'The Mambo Kings', *Sydney Morning Herald*, 12 December: 45.

Caves, R.E. (2002), *Creative Industries: Contracts between Art and Commerce*, Cambridge, MA: Harvard University Press.

Chalmers, J. (2023), 'Capitalism after the Crises', *The Monthly*, February. Available online: https://www.themonthly.com.au/issue/2023/february/jim-chalmers/capitalism-after-crises (accessed 3 February 2023).

Champagne, P. (2005), 'The "Double Dependency": The Journalistic Field between Politics and Markets', in R. Benson and E. Neveu (eds), *Bourdieu and the Journalistic Field*, 48–63, Cambridge: Polity Press.

Chau, D. (2017), 'Billabong Posts $77m Loss on Revenue Wipe-Out'. Available online: http://www.abc.net.au/news/2017-08-30/billabong-posts-77-million-loss/8855378 (accessed 5 August 2018).

Chellew, P. (2014), Interview with Chris McAuliffe, 16 July.

Chessell, J. (2003), 'Up in the Air: How Skate Brothers Fell Out of Fashion', *The Age*, 11 January: 7.

Chesterfield-Evans, J. (1987), 'Mambo Rides a Wave of Success', *Australian Financial Review*, 30 December: 12.

Christie, J. and A. Harris (2013), 'The Sapphires' Stars Sparkle at US Premiere', *Daily Telegraph*, 15 March: 43.

Cleverman (2016–17), [TV series], Goalpost Pictures/Pukeko Pictures/ABC.

Collins, L. (1997), 'Clobbering the Surf Set', *Hobart Mercury*, 29 November: 40.

Connell, R.W., D. Ashenden, S. Kessler and G. Dowsett (1982), *Making the Difference: Schools, Families and Social Division*, Sydney: Allen & Unwin.

Conway, M. (2015), Interview with Mark Gibson, 1 November.

Coombs, A. (1996), *Sex and Anarchy: The Life and Death of the Sydney Push*, Sydney: Viking.

Cornelius, M. (2015), Interview with Tony Moore, 26 June.

Corris, P., K. Bail, L. Jaivin, R. Mombasssa, and L. Graham (1993), 'The Rolling Stone Interview – Paul Keating', *Rolling Stone*, Australian Edition, March (481): 38–47.

Cosgrove, S. (2006), 'Clothing Design: My Experience', *Sydney Morning Herald*, 5 July: 11.

Costikyan, G. (2005), 'Death to the Games Industry: Part I, Dungeons and Dollars', *The Escapist*. Available online: http://www.escapistmagazine.com/articles/view/video-games/issues/issue_8/50-Death-to-the-Games-Industry-Part-I (accessed 30 August 2022).

Countdown (1974–87), [TV series], ABC.

Coupe, S. (2015), *Gudinski: The Godfather of Australian Rock'n'Roll*, Sydney: Hachette.

Craik, J. (2009), 'Is Australian Fashion and Dress Distinctively Australian?', *Fashion Theory* 13(4): 409–41.

Crocodile Dundee (1986), [Film] Dir. Peter Faiman, Australia: Rimfire Films.

Cunningham, S. (1991), *Featuring Australia: The Cinema of Charles Chauvel*, Sydney: Allen & Unwin.

Cunningham, S. (1992), *Framing Culture: Criticism and Policy in Australia*, Sydney: Allen & Unwin.

Cunningham, S. (2002), 'From Cultural to Creative Industries', *Media International Australia* 102(1): 54–65.

Cunningham, S. (2004), 'The Creative Industries after Cultural Policy: A Genealogy and Some Possible Preferred Futures', *International Journal of Cultural Studies*, 7(1): 105–15.

Cunningham, S. (2008), 'Creative Destruction: Lessons for Science and Innovation Policy from the Rise of the Creative Industries', *Cultural Science*, 1(1): 1–5.

Cunningham, S., and D. Craig (2019), *Social Media Entertainment: The New Intersection of Hollywood and Silicon Valley*, New York: New York University Press.

Cunningham, S., T. Cutler, G. Hearn, M. Ryan, and M. Keane (2004), 'An Innovation Agenda for the Creative Industries: Where Is the R&D?', *Media International Australia* 112(1): 174–85.

Dancing in the Street (1997), [TV documentary series], BBC.

Davies, W. (2015), *The Limits of Neoliberalism: Authority, Sovereignty and the Logic of Competition*, London: Sage.

Davis, T. (2014), 'Locating The Sapphires: Transnational and Cross-Cultural Dimensions of an Australian Indigenous Musical Film', *Continuum*, 28(5): 594–604.

Davis, T. (2017), 'Australian Indigenous Screen in the 2000s: Crossing into the Mainstream', in M.D. Ryan and B. Goldsmith (eds), *Australian Screen in the 2000s*, 231–60, Cham, Switzerland: Palgrave Macmillan.

DCA (1994), *Creative Nation: Commonwealth Cultural Policy*, Canberra: Department of Communication and the Arts, Commonwealth of Australia.

DCMS (1998), *Creative Industries Mapping Document 1998*, London: Department of Culture, Media and Sport.

Deadwood (2004–2006), [TV series], Red Board Productions/Roscoe Productions/HBO/Paramount Network Television.

Dempster, Q. (2011), 'Shutting Down ABCTV Production', *News+Views*, Newsletter of the Friends of the ABC (Vic) Inc., Spring (37): 1.

Dent, N. (2011), 'Drama Makes a Reel-Life Horror Story', *Sunday Telegraph*, 27 November: 123.

Denton, A. (2014), Interview with Tony Moore and Mark Gibson, 31 October.

Docker, J. (1988), 'In Defence of Popular TV: Carnivalesque v. Left Pessimism', *Continuum*, 1(2): 83–99.

Dogs in Space (1986), [Film] Dir. Richard Lowenstein, Australia: Central Park Films/ Ghost Pictures.

Dolgopolov, G. (2014), 'Beyond Black and White: Indigenous Cinema and the Mainstream', *Metro: Media & Education Magazine* (181): 78–83.

Don's Party (1976), [Film] Dir. Bruce Beresford, Australia: Double Head.

Donovan, T.G. with B.T. Lorraine (2002), *Media Ethics, an Aboriginal Film and the Australian Film Commission*, New York: Writers Club Press.

Double the Fist (2004–8), [TV series], ABC.

Dow, S. (2009), 'Finding Salvation in Film', *Sun Herald*, 26 April: 8.

Downes, O. (2011), 'Real Life on the Edge', *RealTime*, 104, August–September: 35.

Downie, S. (2002), 'Brothers' Globe Has Darkstar', *Daily Telegraph*, 21 June: 96.

Dreamland (2009), [Film] Dir. Ivan Sen, Australia: Bunya Productions.

Driving Miss Daisy (1989), [Film] Dir. Bruce Beresford, USA: The Zanuck Company.

Drugay, A. (1994), 'Hungry For Hot Labels', *Sydney Morning Herald*, Metro supplement, 18 November: 3.

Dupont, A. (2022), 'The Second Age of Globalisation Is Beginning to Buckle', *The Lowy Institute*, 11 May. Available online: https://www.lowyinstitute.org/publications/ second-age-globalisation-beginning-buckle(accessed 16 December 2022).

Dyer-Witheford, N., and G. de Peuter (2006), '"EA Spouse" and the Crisis of Video Game Labour: Enjoyment, Exclusion, Exploitation, Exodus', *Canadian Journal of Communication*, 31(3): 599–617.

Dyer-Witheford, N., and G. de Peuter (2009), *Games of Empire: Global Capitalism and Videogames*, Minneapolis: University of Minnesota Press.

Eagleton, T. (1981), *Walter Benjamin: Or, Towards a Revolutionary Criticism*, London: Verso.

Eco, U. (1985), *Reflections on the Name of the Rose*, trans. W. Weaver, London: Secker & Warburg.

Edwards, R. (2009), 'Samson & Delilah', *Variety*, 11–17 May: 90.

Elder, B., and J. Wales (1984), *Radio with Pictures! The History of Double Jay AM and JJJ FM*, Sydney: Hale and Iremonger.

Eltham, B. (2015), 'Major Arts Companies Throw Little Guys under the Bus after Brandis' Shake-Up', *Crikey*, 29 May. Available online: https://www.crikey.com. au/2015/05/29/major-arts-companies-throw-little-guys-under-the-bus-after-brandis-shake-up/ (accessed 11 December 2022).

Eltham, B. and A. Pennington (2021), *Creativity in Crisis: Rebooting Australia's Arts and Entertainment Sector after COVID*, Canberra: The Centre for Future Work. Available online: https://australiainstitute.org.au/wp-content/uploads/2021/07/Creativity_in_Crisis-_Rebooting_Australias_Arts___Entertainment_Sector_-_FINAL_-_26_July.pdf (accessed 6 February 2023).

Fashion United (2018), 'Fashion Industry Statistics Australia'. Available online: https://au.fashionunited.com/fashion-industry-statistics-australia (accessed 5 August 2018).

Fast Forward (1989–92), [TV series], Artist Services/Seven Network.

Faulkner, D. (2018), Interview with Tony Moore, 21 February.

Fenech, P. (2014), Interview with Tony Moore and Mark Gibson, 30 October.

Fenton, A. (2010), 'Broome with a View of Life Minus Gloom', *Daily Telegraph*, 7 January: 27.

Fidler, R. (2016), Interview with Tony Moore, 2 May.

Fielke, G. (2016), 'Terry Australis', *The Saturday Paper* (131), 22–8 October. Available online: https://www.thesaturdaypaper.com.au/2016/10/22/melbourne-dolewave-band-terry/14770548003872 (accessed 25 June 2018).

First Australians (2008), [TV documentary series], Blackfella Films/First Nation Films.

First Contact (2014–16), [TV series] Blackfella Films.

Flashez (1976–7), [TV series], ABC.

Flew, T. (2012), *The Creative Industries: Culture and Policy*, London: Sage.

Foley, M. (2017), 'New Arcade Proves Games Are Serious Business, Press Release – Minister for Creative Industries', Government of Victoria, 16 August. Available online: https://www.premier.vic.gov.au/wp-content/uploads/2017/08/170816-New-Arcade-Proves-Games-Are-A-Serious-Business-For-Victoria.pdf (accessed 3 June 2018).

Forster, R. (2017), *Grant and I: Inside and Outside the Go-Betweens*, Melbourne: Penguin Random House.

Foucault, M. (1977), *Discipline and Punish: The Birth of the Prison*, New York: Pantheon.

Foucault, M. (1980), *Power/Knowledge: Selected Interviews and Other Writing*, ed. C. Gordon, New York: Pantheon.

French, L. and M. Poole (2011), 'Passionate Amateurs: The Experimental Film and Television Fund and Modernist Film Practice in Australia', *Studies in Australasian Cinema*, 5(2): 171–84.

Frew, E.A., and J. Ali-Knight (2010), 'Creating High and Low Art: Experimentation and Commercialization at Fringe Festivals', *Tourism Culture & Communication*, 10(3): 231–45.

Friedman, T.L. (2007), *The World Is Flat – A Brief History of the Twenty-First Century*, New York: Farrar, Straus and Giroux.

Frith, S. (1987), 'Towards an Aesthetics of Popular Music', in R. Leppert and S. McClary (eds), *Music and Society: The Politics of Composition, Performance and Reception*, 133–49, Cambridge: Cambridge University Press.

Frith, S. and H. Horne (1987), *Art into Pop*, London: Methuen.

Frontline (1994–7), [TV series], Working Dog.

Full Frontal (1993–7), [TV series], Artist Services/Seven Network.

Galbally, A. (2002), *Charles Conder: The Last Bohemian*, Carlton, Vic.: Melbourne University Press.

Garnham, N. (1987), 'Concepts of Culture: Public Policy and the Cultural Industries', *Cultural Studies*, 1(1): 23–37.

Getz, D. (2002), 'Why Festivals Fail', *Event Management*, 7(4): 209–19.

Gibson, C. (2014), Interview with Tony Moore and Mark Gibson, 22 October.

Gibson, M. (2007), *Culture and Power: A History of Cultural Studies*, Oxford: Berg.

Gill, R. and A. Pratt (2008a), 'Precarity and Cultural Work in the Social Factory? Immaterial Labour, Precariousness and Cultural Work', *Theory, Culture and Society*, 25(7–8): 1–30.

Gill, R., and A. Pratt (2008b), 'In the Social Factory? Immaterial Labour, Precariousness and Cultural Work', *Theory, Culture and Society*, 25(7–8): 1–30.

Ginnane, A. (2008), 'SPAA 2008: Let's Lift Our Game', *Urban Cinefile*, 20 November. Available online: http://www.urbancinefile.com.au/home/view.asp?a=15084&s=features (accessed 2 November 2018).

Gitlin, T. (1987), *The Sixties: Years of Hope, Days of Rage*, New York: Bantam Books.

Giuffre, L. (2009), 'Maintaining Rage: Counting down without a Host for over 20 Years', *Perfect Beat*, 10(1): 39–57.

Golding, D. (2014a), Interview with Mark Gibson and Maura Edmond, 24 September.

Golding, D. (2014b), 'Playing Space: Freeplay Independent Games Festival 2013', *Metro: Media & Education Magazine* 179(1): 110–12.

Goldschmitt, K.E. (2020), 'Favela Chic in Action', in J. Buhler and M. Durrand (eds), *Music in Action Film: Sounds Like Action*, New York: Routledge.

Goldstone (2016), [Film] Dir. Ivan Sen, Australia: Dark Matter Media/Bunya Productions.

Gonzaga, E. (2017), 'The Cinematographic Unconscious of Slum Voyeurism', *Cinema Journal*, 56(4): 102–25.

Gordon, C. (1980), 'Preface', in M. Foucault, *Power/Knowledge: Selected Interviews and Other Writing*, C. Gordon (ed.), vii–x, New York: Pantheon.

Grabher, G. (2004), 'Temporary Architectures of Learning: Knowledge Governance in Project Ecologies', *Organization Studies*, 25(9): 1491–514.

Green Acres (1965–71), [TV series], Filmways/CBS.

Green Bush (2005), [Film] Dir. Warwick Thornton, Australia: CAAMA Productions.

Greene, D. (2008), *Politics and the American Television Comedy: A Critical Survey from I Love Lucy through South Park*, Jefferson, NC: McFarland.

Greenhalgh, L. (1998), 'From Arts Policy to Creative Economy', *Media International Australia*, 87(1): 84–94.

Greer, G. (1986), *The Madwoman's Underclothes: Essays and Occasional Writings 1968–85*, London: Pan Picador.

Greif, M. (2016), *Against Everything: On Dishonest Times*, London: Verso.

Griffin, L., S. Griffin, and M. Trudgett (2017), 'At the Movies: Contemporary Australian Indigenous Cultural Expressions – Transforming the Australian Story', *Australian Journal of Indigenous Education*, 47(2): 131–8.

Hacking, I. (2004), *Historical Ontology*, Cambridge, MA: Harvard University Press.

Haese, R. (1981), *Rebels and Precursors: The Revolutionary Years of Australian Art*, Ringwood, Vic: Allen Lane.

Hage, G. (2009), 'Waiting out the Crisis: On Stuckedness and Governmentality', in G. Hage (ed.), *Waiting*, 97–106, Carlton, Vic.: Melbourne University Press.

Hall, L. (2015), Interview with Tony Moore, 31 July.

Halperin, D. (1995), *Saint Foucault: Towards a Gay Hagiography*, Oxford: Oxford University Press.

Hannah Gadsby: Nanette (2018), [TV special], Netflix.

Hannah Gadsby's Oz (2014), [TV series], Closer Productions.

Hardt, M., and A. Negri (2000), *Empire*, Cambridge, MA: Harvard University Press.

Harry, M. (2015), 'Retail Therapy', *The Age*, 22 August: 15.

Hartley, J. (1992), *The Politics of Pictures*, Abingdon: Routledge.

Hartley, J. (1996), *Popular Reality: Journalism, Modernity, Popular Culture*, London: Arnold.

Hartley, J. (2005a), 'Creative Industries', in J. Hartley (ed.), *Creative Industries*, 1–40, Malden, MA: Blackwell.

Hartley, J., ed. (2005b), *Creative Industries*, Malden, MA: Blackwell.

Hartley, J. (2022), 'Strategic Stories: Weaponising or Worldmaking?', Paper presented to the School of Art, Communication and English, University of Sydney, June.

Hartley, J., and S. Cunningham (2002), 'Creative Industries: From Blue Poles to Fat Pipes (Case Study 1)', in M. Gillies, M. Carroll and J. Dash (eds), *Humanities and Social Sciences Futures: Papers from the National Humanities and Social Sciences Summit held in July 2001*, 15–26, Canberra: Department of Education Science and Training.

Hartley, J., I. Ibrus, and M. Ojamaa (2021), *On the Digital Semiosphere – Culture, Media and Science for the Anthropocene*, New York: Bloomsbury.

Harvey, C. (2009), 'Tale of Two Nations', *Sunday Herald*, 31 May: 30.

Hawker, P. (2002), 'In Full Colour', *The Age*, Culture section, 19 June: 1.

Healy, G. (2022), *The Production of Global Web Series in a Networked Age*, Abingdon, Oxon: Routledge.

Heath, J. and A. Potter (2004), *Nation of Rebels: Why Counterculture Became Consumer Culture*, New York: HarperCollins.

Hebdige, D. (1979), *Subcultures: The Meaning of Style*, London: Methuen.

Hemmings, J. (2013), 'Trading Style: *Weltmode im Dialog*', *Selvedge* 52(1): 86.

Hesmondhalgh, D. (2006), 'Bourdieu, the Media and Cultural Production', *Media, Culture and Society*, 28(2): 211–31.

Hesmondhalgh, D., and L. Meier (2015), 'Popular Music, Independence and the Concept of the Alternative in Contemporary Capitalism', in J. Bennett and N. Strange (eds), *Media Independence: Working with Freedom or Working for Free?*, 94–116, New York: Routledge.

Hesmondhalgh, D., K. Oakley, D. Lee, and M. Nisbett (2015), *Culture, Economy and Politics: The Case of New Labour*, Basingstoke: Palgrave Macmillan.

Hochuli, A., G. Hoare, and P. Cunliffe (2021), *The End of the End of History: Politics in the Twenty-First Century*, Winchester: John Hunt.

Hokenson, J.W. (2006), *The Idea of Comedy: History, Theory, Critique*, Madison, NJ: Fairleigh Dickinson University Press.

Homan, S. (2016), 'SLAM: The Music City and Cultural Activism', *Law, Social Justice and Global Development*, 20(1): 1–12.

Homan, S., S. O'Hanlon, C. Strong, and J. Tebbutt (2022), *Music City Melbourne: Urban Culture, History and Policy*, New York: Bloomsbury.

Horton, S. (2012), 'Schmooze It or Lose It', *Sun Herald*, 12 August: 30.

Hoskin, D. (2009), 'Micro-Budget Aussie Flick Makes No Money', *Overland*, 194: 23–7.

Housos (2011–22), [TV series], Antichocko Productions.

Hoyer, M. (2006), 'Style', *Sunday Telegraph*, 20 August: 116.

Hunter, I. (1992), 'Aesthetics and Cultural Studies', in L. Grossberg, C. Nelson, and P. Treichler (eds), *Cultural Studies*, 94–116, New York: Routledge.

Hunter, I. (2001), *Rival Enlightenments*, Cambridge: Cambridge University Press.

Huntington, P. (2001), 'Australia's Globetrotters', *WWD: Women's Wear Daily*, 21 June: 7.

Hutcheon, L. (1989), *The Politics of Postmodernism*, London: Routledge.

Hynes, E. (2010), 'First Time's the Charm', *Village Voice*, 4 August: 44.

I Manage My Music (2019), promotional video. Available online: https://vimeo.com/315054286 (accessed 2 September 2021).

I Manage My Music (2020), Tejo D'Cruz participant statement. Available online: https://www.imanagemymusic.com (accessed 11 October 2020).

Indie Game: The Movie (2012), [Documentary film] Dir. James Swisky and Lisanne Pajot, Canada: BlinkWorks/Flutter Media.

Inside Retail Australia (2014), 'Globe Cuts Brand Value'. Available online: https://www.insideretail.com.au/news/globe-cuts-brand-value-201408 (accessed 19 July 2019).

'Ivan Sen' (1999), *Vogue*, Australian ed., January: 94.

Jaensch, D. (1989), *The Hawke-Keating Hijack: The ALP in Transition*, Sydney: Allen & Unwin.

Jameson, F. (1991), *Postmodernism, or, the Cultural Logic of Late Capitalism*, Durham, NC: Duke University Press.

Jameson, F. (1993), 'On "Cultural Studies"', *Social Text* 34(1): 17–52.

Jenkins, H. (2008), *Convergence Culture: Where Old and New Media Collide*, New York: New York University Press.

Jimmy Kimmel Live! (2003–), [TV series], Touchstone Television/Jackhole Productions/ ABC Signature/Kimmelot.

Jindalee Lady (1992), [Film] Dir. Brian Syron, Australia: Donobri International Communications.

Jolly, R. (2014a), *Media of the People: Broadcasting Community Media in Australia*, Canberra: Parliamentary Library Research Paper.

Jolly, R. (2014b), *Media of the People: Broadcasting Community Media in Australia*, Canberra: Parliamentary Library, Commonwealth of Australia.

Joslin, S. (2016), Interview with Mark Gibson, 15 July.

'Junior Beat' (2001), *WWD: Women's Wear Daily*, 20 December: 7.

Juul, J. (2014), 'High-tech Low-tech Authenticity: The Creation of Independent Style at the Independent Games Festival', in T. Barnes (ed.), *Proceedings of the 9th International Conference on the Foundations of Digital Games*, Florida: Society for the Advancement of the Science of Digital Games.

Kalina, P. (2009), 'Magic of redemptive tale', *The Age*, Green Guide supplement, 19 November: 12.

Kath and Kim (2002–2007), [TV series], Riley Turner Productions/ABC.

Keast, J. (2018), 'Screen Australia's Indigenous Department turns 25', *Inside Film*, June–July (183): 11–13.

Kennedy-McCracken, C. (2015), Interview with Chris McAuliffe, 4 May.

Kent, M. (2009), 'Back in the frame', *Sunday Age*, Extra section, 10 May: 17.

Keogh, B. (2015), 'Between Triple-A, Indie, Casual and DIY: Sites of Tension in the Videogames Cultural Industries', in K. Oakley and J. O'Connor (eds), *The Routledge Companion to Cultural Industries*, 152–62, Abingdon: Routledge.

Keogh, B. (2023), *The Videogame Industry Does Not Exist*, Cambridge, MA: MIT Press.

Kern, L. (2010), 'No Beast so Fierce', *Film Comment*, July–August: 24–25.

Kerr, A. (2006), *The Business and Culture of Digital Games: Gamework/Gameplay*, London: Sage.

Kilbey, S. (2016), Interview with Tony Moore, 7 November.

King, G. (2005), *American Independent Cinema*, London: I.B. Tauris.

King, G. (2014), 'Differences of Kind and Degree: Articulations of Independence in American Cinema', in J. Bennett and N. Strange (eds), *Media Independence: Working with Freedom or Working for Free?*, 52–70, New York: Routledge.

King, G., C. Molloy, and Y. Tzioumakis, eds. (2013), *American Independent Cinema: Indie, Indiewood and Beyond*, Abingdon: Routledge.

Kirkpatrick, P. (1992), *Seacoast of Bohemia: Literary Life in Sydney's Roaring Twenties*, St Lucia: University of Queensland Press.

Klikauer, T. (2013), 'What Is Managerialism?', *Critical Sociology*, 41(7–8): 1103–19.

Knox, D. (2012), 'Promising Start for Redfern Now, but Nine Wins Thursday', *TV Tonight*, 2 November. Available online: http://tvtonight.com.au/2012/11/promising-start-for-redfern-now-but-nine-wins-thursday.html (accessed 2 November 2018).

Knox, D. (2016a), 'MasterChef Tops the Night, Nine Wins Thursday', *TV Tonight*, 3 June. Available online: http://tvtonight.com.au/2016/06/masterchef-tops-the-night-nine-wins-thursday.html (accessed 2 November 2018).

Knox, D. (2016b), 'First Contact Debate Heats up SBS, Doco Draws Record Numbers for NITV', *TV Tonight*, 2 December. Available online: http://tvtonight.com.au/2016/12/first-contact-debate-heats-up-sbs-doco-draws-record-numbers-for-nitv.html (accessed 2 November 2018).

Knox, D. (2018), 'Factuals Give Seven a Win on Wednesday', *TV Tonight*, 25 October. Available online: http://tvtonight.com.au/2018/10/factuals-give-seven-a-win-on-wednesday.html (accessed 2 November 2018).

Kuipers, R. (2009), 'Dreamland', *Variety*, 13 August: 19.

Laing, D. (1985), *One Chord Wonders: Power and Meaning in Punk Rock*, Milton Keynes: Open University Press.

Lanagan, D. (2011), 'Surfing in the Third Millennium: Commodifying the Visual Argot', *Australian Journal of Anthropology*, 13 (3): 283–91.

Langton, M. (1993), '*Well, I Heard It on the Radio and I Saw It on the Television …*': An Essay for the Australian Film Commission on the Politics and Aesthetics of Filmmaking by and about Aboriginal People and Things, Sydney: Australian Film Commission.

Lawson, T. (1985), 'Last Exit: Painting', in R. Hertz (ed.), *Theories of Contemporary Art*, 142–55, Englewood Cliffs, NJ: Prentice-Hall.

Leadbeater, C. and K. Oakley (1999), *The Independents: Britain's New Cultural Entrepreneurs*, London: Demos.

Lee, H. (2015), Interview with Mark Gibson, Melbourne, 22 January.

Lewis, G.H. (1976), 'The Structure of Support in Social Movements: An Analysis of Organization and Resource Mobilization in the Youth Contra-Culture', *British Journal of Sociology*, 27(2): 184–96.

Lipkin, N. (2013), 'Examining Indie's Independence: The Meaning of "Indie" Games, the Politics of Production, and Mainstream Cooptation', *Loading … The Journal of the Canadian Game Studies Association*, 7(11): 8–24.

Long Way to the Top: Stories of Australian and New Zealand Rock & Roll (2001), [TV documentary series], ABC. Episode 5, 'INXS, in Exile 1976–88'.

Lotz, A. (2021), 'Unpopularity and Cultural Power in the Age of Netflix: New Questions for Cultural Studies' Approaches to Television Texts', *European Journal of Cultural Studies*, 24(4): 887–900.

Loucas, A. (1997), 'Surf's Up', *Sunday Age*, Life section, 11 May: 10.

Lowenstein, R. (2016), Interviewed by Tony More and Chris McAuliffe, 23 June.

Lunn, S. (1998), 'Vizard's $20m England TV Sale', *The Australian*, 11 December, 3.

Mabo (2012), [Film] Dir. Rachel Perkins, Australia: Blackfella Films.

Macey, D. (1993), *The Lives of Michel Foucault*, London: Hutchinson.

Maddox, G. (2009), 'How Learning Became a Dreaming', *Sydney Morning Herald*, 29 August: 19.

Maddox, G. (2011a), 'Darkly Amusing but Dangerously Close to the Bone', *Sydney Morning Herald*, 20 June: 11.

Maddox, G. (2011b), 'Critics' Choice', *Sydney Morning Herald*, 18 November: 3.

Maddox, G. (2012), 'Sapphires Proves an Aussie Box Office Gem', *Sydney Morning Herald*, 13 August.

Maddox, G. (2013), 'Return to Country', *Sydney Morning Herald*, Culture section, 21 September: 6.

Maddox, G. (2014), 'Sapphires Plan', *Sydney Morning Herald*, Short Cuts section, 18 December: 30.

Madsen, V. (2020), '"We Are All Content Makers Now": Losing Form and Sense at the ABC?', *Australian Journalism Review*, 42(2): 243–60.

Mao's Last Dancer (2009), [Film] Dir. Bruce Beresford, Australia: Great Scott Productions.

Marchetto, S. (2001), 'Tune In, Turn On, Go Punk: American Punk Counterculture, 1968–1985', PhD diss., University of Calgary.

Marcus, G. (1989), *Lipstick Traces: A Secret History of the Twentieth Century*, Cambridge, MA: Harvard University Press.

Marsh, I., and L. Galbraith (1995), 'The Political Impact of the Sydney Gay and Lesbian Mardi Gras', *Australian Journal of Political Science*, 30(2): 300–320.

Martin, A. (2012), '*The Sapphires* by Wayne Blair', *The Monthly*, August. Available online: https://www.themonthly.com.au/issue/2012/august/1353967855/adrian-martin/sapphires-wayne-blair-director (accessed 2 November 2018).

Martin, C.B. and M. Deuze (2009), 'The Independent Production of Culture: A Digital Games Case Study', *Games and Culture*, 4(3): 276–95.

Matchett, S. (2015), Interview with Tony Moore, 11 May.

Mathieson, C. (2000), *The Sell-In: How the Music Business Seduced Alternative Rock*, Sydney: Allen & Unwin.

McAuliffe, C. (2017), 'Clothing and Australian Nobrow: Wearable Art for a Global Audience', in P. Swirski and T. Vanhanen (eds), *When Highbrow Meets Lowbrow: Popular Culture and the Rise of Nobrow*, 155–79, New York: Palgrave Macmillan.

McCarthy, T. (2011), 'Toomelah: Cannes Review', *Hollywood Reporter*, 13 May. Available online: http://www.hollywoodreporter.com/review/toomelah-cannes-review-188275 (accessed 29 January 2018).

McCrea, C. (2013), 'Australian Video Games: The Collapse and Reconstruction of an Industry', in N. Huntemann and B. Aslinger (eds), *Gaming Globally: Production, Place, and Play*, 203–7, New York: Palgrave Macmillan.

McElroy, G. (2013), 'Antichamber Passes 100K Sales Mark on Steam', *Polygon*, 20 March. Available online: https://www.polygon.com/2013/3/20/4124946/antichamber-passes-100k-sales-mark-on-steam (accessed 7 February 2020).

McGuigan, J. (2006), 'Book Review: Creative Industries', *Global Media and Communication*, 2(3): 372–4.

McKee, A., C. Collis, and B. Hamley (2012), *Entertainment Industries: Entertainment as a Cultural System*, Abingdon, Oxon: Routledge.

McMaster, M. (2019), Opening Remarks to RMIT Graduate Showcase, Twitter Post, 7 November. Available online: https://twitter.com/mjmcmaster/status/1192193715562921984 (accessed 10 January 2023).

McPherson, S. and M. Pope (1992), *Promoting Indigenous Involvement in the Film and TV Industry*, Sydney: Australian Film Commission.

McRobbie, A. (1999), *In the Culture Society: Art, Fashion, and Popular Music*, London: Routledge.

McRobbie, A. (2002), 'From Holloway to Hollywood: Happiness at Work in the New Cultural Economy', in P. du Gay and M. Pryke (eds), *Cultural Economy*, 97–114, London: Sage.

McRobbie, A. (2004), '"Everyone Is Creative": Artists as Pioneers of the New Economy', in E. Silva and T. Bennett (eds), *Contemporary Culture and Everyday Life*, 186–99, London: Routledge.

McRobbie, A. (2016), *Be Creative: Making a Living in the New Creative Industries*, Cambridge: Polity.

Message Stick (1999–2012), [TV series], ABC Indigenous Programs Unit.

Miles, B. (2010), *London Calling: A Countercultural History of London since 1945*, London: Atlantic Books.

Miller, T. (2009), 'Can Natural Luddites Make Things Explode or Travel Faster? The New Humanities, Cultural Policy Studies, and Creative Industries', in J. Holt and A. Perren (eds), *Media Industries: History, Theory, and Method*, 184–98, Malden, MA: Wiley-Blackwell.

Miller, T. (2016), 'Cybertarian Flexibility: When Prosumers Join the Cognitariat, All That Is Scholarship Melts into Air', in M. Curtin and K. Sanson (eds), *Precarious Creativity: Global Media, Local Labor*, 19–32, Los Angeles: University of California Press.

Mills, B. (2017), *Creativity in the British Television Comedy Industry*, London: Routledge.

Mills, J. (2015), 'First Nation Cinema: Hollywood's Indigenous "Other"', *Screening the Past*, (24). Available online: https://www.screeningthepast.com/issue-24-first-release/first-nation-cinema-hollywood's-indigenous-'other'/ (accessed 2 November 2018).

Milner, A. (1994), 'Cultural Materialism, Culturalism and Post-Culturalism: The Legacy of Raymond Williams', *Theory, Culture and Society*, 11(1): 43–73.

Mombassa, R. (2014), Interview with Tony Moore and Chris McAuliffe, 21 October.

Montgomery, L., J. Hartley, C. Neylon, M. Gillies, E. Gray, C. Herrmann-Pillath, C-K. Huang, J. Leach, J. Potts, X. Ren, K. Skinner, C.R. Sugimoto and K. Wilson (2021), *Open Knowledge Institutions: Reinventing Universities*, Cambridge, MA: MIT Press.

Monty Python's Life of Brian (1979), [Film] Dir. Terry Jones, UK: HandMade Films/ Python (Monty) Pictures.

Moore, T. (2003), 'Hawke's Big Tent: Elite Pluralism and the Politics of Inclusion', in T. Bramston and S. Ryan (eds), *The Hawke Government: A Critical Retrospective*, 112–27, North Melbourne: Pluto Press.

Moore, T. (2005), *The Barry McKenzie Movies*, Strawberry Hills, NSW: Currency Press.

Moore, T. (2012), *Dancing with Empty Pockets: Australia's Bohemians since 1860*, Sydney: Murdoch Books/Allen & Unwin.

Moore, T. (2015), '"Stop Laughing – This Is Serious": The "Larrikin Carnivalesque" in Australia', in C. Nelson, D. Pike, and G. Ledvinka (eds), *On Happiness: New Ideas for the Twenty-First Century*, 146–62, Crawley, WA: UWA Publishing.

Moore, T. (2020), 'Australian Working-Class Art Field: Its Making and Unmaking', in T. Bennett, D. Stevenson, F. Myers and T. Winikoff (eds), *The Australian Art Field: Practices, Policies, Institutions*, 83–97, New York: Routledge.

Morris, M. (1990), 'Banality in Cultural Studies', in P. Mellencamp (ed.), *Logics of Television*, 14–43, Bloomington: Indiana University Press.

Morris, M. (1992a), 'A Gadfly Bites Back', *Meanjin*, 51(3): 545–51.

Morris, M. (1992b), *Ecstasy and Economics*, Sydney: EmPress.

Morrow, J. (2015), Interview with Tony Moore and Mark Gibson, 26 March.

Mother and Son (1984–94), [TV series], ABC.

Mouthing Off (1996–8), [TV series], Artist Services/The Comedy Channel.

Moyse, C. (2019), 'Untitled Goose Game Pinches One Million Sales to Date', *Destructoid*, 31 December. Available online: https://www.destructoid.com/untitled-goose-game-pinches-one-million-sales-to-date-576656.phtml (accessed 10 January 2023).

Music Australia (2016), *National Contemporary Music Plan*, Erskineville, NSW: Music Australia.

My Name's McGooley, What's Yours? (1966–8), [TV series], Seven Network.

My Survival as An Aboriginal (1978), [Documentary film] Dir. Essie Coffey, Australia: Goodgaban Productions.

Mystery Road (2013), [Film] Dir. Ivan Sen, Australia: Mystery Road Films/Bunya Productions.

Mystery Road (2018–22), [TV series], Bunya Productions/Golden Road Productions.

Naglazas, M. (2002), 'Great Black Hope Refuses to Be Labelled', *West Australian*, 21 May: 8.

Nanya, M. (2015), Interview with Mark Gibson, 1 November.

National Gallery of Victoria (2014), *Thirty Years of Shelf Indulgence: Mambo*, museum exhibition. Available online: www.ngv.vic.gov.au/exhibition/mambo/ (accessed 5 August 2018).

Nayna, M. and M. Conway (2015), Interview with Mark Gibson, 2 November.

Neale, S. and F. Krutnik (2006), *Popular Film and Television Comedy*, London: Routledge.

Nehl, A. (2015), Interview with Tony Moore and Mark Gibson, 25 March.

Neil, K. (2014), Interview with Mark Gibson, 8 October.

Neil, K., and M. Westbury (2015), 'Free Play 2004: Co-founders Look Back', *Freeplay Independent Games Festival*, Melbourne. Available online: https://www.youtube.com/watch?v=BFjrmOIVk7I (accessed 9 December 2019).

Newman, M.Z. (2009), 'Indie Culture: In Pursuit of the Authentic Autonomous Alternative', *Cinema Journal*, 48(3): 16–34.

Newman, M.Z. (2011), *Indie: An American Film Culture*, New York: Columbia University Press.

Nicholls, S. (2003), 'Ruddock Fury over Woomera Computer Game', *The Age*, 30 April. Available online: https://www.theage.com.au/articles/2003/04/29/1051381948773.html (accessed 5 June 2018).

Nichols, D. (1997), *The Go-Betweens*, Sydney: Allen & Unwin.

Nichols, D. (2016), *Dig: Australian Rock and Pop Music 1960–85*, Portland, OR: Verse Chorus Press.

Nichols, D. and S. Perillo (2016a), 'Rooms for the Memory: The 30-Year Iconic Legacy of Dogs in Space', in *Icons: The Making, Meaning and Undoing of Urban Icons and Iconic Cities*, Proceedings of the 13th Australasian Urban History Planning History Conference, 302–11.

Nichols, D. and S. Perillo (2016b), 'Rooms for the Memory: The 30-Year Iconic Legacy of Dogs in Space', in Bosman, C. and Dedekorkut, A. (eds), *Icons: The Making, Meaning and Undoing of Urban Icons and Iconic Cities*, Proceedings of the 13th Australasian Urban History Planning History Conference, 302–11, Gold Coast, Qld: Griffith University.

Niesche, C. (2014), 'Hanging 10: Interview with Angus Kingsmill, CEO of Mambo', *Company Director*, 30 (3): 32–4.

Nightmoves (1977–84), [TV series], Seven Network.

No Country for Old Men (2007), [Film] Dir. Joel Coen and Ethan Coen, USA: Scott Rudin Productions/Mike Zoss Productions/Miramax/Paramount Vantage.

Not Quite Art (2007–8), [TV documentary series], ABC.

Not the Nine O'Clock News (1979–82), [TV series], BBC2.

O'Connor, J. (2009), 'Creative Industries: A New Direction?', *International Journal of Cultural Policy*, 15(4): 387–402.

O'Connor, J. (2016), *After the Creative Industries: Why We Need a Cultural Economy*, Platform Papers 47, Strawberry Hills, NSW: Currency House.

O'Connor, J. (2018), *Creative Island Sector Analysis 2017: Creative Island Report*, Hobart: Tasmanian Government.

O'Connor, J. (2020), 'Art as Industry', *wakeinalarm blog*, June 20. Available online: https://wakeinalarm.blog/ (accessed 15 December 2022).

O'Doherty, P. (2014), Interview with Tony Moore and Chris McAuliffe, 21 October.

O'Neil, H. (1996). 'Mambo King', *The Australian*, 27 February: 13.

O'Regan, T. (1992), '(Mis)taking Policy: Notes on the Cultural Policy Debate', *Cultural Studies*, 6(3): 409–23.

O'Regan, T. (1993), *Australian Television Culture*, Sydney: Allen & Unwin.

O'Shea, L. (2020), *Future Histories: What Ada Lovelace, Tom Paine, and the Paris Commune Can Teach Us about Digital Technology*, London: Verso.

Oakley, K. (2004), 'Not So Cool Britannia: The Role of the Creative Industries in Economic Development', *International Journal of Cultural Studies*, 7(1): 67–77.

Oakley, K. (2009), 'The Disappearing Arts: Creativity and Innovation after the Creative Industries', *International Journal of Cultural Policy*, 15(4): 403–13.

One Night the Moon (2001), [Film] Dir. Rachel Perkins, Australia: Music Arts Dance Films.

Oxley, P. (2018), Interview with Tony Moore, 23 March.

Panitch, L., and C. Leys (1996), *The End of Parliamentary Socialism: From New Left to New Labour*, London: Verso.

Pariser, E. (2011), *The Filter Bubble: What the Internet Is Hiding from You*, New York: Penguin.

Parker, F., J.R. Whitson, and B. Simon (2017), 'Megabooth: The Cultural Intermediation of Indie Games', *New Media & Society*, 20(5): 1953–72.

Parkes, S. (2009), 'Bridging the Gaps', *Canberra Times*, 18 April: 23.

Parkinson (1971–2007), [TV series], BBC1/ITV.

Penford, E. (2016), Interview with Mark Gibson, 9 March.

Perkins, R. (2017), Interview with Maura Edmond, 4 December.

Perren, A. (2012), *Indie, Inc.: Miramax and the Transformation of Hollywood in the 1990s*, Austin: University of Texas Press.

Peters, F. (1994), 'The Black Film Unit at the ABC and Aboriginal Filmmaking', in A. Moran (ed.), *Film Policy: An Australian Reader*, 151–4, Brisbane: Institute for Cultural Policy Studies, Griffith University.

Petersen (1974), [Film] Dir. Tim Burstall, Australia: Hexagon Productions.

Petticoat Junction (1963–70), [TV series], Filmways/CBS.

Piris, C. (2016), '"My Girlfriend Has Probably Saved My Life": Courtney Barnett', *The Guardian*, 6 August. Available online: https://www.theguardian.com/global/2016/aug/06/courtney-barnett-when-i-go-into-a-house-i-look-in-all-the-cupboards (accessed 3 September 2019).

Pizza (2000–2021), [TV series], Antichocko Productions.

Pizza Man (1995), [film] Dir. Paul Fenech, Australia: Paul Fenech.

Please Like Me (2013–16), [TV series], Pigeon Fancier Productions/John & Josh International/Pivot/ABC.

Polhemus, T. (1994), *Street Style: From Sidewalk to Catwalk*, London: Thames and Hudson.

Power, L. (1996), 'T-shirt That Surfs around the World', *Sunday Age*, Business section, 21 January: 12.

Poyner, R. (2002), 'Reg Mombassa: Mambo Theology', *Eye* 46(1): 12. Available online: http://www.eyemagazine.com/feature/article/reg-mombassa-text-in-full (accessed 19 July 2019).

Quinn, K. (2012), 'Big Ideas Shape City Life Stories', *Sun Herald*, 28 October: 22.

Rabbit Proof Fence (2002), [Film] Dir. Phillip Noyce, Australia: Rumbalara Film.

Race around the World (1997–8), [TV series], ABC.

Radiance (1997), [Film] Dir. Rachel Perkins, Australia: Eclipse Films.

Rae, G. (2020), *Poststructuralist Agency: The Subject in Twentieth-Century Theory*, Edinburgh: Edinburgh University Press.

Rage (1987–), [TV series], ABC.

Redfern Now (2012–15), [TV series], Blackfella Films.

Reed, A. (2015), Interview with Mark Gibson, 17 November.

Reucassel, C. (2015), Interview with Tony Moore and Mark Gibson, 26 March.

Riley, S. (2017), Interview with Tony Moore, 2 February.

RMIT Music Industry Students (2015), 'Adapt Music Industries Seminar: Kylie Auldist, Mike Callender, Josh Delaney', 24 April, Melbourne: RMIT University.

Rock Arena (1982–9), [TV series], ABC.

Rock around the World (1981–4), [TV series], SBS.

Rosemary, N. (2009), 'Inconvenient Truths', *Weekend Australian*, 27 June: 6.

Ruffino, P. (2013), 'Narratives of Independent Production in Video Game Culture', *Loading … The Journal of the Canadian Game Studies Association*, 7(11): 106–121.

Ryan, M.D. (2015), 'From Aussiewood Movies to Guerilla Filmmaking: Independent Filmmaking and Contemporary Australian Cinema', in D. Baltruschat and M.P. Erickson (eds), *Independent Filmmaking around the Globe*, 71–89, Toronto: University of Toronto Press.

'Saban buys Aussie fashion label' (2018), License Global, 6 April. Available online: http://www.licensemag.com/license-global/saban-buys-aussie-fashion-label (accessed 7 March 2023).

Samson & Delilah (2009), [Film] Dir. Warwick Thornton, Australia: Scarlett Pictures/CAAMA Productions.

'Sapphires playing screens of the globe' (2012), *Daily Telegraph*, 17 October: 22.

Saturday Night Live (1975–), [TV series], NBC/Broadway Video.

Schaffer, G. (2016), 'Fighting Thatcher with Comedy: What to Do When There Is No Alternative', *Journal of British Studies*, 55(2): 374–97.

Schembri, J. (2008), 'Land of Disaster Films', *The Age*, Entertainment Guide, 5 December: 4.

Schembri, J. (2010), 'Bran Nue Era as Indigenous Cinema Enters the Mainstream', *Sydney Morning Herald*, 8 February: 12.

Schlesinger, P. (2007), 'Creativity: From Discourse to Doctrine', *Screen*, 48(3): 377–87.

Scott, T. (2015), 'On the Couch with Royal Headache: Heartache, Torment, and the Perfect Melody', *Vice*, 19 August. Available online: https://www.vice.com/en/article/695qey/on-the-couch-with-royal-headache (accessed 7 November 2020).

Sexton, J. (2001), 'The Face', *Weekend Australian*, Review section, 3 November: 3.

Shirley Thompson versus the Aliens (1972), [Film] Dir. Jim Sharman, Australia: Kolossal Piktures.

Shortt, C. (2015), Interview with Tony Moore, 30 July.

Siemienowicz, R. (2012), 'Timing and Talent: The Secrets behind *The Sapphires*' Success, with Director Wayne Blair', *AFI Blog*, 14 August. Available online: http://blogafi. wordpress.com/2012/08/14/timing-and-talent-the-secrets-behind-the-sapphires-success-with-director-wayne-blair (accessed 2 November 2018).

Siemienowicz, R. (2018), 'Screen Australia crows about 25 years of Indigenous support', *Screenhub*, 30 August. Available online: https://www.screenhub.com.au/news-article/news/policy/rochelle-siemienowicz/screen-australia-crows-about-25-years-of-indigenous-support-256371 (accessed 8 November 2018).

Simon, A. (2011), 'Toomelah', *Variety*, 23–9 May: 23.

Simon, B. (2013), 'Indie Eh? Some Kind of Game Studies', *Loading … The Journal of the Canadian Game Studies Association*, 7(11): 106–21.

Simpson, C. (1999), 'An Interview with Rachel Perkins: Director *Radiance*', *Metro: Media & Education Magazine*, 120(1): 32–4.

Smith, B. (1988), *The Death of the Artist as Hero: Essays in History and Culture*, Melbourne: Oxford University Press.

Sounds (1974–87), [TV series], Seven Network.

South Park (1997–), [TV series], Celluloid Studios/Braniff Productions/Parker-Stone Productions/South Park Studios.

Speed, L. (2005), 'Life as a Pizza: The Comic Traditions of Wogsploitation Films', *Metro: Media & Education Magazine* 146/147(1): 136–44.

Spigelman, J. (2012), 'The Role of the ABC in Australian Culture', Address to the 30th Anniversary of Conversazione, Melbourne', 22 November. Available online: https://about.abc.net.au/speeches/the-role-of-the-abc-in-australian-culture/ (accessed 19 December 2022).

Srnicek, N. (2016), *Platform Capitalism*, Cambridge: Polity.

Stafford, A. (2014), *Pig City: From the Saints to Savage Garden*, St Lucia: University of Queensland Press.

Stallybrass, P., and A. White (1986), *The Politics and Poetics of Transgression*, Ithaca, NY: Cornell University Press.

Stranger, M. (2011), *Surfing Life: Surface, Substructure and the Commodification of the Sublime*, Surrey, UK: Ashgate.

Straw, W. (2015), 'Some Things a Scene Might Be', *Cultural Studies*, 29 (3): 476–84.

Stuckey, H. (2015), Interview with Mark Gibson, 30 July.

Sullivan, J. (2006), *Jeans: A Cultural History of an American Icon*, New York: Gotham Books.

Summer Heights High (2007), [TV series], Princess Pictures.

Sweet Country (2018), [Film] Dir. Warwick Thornton, Australia: Bunya Productions.

Syron, B. with B. Kearney (1996), *Kicking Down the Doors*, Sydney: Donobri International Communications.

Tabrett, L. (2013), *It's Culture, Stupid! Reflections of an Arts Bureaucrat*, Platform Papers 34, Strawberry Hills, NSW: Currency Press.

Taylor, K. (1998), 'Shifting Sands', *The Age*, Entertainment guide, 15 May: 2.

Tetzlaff, D. (1994), 'Music for Meaning: Reading the Discourse of Authenticity in Rock', *Journal of Communication Inquiry*, 18(1): 95–117.

The Aunty Jack Show (1972–3), [TV series], ABC.

The Beverly Hillbillies (1962–71), [TV series], Filmways/CBS.

The Big Breakfast (1992–2002), [TV series], Planet 24.

The Blues Brothers (1980), [Film] Dir. John Landis, USA: Universal Pictures.

The Chaser's War on Everything (2006–9), [TV series], Chaser Broadcasting/ABC.

The Comedy Company (1988–90), [TV series], Media Arts/Network Ten.

The Comic Strip Presents … (1982–2016), [TV series], Channel 4/BBC2/Gold.

The D-Generation (1986–7), [TV series], ABC.

The Hub (1996–9), [TV series], XYZ Entertainment/Arena.

The Larry Sanders Show (1992–8), [TV series], Partners with Boundaries Productions/ Brillstein-Grey Entertainment/HBO.

The Librarians (2007–10), [TV series], Gristmill.

The Mavis Bramston Show (1964–8), [TV series], Seven Network.

The Naked Vicar Show (1977–8), [TV series], Seven Network.

The Paul Hogan Show (1973–84), [TV series], Seven Network/Nine Network.

The Producers (1967), [Film] Dir. Mel Brooks, USA: Crossbow Productions/Springtime Productions/U-M Productions.

The Sapphires (2012), [Film] Dir. Wayne Blair, Australia: Goalpost Pictures.

The Simpsons (1989–, [TV series], Gracie Films/20th Television.

The Wog Boy (2000), [Film] Dir. Aleksi Vellis, Australia: Third Costa/G.O. Films.

The Young Ones (1982–4), [TV series], BBC2.

Thornton, W. (2012), interviewed by M. Langton, Bernard Smith Symposium, Australian Institute of Art History, University of Melbourne, 21 September. Available online: http://www.youtube.com/watch?v=54Ue_hwURFs (accessed 2 November 2018).

Tippet, G. and A. Lawson (2005), 'Rise and Fall of a Dealmaker', *The Age*, 5 July. Available online: https://www.theage.com.au/national/rise-and-fall-of-a-deal-maker-20050705-ge0gly.html (accessed 7 June 2019).

Tonight Live with Steve Vizard (1990–3), [TV series], Artist Services.

Toomelah (2010), [Film] Dir. Ivan Sen, Australia: Bunya Productions.

Top of the Pops (1964–2006), [TV series], BBC.

Torgovnick, M. (1990), *Gone Primitive: Savage Intellects, Modern Lives*, Chicago: Chicago University Press.

Trembath, J.L. and K. Fielding (2020), *Australia's Cultural and Creative Economy: A 21st Century Guide*, Report produced by A New Approach think tank, Canberra: Australian Academy of the Humanities.

Trimboli, I. (2018), 'Amy Shark', *The Guardian*, 3 July. Available online: https://www. theguardian.com/music/2018/jul/02/amy-shark-people-think-im-just-popping-champagne-off-yachts (accessed 3 July 2018).

Turner, G. (2011), 'Surrendering the Space: Convergence Culture, Cultural Studies and the Curriculum', *Cultural Studies*, 25(4–5): 685–99.

Turner, G. (2012), *What's Become of Cultural Studies?*, London: Sage.

Two Laws (1981), [Documentary film] Dir. Alessandro Cavadini and Carolyn Strachan, Australia: Borroloola Tribal Council.

Upper Middle Bogan (2013–16), [TV series], Gristmill.

Vision Street Wear (2018a), 'VSW History'. Available online: http://www. visionstreetwear.com/history/ (accessed 5 August 2018).

Vision Street Wear (2018b), 'Steve Aoki, Electronic Dance Music DJ and Vision Street Wear Ambassador'. Available online: http://www.visionstreetwear.com/history/ (accessed 5 August 2018).

Vizard, S. (2014), Interview with Tony Moore and Mark Gibson, 2 December.

Walker, C. (1996), *Stranded: The Secret History of Australian Independent Music, 1977–1991*, Sydney: Pan Macmillan.

Walker, C., ed. (1982), *Inner City Sound*, Glebe, NSW: Wild & Woolley.

Wark, M. (1992), 'After Literature: Culture, Policy, Theory and Beyond', *Meanjin*, 51(4): 677–90.

Wark, M. (1999), *Celebrities, Culture and Cyberspace: The Light on the Hill in a Postmodern World*, Sydney: Pluto Press.

Warnock, N. (2015), Interview with Tony Moore, 12 May.

Wayne's World (1992), [Film] Dir. Penelope Spheeris, USA: Paramount Pictures.

We Can be Heroes (2005), [TV series], Princess Pictures.

We're Living on Living on Dog Food (2009), [Documentary film] Dir. Richard Lowenstein, Melbourne: Ghost Pictures.

Westbury, M. (2014), Interview with Mark Gibson and Tony Moore, 9 December.

Westwood, M. (2023), 'A New Tune: Arts Minister Tony Burke's First Policy Riff Is Met with Generous Applause', *Weekend Australian*, Review supplement,4 February: 8.

Wilfred (2002), [Film] Dir. Tony Rogers, Australia: Tropfest Festival Productions Pty Ltd.

Wilfred (2007–10), [TV series], Renegade Films.

Wilkinson, M. (2015), 'Royal Headache: High', *New Musical Express*, 18 August. Available online: https://www.nme.com/reviews/reviews-royal-headache-16218-311488 (accessed 22 November 2020).

Williams, M. (2017), 'Rage Is Turning 30, but It Was Never Meant to Last so Long', *The Real Thing*, Radio National, Australian Broadcasting Corporation. Available online: https://www.abc.net.au/news/2017-04-17/rage-was-never-meant-to-last-30-years/8437704 (accessed 3 April 2019).

Williams, R. (1974), *Television: Technology and Cultural Form*, London: Fontana.

Williams, R. (1977), *Marxism and Literature*, Oxford: Oxford University Press.

Wilson, J. (2012), 'Soul Sisters Shine in Gem', *The Age*, 9 August: 15.

Wilson, S. (2001), 'Graffiti Artist Cult Status', *Daily Telegraph*, Sunday Style Magazine supplement, 16 December: 28.

Wolf, G. (2008), *Make It Australian: The Australian Performing Group, the Pram Factory and New Wave Theatre*, Sydney: Currency Press.

Womersley, T. (2006), 'An Outfitter for All Seasons', *The Age*, 28 June: 32.

Zuboff, S. (2019), *The Age of Surveillance Capitalism*, London: Profile Books.

Index